LITERARY WONDERLANDS

LITERARY WONDERLANDS

A Journey Through the Greatest
Fictional Worlds Ever Created

General Editor Laura Miller

BLACK DOG
& LEVENTHAL
PUBLISHERS
NEW YORK

CONTENTS

Introduction   10

ANCIENT MYTH & LEGEND

Previous page: "Heavens. What were these?" from *The Tempest* (III:iii),
from *The Illustrated Library Shakespeare* (1890), see page 64.

2. SCIENCE & ROMANTICISM

3. GOLDEN AGE OF FANTASY

4 NEW WORLD ORDER

1946–1980

5   THE COMPUTER AGE

Introduction

Of all the powerful spells that fiction casts upon us—absorbing plots, believable characters, vivid language—one of the least celebrated is its ability to make us feel transported to another time and place. Most avid readers have had the experience of setting down a book and needing to shake off the sights, smells, and sounds of a world they haven't actually been to, or that may not even exist. We may never have set foot in Victorian London, and we certainly haven't hiked through Middle-earth, but the writings of Arthur Conan Doyle and J. R. R. Tolkien have made those places seem more real, to millions of readers, than cities we've actually visited.

The works described in this book all conjure lands that exist only in the imagination. Some of these places—the America of David Foster Wallace's *Infinite Jest* (1996, page 268), the Japan of Haruki Murakami's *IQ84* (2009–10, page 298)—closely resemble the world we live in. Others—the Alaska of Michael Chabon's *The Yiddish Policemen's Union* (2007, page 294) and the New England of Margaret Atwood's *The Handmaid's Tale* (1985, page 248)—show us how very different our own world might have been, or could become, with only a few tweaks to the course of history. Some of these books, like Ann Leckie's *Ancillary Justice* (2013, page 304), speculate about what life might be like in the distant future, while other works, like Robert E. Howard's original *Conan the Barbarian* story series (1932–36, page 154), postulate a thrilling past that has since been irretrievably lost. Stanisław Lem's *Solaris* (1961, page 194) challenges readers to contemplate a form of intelligent life almost inconceivably alien from ourselves. Satirists like Jonathan Swift and Ngũgĩ wa Thiong'o concoct bizarre yarns about talking horses and child-bearing corpses to confront us with a pointedly familiar reflection of our own behaviors. Then there are those unfettered fantasists, ranging from Italo Calvino to Neil Gaiman, whose great gift is to offer us visions in which the imagination can be set free to roam wherever it desires.

The roots of all these books lie in humanity's oldest stories: myths, fables, and folklore—the tales people made up to explain how the world came to exist and why it is the way it is. While literary criticism tends to valorize the new and the innovative, the literature of the fantastic seeks a connection to tradition, to what persists even as the world changes. The texts in the first section of this book, "Ancient Myth & Legend," are, themselves, often attempts to preserve a fading storytelling culture; *Beowulf* (*c.*700–1100, page 28) and the *Prose Edda* (*c.*1220, page 36) were the works of Christian authors who sought to safeguard a portion of their pagan past. These books have survived in no small part because of their ability to reach across a span of centuries and speak to the inhabitants of new ages and worlds. The messy love lives of Ovid's gods and goddesses; the questing courage of Malory's Arthurian knights; the dauntless faith of Wu Cheng'en's Xuanzang—all remind us of the worst and the best of ourselves. But, along with much that is recognizable, these stories also bewitch us with the rich and strange, the miraculous, the astonishing, and the awe-inspiring. The first tales human beings told each other, the ones that survive from our unrecorded past, were not about everyday life, but about the extraordinary: talking animals, wicked sorcerers, terrifying monsters, and cities built of gold and jewels.

Fantastic literature has always conducted a complex dialogue with the real world. Many of us read it to escape from that world but, more often than not, this fiction aims to make us see our own lives in a new light. Allegories like *The Faerie Queene* (1590–1609, page 54) and epics like *The Divine Comedy* (*c.*1308–21, page 40) offer their readers moral instruction, even if some of those readers prefer to attend only to the lush spectacle that cloaks the lesson. In *Don Quixote* (1605/15, page 62), Miguel de Cervantes impishly used the structure of a chivalric romance to mock the conventions of the "romance" itself, a literary genre that specializes in the wondrous. But with Thomas More's *Utopia* (1516, page 52), the most overtly didactic species of literary wonderland came into its own. In the five hundred years since it was published, utopian tales have used invented worlds and nations to critique and exhort readers to change the world. The utopian strain of fantastic literature springs not from myth but from the great age of exploration, when Europeans set out to discover (and, alas, exploit) previously unknown and unmapped parts of the globe. Travel narratives like Marco Polo's account of his journeys in Asia (c.1300) became immensely popular, starting in the fourteenth century, and travelers' encounters with other cultures naturally encouraged wandering Westerners to contemplate what foreigners did better or worse than the folks back home.

Utopian fiction also arose from Enlightenment thinking itself. If reason and science proved themselves to be superior tools for understanding and mastering the natural world, why not apply them to the engineering of society as well? Writers would continue to produce utopian tales into the twentieth century; women, in particular, wanted to picture what a culture founded on gender equality or even female dominance might look like and, in a sense, Marxism is a utopian dream. By the nineteenth century, however, authors like Samuel Butler had turned to parodying utopian idealism. Utopias, arguably, make for dull reading, but dystopian fiction has demonstrated again and again—right up to *The Hunger Games* (page 296), a 2008 blockbuster intended for teenaged readers—its power to enthrall. Some dystopias, like Yevgeny Zamyatin's *We* (1924, page 138) and Aldous Huxley's *Brave New World* (1932, page 148), are essentially works of social or political criticism—attacks on the dominant ideologies and obsessions of the modern world. Many more simply depict the age-old dilemma of a restless individual at odds with the society into which he or she was born.

Often enough, industrialization and the rise of the mass media provoked this dissatisfaction, and writing a dystopian novel was not the only way to respond to such forces. The "Golden Age" of fantasy, during the first sixty years or so of the twentieth century, was largely a reaction to the wholesale destruction of deeply rooted ways of life in which human beings lived in intimate relation to the natural world. Another source of anxiety was the perceived loss of long-standing folk traditions. (The Brothers Grimm first began collecting fairy tales in the early 1800s, not to compile a book for children, but as an act of ethnographic conservation.) The great, genre-defining fantasies of this period, from *The Lord of the Rings* (1954–55, page 188) to *The Chronicles of Narnia* (1950–56, page 178), were fundamentally nostalgic, celebrating a vanishing, idealized world that existed before machines and market economies defined our lives. This was also a fertile time for children's fiction, and many of the masters of the period, from J. M. Barrie to Tove Jansson, either incorporated the longing for a simpler, Arcadian idyll into their work or saturated everything they wrote with a melancholy lament for the lost innocence of childhood. Meanwhile, literary modernists like Franz Kafka and Jorge Luis Borges deployed surreal, uncanny, and absurd elements in their writings as the ideal tools for portraying the metaphysical paradoxes inherent in a post-religious culture.

The last half of the twentieth century was all about questions, and few literary forms are better suited to fermenting questions than the fantastic. The wonderlands devised by Ursula K. Le Guin, Kurt Vonnegut, Vladimir Nabokov, Samuel R. Delaney, and Octavia E. Butler interrogated long-held assumptions about, respectively, the primacy of European culture, modern warfare, the novel, sexuality, and race. Angela Carter took perhaps the most orthodox of literary forms, the fairy tale, and turned it inside out to reveal the unspoken desires and power of women hidden within. Science fiction became more than just a vehicle for technologically enhanced adventure and began to challenge the rapidly evolving postindustrial world, and to warn us about where it is heading. A few prescient writers—William Gibson and Neal Stephenson, first and foremost—succeeded, largely, in anticipating the central role that linked computers would play in the twenty-first century. Most strikingly, by coining the term "cyberspace," Gibson recognized that our best mental model for understanding the vast and immaterial web of communications perpetually humming all around us is spatial. The Internet, we collectively decided, is a place. Much of it is made up of words. It just might be the ultimate literary wonderland.

We still haven't tired of books, though, even when they come to us via a medium constituted of bits and pixels. The wonderlands being created today and waiting to be created tomorrow will also be the work of graphic novelists, filmmakers, and video-game designers, and they, in turn, will influence the many writers who have stuck with prose text in all its unadorned glory. Novelists like Salman Rushdie, Murakami, and Nnedi Okorafor have raided the toolboxes of science fiction and fantasy in order to tell new stories of their own homelands. A generation of children has grown up saturated in the imaginative liberty exhibited by J. K. Rowling, as well as the trenchant social criticism of Suzanne Collins. They could not be better equipped to build the fictional ships in which all of us will sail off into the unknown, seeking the far horizon and fresh discoveries that will surpass our most extravagant dreams.

Laura Miller
New York City

Briton Rivière, *Una and the Lion* from "The Faerie Queene," 1840, see page 54.

1 ANCIENT MYTH & LEGEND

These legends of kings, knights errant, and epic adventure were the historic and poetic precursors of modern genre fiction.

ANONYMOUS

The Epic of Gilgamesh
(c.1750 BCE)

One of the earliest known works of great literature, this Babylonian poem,
which first emerged c.1750 BCE and found a stable form around 700 BCE,
details King Gilgamesh's feats of valor and vain quest for immortality.

The Epic of Gilgamesh was lost to history until 150 years ago. The text is still incomplete and under reconstruction.

New fragments keep appearing, raising the prospect that the poem will one day be entire again (the tablet above was acquired by the Sulaymaniyah Museum, Iraq, in 2011).

As well as the Babylonian poem, there are five separate Sumerian poems about Gilgamesh, which may be even older.

To the Babylonians, the legendary Gilgamesh was the mightiest hero and greatest king of old. In telling his story the poem touches on many existential questions, such as what it means to be mortal in an eternal world, how human nature differs from animal and divine, and the ethics of political power and military force; these and other universal themes are what make the poem an enduring masterpiece. The poem begins in the ancient Babylonian city of Uruk, where Gilgamesh rules as king, but the narrative shows us imaginary landscapes on the fringes of the known world.

Gilgamesh befriends the wild man Enkidu, and they go on an adventure in search of fame and glory. They run for many days to the Cedar Forest, the realm of the gods, to slay its guardian, the powerful ogre Humbaba, and plunder its timber. There were no forests in Babylonia and the landscape is wholly imaginary—a dense and terrifying jungle that exerts a crushing force on the heroes' strength and will. A piece of the epic reconstructed only in 2012 contains a lively description of the deafening noise that filled the forest canopy: the squawks of birds, buzz of insects, and yells of monkeys form a cacophonous symphony to entertain the forest's guardian.

Humbaba is a king with an unfamiliar court. He is partly the personification of the eternal life-force of the ancient trees themselves, but he also has elephantine features: His trumpeting is heard from afar, he leaves great tracks in the undergrowth, his face is ugly with wrinkles, and he has tusks. In the episode of Humbaba and the cedars, familiar human responses react to imposing forces of nature: terror and wonder, cupidity and remorse. Humbaba is awesome and dangerous, but killing him, stealing his tusks, and felling his cedars are momentous acts, not done without prevarication, pity, and shame. The forest is a "Heart of Darkness" presenting contemporary moral dilemmas. May invaders kill a ruler and steal his resources in the name of civilization? The episode expresses the heroes' ambivalence to the destruction of the forest. "My friend," says Enkidu to Gilgamesh, "we have reduced the forest to a wasteland; how shall we answer our gods at home?" The gods accounted the slaughter of Humbaba a sin, one reason why, eventually, Enkidu must die.

Alabaster statue from Sargon II's palace at Khorsabad, Northern Iraq (eighth century BCE), supposedly depicting Gilgamesh, King of Uruk.

Enkidu's death precipitates in Gilgamesh an unbearable grief, but also a terrible fear for himself. Must he, too, die like his friend? He travels to the ends of the earth in search of the only man known to have escaped the mortal doom that the gods laid on humankind after the great flood. The scenes are truly bizarre: a mountain-top cave whose entrance is guarded by monstrous beings, part human, part scorpion; a magic garden where trees and their fruits are precious stones; a grove where docks a ferry whose crew of stone propel it across the Waters of Death.

The poet uses imaginary landscapes to confront his hero with realities that looked unproblematic from home, things that were easier said than done. The poem's end brings the audience back to the familiar city of Uruk. Enclosed within its wall the observer can see the multifarious activities of mankind and know that, while the individual perishes, the race is eternal. To understand this simple truth, Gilgamesh had first to acquire wisdom in exotic and imaginary places.

HOMER

THE ODYSSEY (C.725–675 BCE)

One of the most celebrated and influential stories ever told, this epic poem describes Odysseus's long voyage home, beset by fantastical creatures and mythic foes in a grand evocation of the human journey through life.

The oldest known works of European literature are the Greek epics the *Iliad* and *The Odyssey*. Nothing is known for sure about their author, known from antiquity as "Homer." Many places have claimed the honor of his birth, including the island of Chios, a few miles off the coast of Asia Minor, but he may also have come from the mainland, in what is now Turkey. The poems were first written down in Athens in the sixth century BCE, but were orally composed probably two centuries earlier, while the events they describe—the Greek expedition against Troy and the hero Odysseus's return from it—are set in an age even older, before the fall of the great civilizations of Crete and Mycenae.

The main subject of the poem is the journey home of the Greek hero Odysseus after the fall of Troy. He is away so long (the war itself lasts ten years and the voyage another ten) that it is assumed he is dead, but his wife Penelope remains faithful and fends off an army of suitors.

Odysseus recounts eleven different adventures, as well as his long detention on the island of the nymph Calypso. The third is his encounter with the Cyclops Polyphemus. The one-eyed giant–shepherd captures the hero and his companions by trapping them with his sheep in his cave, which is closed every evening by an enormous rock. Polyphemus eats one or more of the companions every night. Odysseus and his men cannot kill the giant, because they need him to roll the stone aside in the morning; so Odysseus takes an olive branch, sharpens it, and—having given Polyphemus strong wine to make him sleep—drives it into the giant's eye. In the morning, the blinded giant rolls the stone aside to let his sheep out, and Odysseus and his men escape, clinging to the underside of the sheep as Polyphemus runs his hands over them.

In another version that must have predated Homer, the giant roasts his victims on an iron spit and Odysseus uses that to blind him. This other version seems to run a little more naturally and hints of it within Homer serve to illustrate that he was not inventing the story, but repeating it, and likely conflating details from various versions as he did so.

Several of Odysseus's other adventures have the same sort of ancestry. The story of the Cyclops is followed by that of Aeolus, who gives Odysseus a magic bag of winds to help him on his journey. This works well until—as in many versions of the tale—the disobedient crew decide to open the bag to see what's in it. Odysseus is blown back to the land of the Laestrygonians, another set of cannibal giants, where his ship is the only one to escape as the giants hurl stones into the bay. Homer then tells the tale of Circe, the witch who turns men into swine. Odysseus's crew is transformed, but he rescues them, protected by the magic herb "moly," which is brought to him by Hermes, messenger of the gods, by order of Odysseus's protector, the goddess Athene.

Homer not only drew upon handed-down myths, but also delved into accounts of foreign lands brought back by early Greek travelers. In Homer's time, Greeks were already familiar with the Near Eastern coastline, from Turkey to Egypt, and were probing east into the Black Sea, and west across the Mediterranean to Italy and even Spain. There are traces of all these, locations suitably exaggerated and embroidered, in Odysseus's long narration, and scholars have tried for many centuries to pin down exact references.

One clear case is Odysseus's tale of "the Lotus-eaters." These are perfectly harmless themselves, but anyone who eats the lotus-fruit loses all interest in anything else and no longer wants to return home. There is a hint here of the traditional fairy-tale caution against eating or drinking in unknown climes, but the fruit of two kinds of lotus are eaten in both India and Egypt and

Jacob Jordaens,
*Odysseus in the Cave
of Polyphemus*, 1635.

Homer had probably heard of the latter. When Circe gives Odysseus sailing directions, she warns him against "the Clashing Rocks" and says specifically that the only ship ever to traverse them was the *Argo* commanded by Jason. Homer knew, then, of the voyage of the Argonauts to find the Golden Fleece, which has often been explained as a trip into the then-unknown waters of the Black Sea, where the inhabitants used sheepskins to pan for gold.

Circe also warns about the twin dangers of Scylla and Charybdis. Scylla is a barking, many-headed monster who snatches sailors from her cliff, while those who steer to avoid her run the risk of the giant maelstrom Charybdis, which would suck their ship down. The currents in the Straits of Messina between Italy and Sicily still create whirlpools dangerous to small craft, and Scilla is still the name of a village on the facing Italian shore, by cliffs honeycombed with caves, where the wind creates strange cries. The Sirens, who draw men to destruction by their song, have often been located not far off in the Bay of Capri; Odysseus survives them by plugging his sailors' ears with beeswax, having himself lashed to the mast, and ordering them not to release him no matter how hard he struggles.

The gods of Greek myth play a prominent and active part in Homer's imaginary world in both *The Iliad* and *The Odyssey*. Poseidon the sea-god persecutes Odysseus for blinding his son Polyphemus, and Helios the sun god troubles them, too, because Odysseus's men ate his sacred oxen. He is, however, protected by Athene, who intercedes for him with the supreme deity Zeus, and sends her messenger Hermes to guide and advise him and his son Telemachus. Humans, nymphs, gods, and goddesses interact on a basis, not of equality, but something closer to it than in later mythologies. The deities appear as a constant presence in heroic life.

Study of the Homeric poems has formed the basis of a Classical education from postmedieval Europe to the present day. Their poetic power, arguably never matched in almost 3,000 years, has had a perennial and immeasurable influence on Western art and literature. The stories have infiltrated numerous works of celebrated literature; Dante, for example, revisits the tale in *The Divine Comedy* (c.1308–21, page 40), but perhaps the greatest evocation in the twentieth century belongs to James Joyce's modernist masterpiece *Ulysses*, which assigns a chapter to each adventure in *The Odyssey*.

John William Waterhouse, *Circe Offering the Cup to Ulysses*, 1891.

METAMORPHOSES (c.8)

Ovid's fifteen-book poem weaves a kaleidoscope of colorful narratives from Greek and Roman myths on the theme of change and transformation, in which the fates of both man and gods echo the never-ending mutability of life itself.

Metamorphoses contains fifteen books and covers more than 250 myths.

In CE 8 Ovid was banished from Rome and exiled to what is now Romania for reasons that remain unclear.

Metamorphoses was first printed in English by William Caxton in 1480.

Opposite: Michelangelo da Caravaggio, *Narcissus*, 1599.

Overleaf: Titian, *Perseus and Andromeda*, c.1554–56.

The *Metamorphoses* of Publius Ovidius Naso (43 BCE–CE 17/18), or Ovid, is a long Latin poem of almost 12,000 lines. It was written in the first years of the Christian era, and completed about CE 8. Each book tells stories—more than a hundred in total, casually linked and with no obvious chronological order—which together form our best surviving guide to the world of Greek and Roman mythology.

It is, however, a skewed selection, for Ovid announces that he purposefully chose stories that ended in metamorphosis or transformation. Many of these remain familiar, and have even brought words to modern language. The story of Echo and Narcissus, in Book III, tells of how the nymph Echo was punished by the goddess Juno for continually delaying her with chatter while Juno was trying to catch her husband Jupiter with other nymphs. She decreed that from then on Echo would only be able to repeat the last few words of whatever was said to her. Echo fell in love with the handsome boy Narcissus, who scorned her, and she wasted away until only her voice was left—leaving only the "echo" we know today. Narcissus was then in turn cursed to fall in love only with himself, which he did gazing at his own reflection in a pool until he too wasted away, and his body turned into a flower—a bloom that we still call the narcissus. One more character name that has become a modern word is that of the youth Hermaphroditus. The water nymph (or Naiad) Salmacis fell in love with him, came upon him while bathing, and dived in to join him. Her embrace was so fierce that they fused together, becoming both male and female—a "hermaphrodite."

These three stories show several things about the world of the *Metamorphoses*. It is a Mediterranean world, but seems much lusher, greener, and far less populated than the one we know. Events commonly take place in the forest, by streams, and pools, where gods and men hunt deer and boar. And in this world humans and divinities mix freely, along with the nymphs, fauns, and goat-legged satyrs that populate the tales. Furthermore, most of the stories are love stories, and the most powerful deity in the *Metamorphoses* seems not to be Jupiter, father of gods and men, but Amor—a

personification-turned-deity, who rules all the others and continually involves them in frustration, disaster, or disgrace.

The work also contains extended hero stories, such as those of Perseus, son of Jupiter and Danaë; the Athenian Theseus, conqueror of the Minotaur; Jason the Argonaut and his disastrous affair with the Thessalian witch Medea; and Hercules, Orpheus, Aeneas, and Romulus and Remus, the founders of Rome. Near the end, Ovid includes some judicious flattery, introducing Julius Caesar and the Emperor Augustus himself.

Many of Ovid's heroes are still the subject of film and literary adaptations today and persist as household names—and naturally so are the monsters that they must defeat. Perseus must battle the snake-haired Gorgon Medusa, whose eyes can turn men to stone. A feat he follows up by rescuing the maiden Andromeda from the Godzilla-like sea-monster Cetus. Theseus defeats the bull-headed Minotaur and is also involved in the wedding feast turned bloody battle between Lapiths and Centaurs, the latter half-horse, half-man. Among the many feats of Hercules are the chaining of Cerberus, the three-headed dog who guards the gates of Hell.

The irreverence of Ovid's tales caused anger and uncertainty among pious pagans of his own time (and pious Christians in later eras); he was eventually exiled to the shores of the Black Sea by the Emperor Augustus. Another response to the *Metamorphoses*, however, was to regard the whole collection as an allegory that would teach morality, resulting in the medieval French *Ovide Moralisé*, or "Moralized Ovid," the form in which the work was best known throughout the Middle Ages and into the Renaissance.

The overall effect of the work has been incalculable. In one form or another, often censored or allegorized, his stories became part of the school curriculum for many centuries. Chaucer's poem *The House of Fame* derives from Ovid's home of Fama (the source of all rumor), while *The Manciple's Tale* derives from the story of Phoebus and the crow. Shakespeare's poem "Venus and Adonis" draws on several stories from the *Metamorphoses*. In *A Midsummer Night's Dream* the comic workmen attempt to put on their play of Pyramus and Thisbe before Theseus and his Amazon bride-to-be, Hippolyta.

Ovid's dramatic and provocative scenes also made him a favorite for painters, including Caravaggio, Tiepolo, and Velázquez. In the sixteenth century, Titian painted *Diana and Actaeon* and *Diana and Callisto*, while in the seventeenth century Rembrandt chose *The Rape of Ganymede* and *The Abduction of Europa*. In England, in the nineteenth and early twentieth century, John Waterhouse more decorously painted *Circe* and *Thisbe*.

In later years the stories that draw on Ovid are too numerous to list, especially when mingled with second- or third-hand references. C. S. Lewis's *The Lion, the Witch, and the Wardrobe* (1950, page 178) for example, mentions fauns, dryads, centaurs, the god Bacchus, and the goddess Pomona. George Bernard Shaw's play *Pygmalion* (1912)—inspired by Ovid's tale of a king who fell in love with a statue—later became the 1964 musical *My Fair Lady*. And in the twenty-first century, J. K. Rowling draws heavily from Ovid's mythology

in the Harry Potter series (1997–2007, see page 272): Dudley Dursley sprouts the tail of a pig, Centaurs roam the Forbidden Forest, and a three-headed dog ("Fluffy") guards the Philosopher's Stone, to name but three examples.

> My soul would sing of metamorphoses.
> But since, o gods, you were the source of these
> bodies becoming other bodies, breathe
> your breath into my book of changes: may
> the song I sing be seamless as its way
> weaves from the world's beginning to our day. (1:1–5)

ANONYMOUS

BEOWULF (C.700–1100)

The oldest surviving epic poem in Old English centers on three battles pitting the Scandinavian hero Beowulf against monstrous giants and a dragon in a classic depiction of the ambiguous triumph of good over evil.

The full poem, more than 3,000 lines, survives as a single manuscript located in the British Library, London. Opinions on its exact age vary, but the manuscript must be approximately 1,000 years old.

There have been numerous translations of the text, including a recent well-known example by Seamus Heaney, then Nobel laureate in Literature, which won the Whitbread Book of Year Award in 1999.

The 3,000 lines of the epic poem *Beowulf* (composed in Old English between the eighth and eleventh centuries CE) are dense with meaning and give rise to multiple interpretations; some see early appreciation of Christian values, while others observe a gripping tale of pagan heroism. Its position in the canon of English literature, however, is in no small part due to the novelist and scholar J. R. R. Tolkien, who argued the poem's powerful value as a work of art to the British Academy in 1936.

Beowulf is set in southern Scandinavia around CE 400 to 600, at the start of the Dark Ages and at the heart of the Northern Heroic Age. As such, *Beowulf* is a period piece, and readers today listen in on a sophisticated tale told to a Christian Anglo-Saxon audience about their heroic, pagan predecessors living in violent lands terrorized by warrior bands and (sometimes) monsters. In the world of the poem, the monstrous Grendel, his vengeful mother, and the dragon are characters as real as Beowulf; for audiences more recent than the Dark Ages, these monsters remain "fantastically real" but take on symbolic possibilities. We are told that Grendel and his mother are descendants of the biblical first murderer, Cain; and for educated Christian listeners the terrifying dragon might suggest "that ancient serpent" described in Revelation 20:2, "who is the devil and Satan."

The poem also alludes to history and legends that audience members would have known well, and looks back to a time of military aristocracy where a real man is a professional warrior who serves and protects his lord, a lord who protects him in turn and equitably distributes the bloodily won loot. In the twenty-first century, we have not outgrown warlords, nor social ranks nor machismo, but we may look back at Norse- and Germanic-age heroes as being part of a time of both barbaric splendor and squalor. At the courts of King Alfred the Great (CE 849–99) or King Canute (CE 99–1035), Beowulf would have described a world that was still familiar, but more parochial and basic (and more bothered by monsters).

The first great battle of the poem sees Beowulf, a prince of the Geats (a northern Germanic tribe occupying part of what is now Sweden) defeat the horrifying Grendel who has terrorized a neighboring land ruled by King Hrothgar. After the defeat, there is much celebrating in King Hrothgar's great hall, Heorot, but Grendel's mother (never awarded her own name) wreaks a brutal attack on the hall in revenge for her son's death. Beowulf once again seeks out and slays the monster in the poem's second battle and his bravery is rewarded with gifts and celebration from Hrothgar's people. Beowulf's grand heroic actions, however, are set against a background of human betrayal and warfare that will eventually destroy Heorot and Hrothgar's dynasty.

In the final episode, fifty years later, when Beowulf is now King of the Geats, a dragon attacks his kingdom. Against good advice, Beowulf chooses to fight the dragon alone. When he falters, only one of his followers, Wiglaf, comes to his aid. At that exciting moment, the poem pauses to remind listeners of the history of Wiglaf's sword—inherited from his father, Weohstan, who had taken it and other war gear, from the body of a Swedish prince he killed in battle—and hints at a feud between the Swedish king and whoever owns the sword, shield, and armor. The action then resumes for Beowulf to kill the dragon, but leaves Beowulf mortally wounded.

A twentieth-century interpretation of Beowulf slaying the dragon.

Wiglaf succeeds Beowulf, and in the conclusion of the poem it's clear that in addition to traditional Swedish hatred of the Geats, now made personal against Wiglaf, there is the enmity of the powerful Franks, attacked by Beowulf's predecessor. Like Beowulf's heroism and generosity, Wiglaf's will be futile; like Heorot and Hrothgar's line, the Geats are also doomed.

The poem ends as it begins, with a pagan funeral, this time Beowulf's: mourned as mild and good, a heroic warrior of the old time, striving for fame. But Beowulf's heroic deeds in life will be undone, and in any life to come he may be damned as a pagan, of all men *lofgeornost* (the last word of the poem): proudly, hence sinfully (for hard-nose Christians), yearning for glory.

In the worlds of poem and poet, Beowulf in his doomed struggles may be the purest of heroes; in present debates whether one can be a hero and lose, in popular cultures awash in flawed (super)heroes—for us, too, *Beowulf* remains relevant.

ANONYMOUS

THE THOUSAND AND ONE NIGHTS (c.700–947)

This vastly influential collection of folktales was compiled more than 1,000 years ago and is framed by the narrative of King Shahriyar and the many tales told by his wife Shahrazad.

The Oriental Institute at the University of Chicago holds the earliest example of the tales in manuscript.

It is one of the oldest existing Arabic literary manuscripts. A legal document over-written on one side of the manuscript gives a likely date of CE 879.

Spellings for King Shahriyar and Shahrazad (or Shahryar and Scheherazade) vary in English transliterations, and there is still some dispute between scholars over which is more accurate.

The Thousand and One Nights, or *The Arabian Nights* (the first English translation, 1706), is a compilation of tales from many sources—Persian, Indian, Chinese, and Egyptian—put together in Arabic more than a thousand years ago. It first became known in Europe when Antoine Galland published a twelve-volume French translation between 1704 and 1717. The best-known English version, by the explorer Sir Richard Burton, came out in sixteen volumes between 1885 and 1888. Two of the most famous tales in the collection, "Aladdin's Lamp" and "Ali Baba and the Forty Thieves," were added by Galland, who claimed to have been told them by a Syrian storyteller named Hanna Diab. They appear to be genuine Middle Eastern folktales, so his claim is probably true, and they are now regularly added to translations.

When the collection first became known in Europe, it struck its audience as completely novel on many levels. The framing concept sees King Shahriyar, horrified by the infidelity of his wife, deciding that the only way to be safe from female betrayal is to marry a virgin every evening, and have her executed the next morning. He continues this custom until Shahrazad, or Scheherazade, the wily daughter of the king's vizier (a high official), hits on a plan. Every night she begins to tell a story, but leaves it unfinished, so that her life is spared until the next day to complete the tale, whereupon she begins another one. Often tales are inserted one inside the other, so that endings continually recede, although in the end, after a thousand and one nights (and three children) Shahrazad persuades Shahriyar to trust her and spare her life permanently.

From the start we are in a world of despotic power and cruelty, but also enormous wealth and generosity. Kings and Caliphs award thousands of gold pieces and camel-loads of treasure to deserving young men, so much money sometimes that "no-one could count it but God." A merchant may spend a million dinars in pursuit of a beautiful woman and bankrupt himself, to be saved by a turn of fortune that brings him a sack of jewels, and among the jewels a magic amulet, priceless because it holds the cure of the daughter of the king of India (tales 946–52).

Wealth is abundant even on a less miraculous level, for the tales are set within the immense civilization of medieval Islam, with its connections to Africa, India, China, and Central Asia, and its great cities of Cairo, Damascus, Aleppo, Basra, and above all Baghdad, home of the Caliphs, where city markets are stuffed with goods of which Europeans in Galland's time had barely heard: quinces, peaches, jasmine from Syria, raisins of Tihama, pomegranate blooms, and pistachios.

Also totally novel to Westerners, and perhaps even more influential for imitators of the *Nights*, was the cast of supernatural creatures who figure continually. Shahrazad's first tale begins with a fearsome *'ifrit*, who appears with a drawn sword to kill a merchant who has carelessly thrown away the pit of a date. Other menaces include the man-eating tomb-haunting *ghuls*, all too capable of disguising themselves as beautiful women, or even *houris*, the nymphs of the Muslim Paradise. But most prominent of all in the tales are the *jinn*, or genies, often trapped inside a lamp or bottle or ring, and when released bound to fulfill every wish of their new master. Sometimes the power that constrained them was that of the great magician Suleiman, in whom Christians could recognize the Old Testament's King Solomon, son of David.

"The Seven Voyages of Sindbad the Sailor" (tales 536–66) introduced the *rukh*, or roc, a bird so enormous it caught elephants to feed its chicks, as well as the elephants' graveyard from which Sindbad takes a fortune in ivory. In his travels across the Indian Ocean, Sindbad also encounters a diamond mountain, the City of the Apes, giants and cannibals, and the Old Man of the Sea. Oddly enough the magic carpets—now a classic component of Middle Eastern tales—appear only fleetingly in the *Nights*.

The final and most alluring novelty for eighteenth- and nineteenth-century Western readers, was the presentation of sex and love. Every king, caliph, emir, and vizier has his harem of beautiful wives and concubines, graceful as gazelles, with their eunuch guards. The ladies, however, do not seem to be strictly cloistered and are as passionate for adventure as their admirers—which, of course, is what causes King Shahriyar's murderous custom. Both men and women fall in love readily and, far more than in medieval European tales, consummate their love without feelings of guilt. Although respect for the Prophet and the Koran is everywhere in *Nights*, expressed even by the *jinn* and the creatures of the sea, the characters' religious devotion contains nothing of the asceticism that often accompanies Christian piety. While women are in theory controlled and all but enslaved, their intelligence often gives them the upper hand.

One final charm is the elaborate style in which the tales are told and in which the characters speak. The tales are studded with poetry and with set-piece descriptions using rhyme and rhythm, much appreciated in Arabic culture, all of which translators have struggled to reproduce.

The *Nights* soon became as familiar to Western children, in censored and selected form, as "Jack and the Beanstalk" or "Cinderella." Many classical authors mention them, from Stendhal to Tolstoy. Dickens makes several explicit references to them, and his London, where disguised figures walk the streets and uncover strange tales, seems a transmuted Baghdad, as is the London of Robert Louis Stevenson's *New Arabian Nights* (1882). The Brontë family was especially fond of a moralized version of some of the tales, published as *Tales of the Genii* by James Ridley in 1764.

The effect of the *Nights* on children's literature has probably been even greater than on the classics. *Aladdin* is now a staple of children's theater, and everyone knows "Open Sesame" and Sindbad the sailor. E. E. Nesbit's trilogy, *Five Children and It* (1902), *The Phoenix and the Carpet* (1904), and *The Story of the Amulet* (1906), uses props derived from the *Nights*, although the Psammead is her own invention. C. S. Lewis's *The Horse and His Boy* (1954) starts like a tale from the *Nights* with a poor fisherman called Arsheesh, and the hot country of Calormen to the south of Narnia, with its despotic ruler, groveling vizier, and insincerely flowery language, is a parodic version of the *Nights*'s Arabia. The world of the *Nights* is now so familiar that references to it may be third-hand, or even more indirect. It has become as much a part of Western popular culture as Middle-earth or Sherwood Forest.

As a result of its popularity *Nights* has inspired many film adaptations, including three versions of *The Thief of Baghdad* (1924, 1940, 1978), and the animated *Seventh Voyage of Sinbad* (1958). The most successful was Disney's *Aladdin* of 1992, which won two Oscars. In recent years Salman Rushdie has turned to the treasure trove of *Nights*, causing Ursula K. Le Guin to remark of his *Two Years Eight Months and Twenty-Eight Nights* (2015, page 308): "Rushdie is our Scheherazade."

An hour before daybreak Dinarzade awoke, and exclaimed, as
she had promised, "My dear sister, if you are not asleep, tell me
I pray you, before the sun rises, one of your charming stories.
It is the last time that I shall have the pleasure of hearing you."
Shahrazad did not answer her sister, but turned to the Sultan.
"Will your highness permit me to do as my sister asks?" said she.
"Willingly," he answered. So Shahrazad began . . .

THE MABINOGION
(12th–14th century)

A blend of Celtic mythology and Arthurian legend in eleven atmospheric tales, playing out in the forests and valleys of Wales as well as the shadowy "otherworld," where dragons and giants roam, and virtuous heroes quest for honor.

The tales of *The Mabinogion* were preserved in the *White Book of Rhydderch* (mid-thirteenth century, now in the National Library of Wales) and the *Red Book of Hergest,* (c.1382–1410, now held in the manuscript collection of Jesus College, Oxford).

Lady Charlotte Guest's (1812–95, below) translation of *The Mabinogion* became the standard for nearly a century. The first volume was published in 1838, and by 1845 the tales had appeared in seven parts.

The Mabinogion (mabbi-*nogue*-yon) is the name given to a collection of eleven medieval Welsh tales, which form our best guide to the world of early Welsh mythology. The manuscript dates from the fourteenth century, but the stories themselves were composed well before that. The meaning of *Mabinogion* is not known, and the word may be an old scribal error. It was probably intended to mean "tales of youth," a Welsh equivalent of the French *enfances*. Some have suggested the word *mabinogi* may have meant "tales of Maponos," the mythological Divine Son, who perhaps underlies the figure of the hero Pryderi in some of the stories.

In the world of *The Mabinogion*, myth and legend co-exist with history and reality, and they are not easy to tell apart. The geographical world of the tales looks like medieval Wales, divided into separate kingdoms such as Gwynedd, Powys, and Dyfed, but this imagined Wales also contains giants, monsters, and strange beasts, and is in contact with supernatural dimensions.

The society, meanwhile, is that of the medieval Welsh aristocracy—still independent and unconquered by English or Normans, proud of their native traditions as sung or told by bards—and their sense of history reaches back surprisingly far. In "The Dream of Macsen Wledig," Macsen is thought to be the Roman general Maximus, who led his British legions into Gaul in CE 383 to fight unsuccessfully for the imperial throne. The Welsh tale makes him an Emperor of Rome, who originally came to Britain led by a vision of a beautiful Welsh princess.

Two other tales are stories of Arthurian legend. "Culhwch and Olwen" tells how Arthur assisted his cousin Culhwch in winning the daughter of the chief giant Ysbaddaden, by acquiring an extensive list of magic objects, including the blood of the Black Witch of the Valley of Grief; the comb and shears between the ears of Twrch Trwyth, the giant boar; and a leash made from the beard of Dillus the Bearded, to hold the hounds that hunt the boar. Both "Culhwch" and "The Dream of Rhonabwy" list many members of Arthur's court, including some who became widely known, such as Cei (Sir Kay), already as disobliging as he is in later stories.

A detail from *Kilhwych* [Culhwch], *The King's Son* by Joseph Gaskin, 1901. Culhwch employs the help of his cousin Arthur in order to secure the hand of the beautiful Olwen, daughter of the chief giant Ysbaddaden.

Pride of place, however, must go to the four tales designated as the four "branches" of the *mabinogi*, loosely connected by the hero Pryderi. Their humor and imagination set them apart from any other wonder-tales known anywhere in the world. Their characters are paradoxical: passionate but polite, wordy and taciturn courteous but rough. Women are valued highly and treated respectfully, but when the lady Rhiannon is falsely accused of murdering her son (who will become the hero Pryderi, and has actually been carried off by a giant claw) her punishment is to sit by a mounting-block and carry visitors on her back to the court. She is later exonerated, but such vulgarities would likely have been forgotten in later courtly romance tales.

With their cast of colorful characters, high drama, philosophy, and romance, it is no surprise these Celtic stories have proved an irresistible inspiration, first to French romancers and then through eight centuries of further storytellers. The stories are especially treasured in Wales as foundations of national culture. They have been retold in novelistic form several times in recent years, in Lloyd Alexander's six-volume *Chronicles of Prydain* (1964–73) and in Evangeline Walton's four-volume sequence begun with *Prince of Annwn* (1970) and re-issued as *The Mabinogion Tetralogy* in 2002. Alan Garner's *Owl Service* (1967) retells the tragic love-story of Lleu, Gronw, and Blodeuwedd, with a happier ending.

SNORRI STURLUSON

THE PROSE EDDA (c.1220)

A remarkable written preservation of Norse mythology, detailing the adventures of gods, heroes, warrior kings and queens, giants, dwarves, and elves. It is the most renowned and influential work of all Scandinavian literature.

Seven manuscripts of *The Prose Edda* still survive —six from the Middle Ages and one from 1666 (above).

As no manuscript is complete, *The Prose Edda* has been pieced together over many years.

A statue of Snorri Sturluson (below) by Gustav Vigeland was gifted to the Icelandic nation in 1947 by the Norwegian government, and is located at Reykholt.

Opposite: A seventeenth-century illustration depicting Odin, with his two crows, Hugin (thought) and Munin (memory).

Iceland had been Christian for two centuries by the time of Snorri Sturluson (1179–1241), and the old pagan traditions were fading. Snorri's main purpose in writing *The Prose Edda* was to provide a guide to poetic diction and allusion for future poets. He drew on and quoted older poems, both heroic and mythological, of which many survive as a group called *The Poetic Edda*.

Snorri's text describes a variety of interrelated worlds: The gods (or Æsir) live in Asgard; the giants in Jötunheim; Svartalfaheim is home to the dwarfs; Alfheim is where the "light-elves" live; and Niflheim is a dark world of primeval chaos. The world of humans is a flat disk encircled by ocean, with girdling walls erected by the gods to keep out the giants, called *Mithgarthr* in Old Norse, usually Anglicized as Midgard. At the center of the cosmos is the great ash-tree Yggdrasil. Its three roots extend to Asgard, to Niflheim, and to the land of the frost-giants. In the ocean around Midgard lives the dreaded Midgard Serpent, also known as Iörmungand.

Perhaps the most striking thing about this Northern cosmology is its sense of grim threat. The dragon Nidhögg eternally gnaws the root of Yggdrasil. The squirrel Ratatosk runs up and down conveying messages of hate and defiance between Nidhögg at the bottom and an eagle at the top. The sun and moon move across the sky constantly pursued by two great wolves called Sköll and Hati: and one day it is expected that they will catch up. Gods and men are under constant threat from the monster-world, and this will end in Ragnarök, "the doom of the gods," when gods and heroes will fight a final battle against the giants and the monsters—and it is known to all that they will lose, hoping only to lose gallantly and destructively.

Furthermore, the universe of *The Prose Edda* is one of moral neutrality, or even moral indifference. Humans are on the gods' side against the monsters, but no one can trust Odin, the All-Father, who betrays heroes on the battlefield in order to bring them to Valhalla and swell his armies. Thor, the thunder-god, and Frey, a god of fertility, may seem friendlier, but another lurking presence among the Æsir is the god Loki, who continually brings trouble.

i tueir ok þr̄. en þi heto þicta m̄ oskyllt ar hā . neā kuez̄ set
an here h̄ran þyrnir heið þyrnir leþr hrioð vid blaiñ.
þnıñ s̄t keña himinin. kalla h ỹnuſ hauſ z erpið z bꝩre
dꝛꝩst hrahm auftra veſtra noꝛꝥa supꝛa . ꝥ ſolar z uñgls
z himtugla var ꝥa enuezꝛa hꝛalꝛ . . hꝩ lopꝺz z uꝛbar

Heſſ ero noꝛꝩ ſtundana . aulld ꝺçtum
alldc. þꝩr � longu. opiſſerꝛ. uecꝺ ſumar hauſt var manꝺꝺ . uika
ꝛ nor oçꝛgin artañ. olld arla. ſneꝺma ſibla. Iſiñ pyꝛꝛ dag
necꝺ igeꝛ ꝛꝛaþerꝺ   ſi cꝺ here nœtruꝛa̅r ı ꝺluiſ malum
þc hcꝺ mꝩ mꝩn. þriota helio. kallud er grima mꝩ gupꝺ . oldg
kalla rœꝛaꝛ. Qꝛar ſuꝛꝛngaiꝛan ꝺluar ꝺꝛauim
 b̄ unꝺgſt narıñ muluñ mꝩluñ ny hꝩꝥ arꝺlt
þengꝛor kloꝛ ſꝩꝩndir ſkoalgꝛ ſkranir.
Sꝩol ſeꝛꝛa aꝛaubull eꝛaloa an ſkip ſyin þaꝺ hꝩel lıno ſtan
ꝺuilõſteıꝛa alþꝛaubull . hũıg ſt keña ſol kalla hꝺꝺuꝛ
munꝺulþeꝛa . ꝺ mana . koıꝛ olcſ ellde hıꝛꝛꝥ z lꝩꝩꝥ

Heꝛuıꝛꝛ
cıaıꝛꝯ
ꝺon hꝩꝥ

The other side of Norse myth, surprisingly, is its sense of (sometimes cruel) humor. Thor, with his powerful hammer, Mjöllnir, which always returns to his hand, is at once the hero and the butt of several tales. Snorri gives an extended account of the visit made by Thor and Loki to the giant Utgarda-Loki. The giant challenges Thor to an easy test of strength. He is asked to drain a drinking-horn, but fails even after three drafts; to pick a cat off the floor, but can only raise one of its paws; and to wrestle with an old woman called Elli, who forces him to one knee. Thor is humiliated, but the tests were not as they seem. The drinking horn was connected to the ocean, and Thor has just created the tides. The cat was really the Midgard Serpent, and the old woman's name, Elli, means "Old Age," which as the Eddic poem *Hávamál* says, "gives no-one mercy."

Snorri tells some twenty stories of this nature in *The Prose Edda*. The most influential of them in the modern world is the long tale of the Völsungs and the Nibelungs. The tale centers on a ring belonging to the Nibelungs, which Loki extorts from the dwarf Andvari in order to pay restitution to the giant Hreidmar (Loki having mistakenly killed and flayed Hreidmar's son, Otr, when he was in the form of an otter). The ensuing story of the ring brings in the dragon Fafnir, the hero Sigurd, and eventually the historical kings of the Burgundians, wiped out by the Huns in the year 437. Richard Wagner famously re-created the story in his four-opera cycle *Der Ring des Nibelungen* (1876, see page 96), and J. R. R. Tolkien attempted to re-create the lost original poetic version—on which he thought all others must have been based—in his posthumously published *Legend of Sigurd and Gudrún* (2009).

The fact that the legend caught the imagination of the greatest re-workers of medieval themes in both the nineteenth and twentieth centuries testifies to its abiding power. Indeed, the whole mythology of *The Prose Edda* has since become a favorite source for authors of fantasy. Tolkien's Middle-earth represents his highly eclectic re-imagining of Midgard, with elves, dwarves, and other creatures, but without the pagan gods. A somewhat similar, but independent work by the prominent science-fiction author Poul Anderson, *The Broken Sword* (1954), tells the story of a human changeling brought up by the elves and a half-troll reared by humans, both embroiled in human and also elf-troll warfare unscrupulously fomented by Odin. Northern (and other) deities are brought into the contemporary American world in Neil Gaiman's *American Gods* (2003) and Joanne Harris retells the tale of the ultimate trickster in *The Gospel of Loki* (2014).

The most popular mode of modern retelling has, however, been the comic book industry. Marvel Comics have published more than 600 issues of *The Mighty Thor* since 1962, in which a modern American discovers that he is an avatar of Thor, able to move between our world and the world of Asgard. In 2011 the comic book adventures of Thor and Loki were brought to the big screen by director Kenneth Branagh, and today Northern mythology, once almost forgotten, is probably better known in the Western world than many classical or Biblical myths.

Opposite: A page from a fourteenth-century illustrated manuscript of *The Prose Edda*.

DANTE ALIGHIERI

THE DIVINE COMEDY
(C.1308–21)

Dante's epic poem is celebrated as one of the greatest and most influential works of medieval Europe. This spiritual journey takes us from the darkness of the Inferno to the mountain of Purgatory to Paradise, during which reason and faith bring moral and social chaos into order.

The Biblioteca Riccardiana in the Palazzo Medici Riccardi, Florence, Italy, holds a remarkable manuscript of the *Commedia* containing the complete text of the *Inferno, Purgatorio,* and *Paradiso* written in the hand of Giovanni Boccaccio (1313–75).

Dante wrote in angry criticism of the Florentine government and was permanently exiled from the city around 1308.

La Divina Commedia (The Divine Comedy) was written between 1308 and the poet's death in 1321. It consists of 100 cantos, each around 140 lines, in which Dante travels successively through Hell (*Inferno*), Purgatory (*Purgatorio*), and Heaven (*Paradiso*). The whole work presents the medieval Catholic image of life after death, as codified in the generations before Dante by the great theologians Thomas Aquinas and Bonaventure. Yet Dante's (*c.*1265–1321) particular vision is enriched by his classical learning: His guide through Hell and most of Purgatory is the Roman poet Virgil, who had presented a "descent into Hell" in Book VI of his epic *Aeneid*. And throughout *The Divine Comedy* figures appear from the confused and bloody world of contemporary Italian politics, in which Dante was deeply and dangerously immersed.

Especially haunting to the imagination is Dante's description of Hell, which is famously entered through a gate marked with an inscription ending: "Abandon all hope, you who enter here." Beyond are nine circles in which the punishments that sinners endure are matched to their sins. The lustful are whirled forever around the Second Circle by a mighty wind. Tyrants scald forever in lakes of boiling blood in the Seventh Circle. False prophets in the Eighth Circle shuffle endlessly around, unable to see where they are going because their heads have been turned backward on their shoulders, and Flatterers forever drop filth from their mouths. The Ninth Circle is reserved for the treacherous, with the deepest division named Judecca after Judas Iscariot, the apostle who betrayed Jesus.

Not only sinners are to be found in Hell. Dante also imagines many strange creatures with roles to play there. As in Classical mythology, Charon is the ferryman who takes the souls across the river of Acheron. Minos judges each soul and wraps his tail around them, the number of coils corresponding to the circle to which they are assigned, and flings them to their place. In Canto XII Dante and Virgil meet the centaurs who guard the lake of boiling blood, and who give them further guidance. Very different are the horned demons that plague the barrators (corrupt judges and politicians) in the Eighth Circle. The demons there have names like Evil-tail, Swineface, and

Joseph Anton Koch,
Dante and Virgil Riding on the Back of Geryon, c.1821.

Overleaf: Sandro Botticelli,
The Abyss of Hell, c.1485.

Scratchdog. They haul the sinners out of the boiling pitch with their hooks and are barely under the control of their commanders. The monstrous Geryon carries the travelers down from the Seventh Circle. With a human face, a lion's paws, and a scorpion's poisonous sting in his tail, Geryon is the personification of Fraud.

Purgatory, like Hell, is organized in levels that correspond to the sins being expiated. The stiff-necked proud have their necks weighed down by stones, the envious have their eyes stitched up, the gluttonous are disciplined by thirst and hunger, the lustful learn to greet with no more than a holy kiss. The demons and monsters of Hell are, however, replaced by angel-pilots and guardian angels. Near the peak of Purgatory, Dante enters the earthly Paradise. Here, Virgil cannot enter and must return to First Circle of the virtuous heathen. Dante's guide to the celestial spheres is Beatrice, a personification of theology in the form of idealized beauty. In Heaven, finally, Dante meets those who show the virtues of their spheres. In the sphere of the Sun are the wise and the theologians, Mars has the brave commanders and Jupiter the just rulers, rising upward to the Church Triumphant in the Eighth Sphere, the Angelic Orders in the Ninth, and the Beatific Vision of the Tenth.

The vivid description and poetic craftsmanship of *The Divine Comedy* has ensured that it remains in the collective conscience today. Its influence within Western art and culture is simply immeasurable, inspiring numerous writers, from Chaucer and Milton to Balzac, T. S. Eliot, and Samuel Beckett.

THOMAS MALORY

LE MORTE D'ARTHUR (1485)

Malory's evocative and enthralling text provides the touchstone for all later explorations of Arthurian legend, charting the ancient king's ascendancy to the throne and the adventures of the Knights of the Round Table.

William Caxton, the man who first introduced the printing press to England, printed *Le Morte d'Arthur* in 1485.

The discovery in 1934 of the "Winchester manuscript" (c.1471–81, now held in London's British Library) made it possible to identify Malory as the author of *Le Morte d'Arthur*, who had previously been described only as "a knyght presoner."

There are no known portraits of Malory and the Winchester manuscript is the sole surviving written version of his text.

If there was a historical King Arthur, he would have lived in the centuries after the withdrawal of the Romans from Britain (CE 407), a period for which we have almost no documentation. A Welsh author, writing in Latin and known as Nennius, provides an account of the king that can be dated to around 830, and Arthur is given an impressive, if bogus, biography in Geoffrey of Monmouth's *History of the Kings of Britain* written in the 1130s. The enduring legend of quests, castles, and tournaments that we know so well today, however, was not cemented in the collective imagination until the fifteenth century with Sir Thomas Malory's *Le Morte d'Arthur* (written around 1469 and published in 1485).

Malory's main source was the long sequence of French prose romances known as "the Vulgate Cycle," themselves the culmination of centuries of Arthurian invention. In Malory these monastic works were given a strong personal slant. He was not a monk, but a knight, and seems to have written the *Morte* while in prison for a whole string of violent crimes during an eventful career dating as far back as the 1430s. The extent of his guilt is unknown since his accusers could have been politically motivated—the Wars of the Roses were raging at the time, new grudges were created daily, and ancient affiliations were frequently tested. The work was printed in 1485, and is one of the few medieval English works to have remained continuously familiar ever since.

Le Morte d'Arthur gives us a full account of the whole Arthurian legend, including Arthur's sinful conception, the incestuous birth of his son Mordred, Excalibur the "sword in the stone," Merlin the magician advisor, and introduces the many Knights of the Round Table, among them Sirs Lancelot, Gawain, Geraint, Percival, Bors, Galahad, and Tristan. Despite, or possibly because of, the bloody upheavals, factionism, and opportunism of the Wars of the Roses, there was a strong interest in chivalric legend and history at the time. Arthur's knights were symbolic of virtues—such as loyalty,

bravery, honor, and gallantry—that were seen as being eroded by the political infighting of the Wars.

Yet there is far more to the enduring appeal of Malory's text than contemporary relevance. The tales are filled with a heady mix of prophesy, predestination, sex, danger, and magic; and the bucolic English settings of streams, lakes, meadows, and castles are at once both familiar and strange. In numerous stories the knights arrive at unknown castles where unusual practices and customs are the norm, their virtues are put to the test, and complexity of character is revealed.

The core of the story is the tragic, romantic triangle of Arthur, his wife Guinevere and the noble knight Sir Lancelot, which is made even more strained by the mystical presence of the Grail—the cup that, according to legend, was used by Christ at the Last Supper and in which his blood was collected at the Cross. The Grail mysteriously appears at Camelot, Arthur's

The Arming and Departure of the Knights, a tapestry based on *Le Morte d'Arthur* and designed by Edward Burne-Jones. It was woven by Morris and Co., 1895–6.

¶Chere foloweth the syxth boke of the noble and wozthy pzynce kyng Arthur.

¶How syr Launcelot and syr Lyonell departed fro the courte for to seke auentures / ¶ how syr Lyonell lefte syr Launcelot slepynge ⁊ was taken. Capitulm .j.

Anone after that the noble ⁊ wozthy kyng Arthur was comen fro Rome into Englande / all the knyghtes of the rounde table resozted vnto ð kyng and made many iustes and turneymentes / ⁊ some there were that were good knyghtes / whiche encreased so in armes and wozshyp that they passed al theyr felowes in prowesse ⁊ noble dedes ⁊ that was well pzoued on many. But in especyall it was pzoued on syr Launcelot du lake . Foz in all turneymentes and iustes and dedes of armes / bothe foz lyfe and deth he passed all knyghtes ⁊ at no tyme he was neuer ouercomen but yf it were by treason oz enchauntement. Syr Launcelot encreased so meruaylously in wozshyp ⁊ honour / wherfoze he is the first knyght ð the frensshe booke maketh mencyon of / after that kynge Arthur came from Rome / wherfoze quene Gueneuer had hym in grete fauour aboue all other knyghtes / and certaynly he loued the quene agayne aboue all other ladyes and damoyselles all the dayes of his lyfe / and foz her he court, and provides sustenance for a feast, beginning a series of quests by knights hoping to recover the lost vessel. Lancelot's own attempt to approach the Grail is prevented by a fiery breath and unseen hands: his sinful love for Guinevere has made him unworthy.

Lancelot's relationship with Guinevere then becomes uneasy, as if he blames her for his failure, but she continues to need him as a protector, in circumstances of increasing doubt and guilt. When Sir Mellyagaunce accuses Guinevere of adultery, Lancelot challenges him, which, given Lancelot's prowess, comes close to murder. Finally, Lancelot is caught in Guinevere's room and although he fights his way out, she is sentenced to death. In the rescue he kills his friends, Sir Gawain's brothers Gareth and Gaheris. Gawain vows eternal revenge, the Round Table breaks up, and in the confusion Mordred, Arthur's son and nephew, tries to seize the throne, leading to the Last Battle and Arthur's removal, badly wounded, to Avalon. Lancelot and Guinevere die as penitents.

Christian interpretations of the Grail and Lance compete with pagan ones, which see them as fertility and phallic symbols, and the Christian moral that chivalry is irrevocably made imperfect by lust and pride ran counter to Malory's evident sympathy with his main hero, Sir Lancelot. Malory portrays Lancelot as a man caught between love of Guinevere, loyalty to Arthur, and a desperate attempt to be worthy of the Grail, in all of which endeavors he ultimately fails. The *Morte* is remarkable for its acute psychological insights, expressed in original scenes of great tension.

The legends of Arthur, Merlin, Excalibur, the Lady of the Lake, and the brave and valorous knights continue to be re-told by novelists and by moviemakers. The numerous adaptations range from Mark Twain's fusion of time travel and legend *A Connecticut Yankee in King Arthur's Court* (1889, page 108), to T. H. White's *The Once and Future King* (1958), which reinterprets the story for a postwar audience, and the surreal humor of *Monty Python and the Holy Grail* (1975).

Opposite: A woodcut from Wynkyn de Worde's 1529 edition of Malory's *Le Morte d'Arthur* shows Sir Lancelot competing in a courtly tournament (colored later).

LUDOVICO ARIOSTO

ORLANDO FURIOSO
(C.1516/32)

A playful Renaissance fantasy that adds the theme of passionate love to the old stories of the paladins of Charlemagne, while also employing a host of enchanters, magic rings and lances, hippogriffs, and sea monsters for pure imaginative entertainment.

Ludovico Ariosto was born in Reggio Emilia, but his family moved to Ferrara when he was fourteen. In 1518 Ludovico entered the service of the great patron of the arts, Duke Alfonso d'Este.

Orlando Furioso went through three major revisions or versions (1516, 1521, and 1532) before Ariosto's death in 1533.

The finished version, published in Ferrara in 1532, served as inspiration to Cervantes, Spenser, and Shakespeare.

The main rival to the great cycle of Arthurian romances was the body of legends centered on Charlemagne and his paladins (his foremost knights). Their historical basis is clearer than the Arthurian stories, with the defining incident being the death of Roland, Count of Brittany, at the battle of Roncevaux Pass in 778. The stories never achieved the popularity of the Arthurian legends, and the Italian Renaissance poet Matteo Maria Boiardo (1441?–94) proposed this was because they lacked lust and passion. His long poem *Orlando Innamorato* ("Roland in Love") set out to resolve the issue, but Boiardo died leaving his work incomplete. Around ten years later, the poet Ludovico Ariosto (1474–1533) continued the story in his epic *Orlando Furioso* ("The Frenzy of Roland"), first published in 1516, with a final version in 1532.

The background for the poem is the clash between Christians and Muslims, which had continued in Spain and the Balkans up to the time of both authors. This real-world scenario, however, is overlaid with centuries of magnificent romance and magic. Keeping track of the plot is difficult because it moves at a furious pace, with one narrative thread after another being followed and dropped, frequently in cliff-hanger style. The backdrop of war is offset by honorable missions and magic props, such as the beautiful maiden Angelica's ring that defends her from enchantment; the shining shield of the magician Atlante, which strikes everyone who sees it unconscious; the magic horn of the English paladin Astolfo, which fills all hearers with terror; heroine Bradamante's invincible lance; and Atlante's winged steed the hippogriff, which Ruggiero the pagan champion rides when he rescues Angelica from the "orc" or sea-monster to whom she is to be sacrificed in one of many damsel-in-distress sequences.

The characters' main motivations are love, lust, or infatuation, but these threads are, however, perhaps less significant than the digressions. The poem is designed as pure entertainment, with a constant flow of marvels and surprises. Its world is one where anything can happen, exciting, horrifying, sexually explicit, gruesome, but above all unexpected. Characters may travel anywhere—to Cathay, Taprobane, the Moon, Hell, or a Terrestrial Paradise;

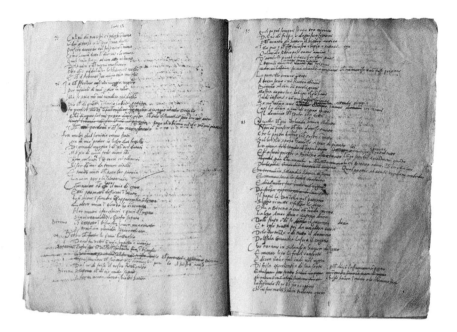

be threatened by demons and monsters, including the terrible creature born of necrophilia in Boiardo's "Castle Cruel"; and are protected or attacked by a gallery of good and bad magicians. The author C. S. Lewis declared that the poem made for ideal convalescent reading: always amusing, light-hearted, and never too difficult or morally taxing—the ancestor of a whole modern genre of romantic fantasy.

Much of the success of *Orlando Furioso* springs from its air of freewheeling irresponsibility, enlivened by constant sexual allusion. In 1591 Sir John Harrington translated an improper tale from canto 28 to amuse the maid-attendants of Queen Elizabeth, was caught by the Queen, and banished from court. The poem proved highly influential to Edmund Spenser's *Faerie Queene* (1590–1609, page 54) and a few years later Shakespeare would find inspiration in it for the plot of *Much Ado About Nothing* (1612). Cervantes also makes reference to *Orlando Furioso* when detailing the romances that have so enchanted *Don Quixote* (1605/15, page 62).

In the twentieth century, the poem inspired the "Incomplete Enchanter" fantasy series written by L. S. de Camp and Fletcher Pratt (1940), in which two American academics gain the ability to travel into imaginary worlds and become magicians. In recent years the novelists Italo Calvino, Jorge Luis Borges, and Salman Rushdie have all turned to Ariosto for inspiration and, more specifically, Chelsea Quinn Yarbro's *Ariosto: Ariosto Furioso, a Romance for an Alternate Renaissance* (1980), also plays with the idea of moving between worlds, including the world of the poem, an imagined Renaissance Italy, and a fantasy America.

The manuscript for *Orlando Furioso* is held by the Biblioteca Comunale Ariostea, Ferrara.

Overleaf: Jean-Auguste-Dominique Ingres, *Ruggiero Rescuing Angelica*, 1819.

THOMAS MORE

UTOPIA (1516)

More's vision of a faraway island where society is perfected and people live in harmony gave rise to the entire genre of Utopian fiction. Utopia, however, means "no place," revealing the work as a criticism of the failings and corruption he observed in society.

Utopia was first published in Louvain, Belgium, in 1516.

More's learning and wit attracted the attention of King Henry VIII, who made him Lord Chancellor in 1529.

He resigned in 1532 when he refused to acknowledge the king as the head of the Church of England and was confined to the Tower of London.

He was beheaded on July 6, 1535, announcing to the crowd that he was dying as "the King's good servant, but God's first."

Utopia, written in 1516 by the English humanist Thomas More (1478–1535), has been so influential as to give its name to an entire literary genre, and the notion of a civilization perfected by social engineering has fascinated writers and artists ever since. More's intentions in creating his idealized land, however, are far from straightforward.

Utopia is divided into two books. The first begins with More on official business in Antwerp, where he is introduced to Raphael Hythlodaeus. Hythlodaeus describes his travels to More and a colleague, and their talk turns to rules of governance and issues such as poverty, the death penalty, and enclosure laws (where arable land is closed off and converted for more profitable sheep farming to the detriment of agricultural workers). In the end, Hythlodaeus announces abruptly that the only satisfactory arrangement is to abolish private property altogether. How this would work is then set out in Book II, as being already practiced by the citizens of Utopia.

Utopia is an island around the same size as England. It has fifty-four towns, all built to the same plan. Citizens live in houses that are all the same, and every ten years they are re-allocated, so no one comes to feel ownership. Farms produce enough food to sustain the entire country. Everyone works, but only for six hours a day. Food is drawn from central stores, and like everything else, is handed over without payment. Everyone wears the same serviceable clothes, silver and gold are despised, and only babies play with jewels.

Later verdicts on the Utopian system have been negative: dull, uniform, harsh, and regimented. Utopians keep domestic or foreign criminals as slaves. Anyone engaging in premarital sex is sentenced to a lifetime of celibacy. Marriage is for life, and adulterers are punished by slavery. Divorce is possible, but only under strict conditions. Utopians are allowed to play, but the games described seem drearily educational. You need a passport to travel inside the country; improper documentation results in enslavement.

These monastic arrangements might have seemed more tolerable in a time when many starved to death or were hanged for theft of food, and where there was little social provision for the poor; but seen through the lens of the

Ambrosius Holbein (elder brother of Hans Holbein, court painter to Henry VIII) made woodcuts for an edition of *Utopia* that was published in Basel in 1518. This detail shows the island's capital Amaurotum ("Mist Town") surrounded by the river Anydrus ("Waterless"). The river's source (*Fons Anydri*) and mouth (*Ostium Anydri*) are labeled.

twenty-first century More's island seems alarmingly totalitarian and authoritarian. More's reason for inventing *Utopia* is a question that has plagued scholars for centuries. More is aware his ideal society could never exist, since the island's name is created from the combination of the Greek words *ou*, "no," and *topos*, "place." *Utopia* is satirical in places, and some of the practices in Utopia, such as euthanasia and married priests, actively contradict More's own Catholic faith. More repeatedly invites comparison between Utopia and the failings of the real world. His overriding purpose is perhaps not to provide an answer, but to ask the simple question: Can we not do better than we do?

H. G. Wells tried to update More in *A Modern Utopia* (1905) and *The Shape of Things to Come* (1933), but his ideas were soon discredited by war and Stalinism. George Orwell's *Nineteen Eighty-Four* (1949, page 174) presents a kind of Communist Utopia gone horribly wrong, while Aldous Huxley's *Brave New World* (1932, page 148) satirizes a consumerist technological utopia. The most thoughtful fictional comment is perhaps Ursula K. Le Guin's *The Dispossessed* (1974), which describes a community that follows many of the rules of More's Utopia, including abolition of money and private property, and which, like More's vision, was triggered by poverty and injustice. But this society is shown as beginning to crumble, unable entirely to suppress human nature.

EDMUND SPENSER

THE FAERIE QUEENE (1590–1609)

An extended allegorical poem by one of the finest writers of Elizabethan England presents a grand vision of an Arthurian courtly landscape populated by the gods and monsters of classical and British legend.

Spenser wrote this long, but still unfinished, poem in honor of Queen Elizabeth I, but, apart from an annual pension awarded by the crown, he received little recognition during his lifetime.

He spent much of his life in Ireland as the English sought to establish rule over the country, but Irish insurgency forced him to flee in 1598 and he returned to England.

After his death in 1598 Spenser's body was interred in Poet's Corner in Westminster Abbey.

In a 1590 letter to his friend Sir Walter Raleigh, Edmund Spenser (1552–98) described how he planned for *The Faerie Queene* to comprise twenty-four books, but the project was never completed. Three books were published in London in 1590 and three more in 1596, with a part of a seventh appearing in 1609, ten years after Spenser's death. All are set in what Spenser calls a "delightfull land of Faery," which combines the castle-studded forests of Malory's *Le Morte d'Arthur* (1485, page 44) with the enchanted whirl of Ariosto's *Orlando Furioso* (c.1516/32, page 48).

Indeed, Spenser's epic poem imitates *Orlando Furioso* in many ways: His maiden-knight Britomart closely resembles Ariosto's heroine Bradamante, and her rescue of Sir Artegall, Spenser's Knight of Justice, parallels Bradamante's rescue of the hero Ruggiero; Ariosto's fair lady Angelica, always seen in flight from would-be ravishers, is echoed by Florimell; and both romances have the same supporting cast of enchanters, giants, dragons, damsels, and tournaments.

There is also a strong influence of English folklore and the Arthurian tradition. Prince Arthur (not yet king) appears in each completed book, along with, in the last of them, the Blatant Beast, modeled on Malory's Questing Beast. In his letter to Raleigh, Spenser claimed to be in the tradition of Homer and Virgil, but an even more prominent debt is owed to the Bible. The hero of Book I for example, the Red Cross Knight, is undeniably emblematic of Saint George, the patron saint of England, but, as Spenser stated in the Raleigh letter, the armor he wears is the "armor of God" (Ephesians 6:10–18). Even without the letter, it is clear that Red Cross represents the idealized Christian, since the book is dedicated to the virtue of Holiness and contains many hints toward religious conflicts such as the defeat of the Spanish Armada in 1588, just two years before Books I–III were published. In addition, Spenser's deceitful sorceress Duessa bears comparison to the Whore of Babylon (Revelations 17) and Protestant commentators saw allegorical parallels between Duessa and the Catholic Mary Queen of Scots.

But full of fire and greedy
hardiment,
The youthfull knight could
not for ought be staide,
But forth vnto the darksome
hole he went,
And looked in: his glistring
armor made
A litle glooming light, much
like a shade,
By which he saw the vgly
monster plaine . . .

Acrasia by John Melhuish Strudwick, 1888. The painting depicts Acrasia, the magical seductress described in Book II with an enchanted knight in the Bower of Bliss.

The Faerie Queene differs from Ariosto in its closer focus and tighter structure, imposed by Spenser's much more serious purpose. Each book has a single virtue personified by a hero or heroine (or a double hero in the form of Cambell and Triamond in Book IV), and their adventures illustrate that virtue and the potential traps that lie in store. In Book II, Sir Guyon, who personifies temperance, goes to the rescue of a young man being beaten by the lunatic Furor. Guyon struggles in the fight until his adviser, the Palmer, tells him he first has to bridle the old hag, named Occasion, who accompanies Furor. The moral being that one can defeat fury by not giving it an opportunity to grow strong.

Spenser's epic is also informed by Classical mythology. The imprisonment of the beauty Florimell beneath the sea by shape-shifting god Proteus resembles the myths of Persephone or Eurydice held in the Underworld. The contemporary philosopher Francis Bacon took Proteus to represent Matter—always ripening, rotting, and returning like fruit on a tree.

The Faerie Queene is remarkable for its descriptions: of the Bower of Bliss, complete with naked damsels and knights-turned-beasts; the Garden of Adonis, a place of pagan amoral fertility; the Dance of the Graces, with its pastoral setting; and the declamations of Change and Nature in the unfinished Book VII. In such colorful, sensuous settings Spenser adds new psychological and emotional depth to the charm of fantasy found in the Italian Orlando romances, as well as an insistent sense that more is meant than meets the eye.

A study for *The Red Cross Knight* (*c*.1793) by John Singleton Copley, in which the knight encounters two personifications of virtue. Faith (left) holds a chalice with a serpent and Hope (right) carries a small anchor.

WU CHENG'EN

JOURNEY TO THE WEST (XIYOUJI) (C.1592)

A late sixteenth-century take on an ancient Chinese legend of dragons, bandits, demons and wizards that adds dazzling layers of comedy and profundity to spiritual wisdom.

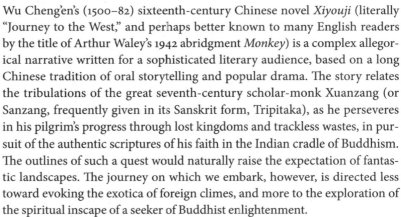

Journey to the West was originally circulated anonymously, and the subject of the text's authorship is still debated.

Centuries later, the tale was made into the television series *Monkey* in 1986, starring Masaaki Sakai in the title role, which has come to be regarded as a cult classic and still enjoys wide popularity.

Wu Cheng'en's (1500–82) sixteenth-century Chinese novel *Xiyouji* (literally "Journey to the West," and perhaps better known to many English readers by the title of Arthur Waley's 1942 abridgment *Monkey*) is a complex allegorical narrative written for a sophisticated literary audience, based on a long Chinese tradition of oral storytelling and popular drama. The story relates the tribulations of the great seventh-century scholar-monk Xuanzang (or Sanzang, frequently given in its Sanskrit form, Tripitaka), as he perseveres in his pilgrim's progress through lost kingdoms and trackless wastes, in pursuit of the authentic scriptures of his faith in the Indian cradle of Buddhism. The outlines of such a quest would naturally raise the expectation of fantastic landscapes. The journey on which we embark, however, is directed less toward evoking the exotica of foreign climes, and more to the exploration of the spiritual inscape of a seeker of Buddhist enlightenment.

If we leap to the conclusion that this allegorization of one of the great peregrinations of human history reflects some sort of cultural blinkers constricting the literary imagination of the "Central Kingdom," we would be quite far from the truth. From a very early time, Chinese readers have been fascinated by the bizarre lands and creatures cataloged in works such as the "Classic of Mountains and Seas" (*Shanhaijing*). In more recent centuries of the late-Imperial period, fictionalized accounts of expeditions to the Chinese periphery continued to cast the spell of unknown lands and peoples. Closer to home, one of the more abiding themes of the Chinese poetic imagination has long been the serendipitous discovery of hidden valleys where people live in perfect peace and harmony, far from the injurious pursuit of fame and wealth in the outside world—perhaps the best known example being Tao Yuanming's "Peach Blossom Spring."

In *Journey to the West*, however, primary literary interest is focused not on the imaginary worlds through which the pilgrims pass, but on the narrative figures that people these lands, both the more "human" inhabitants—from rustic woodcutters to enlightened or benighted kings, and the demonic denizens who typically masquerade as benign rulers in order to ensnare

the unsuspecting monk. As for the lost cities or uncharted wilderness through which our heroes move, these are for the most part fully domesticated in line with the pictorial and iconographic conventions of Ming landscape. These worlds are almost always identified as "mountains," beautiful yet forbidding venues in whose hidden fastnesses and caves there lurk a variety of maleficent forces. With the exception of the topsy-turvy "Kingdom of Women at Xiliang" (where women assume virtually every form of male domination), we get little sense of realms in which alternative modes of existence hold sway, and—with few exceptions—all attention is focused on the evil intentions and bizarre weaponry of their demonic rulers.

One exception to this observation does materialize, however, in the full-blown literary tableau of a lost world of perfection (initially, at least) that is put before our eyes at the very start of the book. Here the narrative of the Tang monk's "epic" journey is prefaced by a series of episodes on the pre-history of the "Monkey King," depicting his spontaneous emergence as the insouciant founder of an enclosed paradise for his monkey-brethren on the "Mountain of Flowers and Fruit," a land of unfettered freedom and undiminished plenty located, quite pointedly, in the "Land of Burgeoning Pride." It is only a matter of time, however, before the hubris of self-containment leads him to abandon his circumscribed existence and to rebel against the powers of Heaven, until he is ultimately subdued and subordinated—now in the guise of a simian figure with the monkish name Sun Wukung—to the exalted aims of a quest journey beyond the bounds of Self.

An early twentieth-century illustration showing the cunning demons of Blackwater River disguised as boatmen attempting to carry away the master Xuanzang, before Sun Wukung ("the Monkey King") comes to the rescue.

THE CITY OF THE SUN (1602)

A theocratic utopia in which everything is shared. Solarians benefit from free universal education; they work only six hours daily, and live for a minimum of one hundred years.

Although written in 1602, *La città del Sole* was first published in Frankfurt in 1623.

Campanella lived in France from October 1634 until his death, and was delighted to prepare a horoscope for the future King Louis XIV.

The child was born September 5, 1638, the same day Campanella was born some seventy years earlier.

Dominican friar and polymath Tommaso Campanella (1568–1639) was in prison (for leading a conspiracy against Spanish rule in Naples) when he put the finishing touches to his 1,100-page utopian manifesto *Philosophia Realis* in 1602. Buried within it is an appendix entitled *La città del Sole* (*The City of the Sun*) that was to become his best-known work. The story appears within the literary frame of a traveler's tale, a device perhaps drawn from Thomas More's *Utopia* (1516, page 52), although Campanella makes no explicit reference to the English humanist in his text, preferring instead to underline the influence and ideas of the ancient Greek philosopher Plato.

In the story, a recently returned sea captain is asked by a Grand-Master of the Knights Hospitallers (a Roman Catholic military order) to describe his visit to the faraway "City of the Sun." The city, explains the captain, is located on the Island of Taprobane (known to the ancient Greeks and thought to be modern-day Sri Lanka or Sumatra) and its inhabitants had fled there from India. The captain reveals an array of intricate detail about the place and its people, the Solarians, and from this we can assume that Campanella wanted his utopia to be less illusory than other examples in the genre. It is *somewhere*, and therefore not purely speculative, as was Plato's Republic, nor as brimming with negation as More's Utopia.

While some details given by the captain are rather prosaic, the most important elements—governance, education, religion, and personal liberty—reflect Campanella's own views and his leanings toward astrology and numerology (for instance, we learn that the city is walled by seven, heavily-fortified concentric circles and each circle is dedicated to a planet). At the very center of the city, on top of a hill, is a circular temple around which dwell forty-nine priests. Within the temple is an altar supporting two globes, one terrestrial and one celestial, depicting the heavenly bodies. On the vaulted side of the upper dome hang seven golden lamps, always lit and each bearing the name of a planet. Unsurprisingly, education is a central tenet and crucial in the perfection of the inhabitants. Thus, the inner and outer walls of each circle contain illustrations of all

Pio Sanquirico, *Tommaso Campanella in Prison*, 1880. The Dominican friar was imprisoned for leading a conspiracy against Spanish rule in Naples, and finalized his text for *The City of the Sun* from his cell.

knowledge, and this is where all children take compulsory classes from the ages of three to ten.

The city is governed by a supreme leader; a priest called Hoh. He will retain the position for life and must have a greater understanding of metaphysics and theology than anyone else. A triumvirate of three princes, each of whom in turn is assisted by a number of magistrates, aids Hoh in his responsibilities. First, there is Pon (power), who is charged with affairs of war and peace; next, Sin (wisdom) the "ruler of the liberal arts, of mechanics, and of all sciences"; and finally there is Mor (love), who attends "to the charge of the race," which means he ensures a long life for all and "sees that men and women are so joined together that they bring forth the best offspring."

While the seeds of dystopian alternatives lie just beneath the surface in *The City of the Sun*—ideas of proto-eugenics and totalitarianism come to mind—Campanella's text reflects important philosophical themes of equality emerging in the late Renaissance period and strives to promote intellectual freedom. The doctrine of state-controlled procreation and the view that fornication was not a sin created much of the sensation surrounding the text on its publication in 1623, and raised allegations of heresy.

MIGUEL DE CERVANTES

DON QUIXOTE (1605/15)

Cervantes paints a subversive portrait of imperial Spain in this epic masterpiece, charting the comic adventures of a knight deluded by legends of chivalry and romance in which the real becomes imaginary and the imaginary in turn symbolizes the real.

Cervantes was christened on October 9, 1547, but his actual birth date is unknown. It has been suggested that his first name implies he was born on Michaelmas Day, September 29.

Since publication of the novel, "quixotic" has become a word in its own right, meaning an impractical pursuit of rash or romantic ideals without consideration of consequences.

Volume I of *Don Quixote* was first published in Madrid by Francisco de Robles in 1605.

Don Quixote is a book (considered by many to be the very first example of the modern novel) in which contraries coexist, and imaginary and real landscapes merge. And this very complexity is precisely why Cervantes's (1547–1616) visionary epic has remained as a classic to the present day.

Cervantes's writing was highly informed by his own life of travel and adventure. He was variously: a servant of an Italian Cardinal, a soldier of the Spanish empire, a prisoner in Algiers, a playwright, a poet, and a tax collector. He was also detained in several Spanish prisons for financial irregularities and was far from wealthy even after the startling popularity of *Don Quixote*.

As the protagonist's name, "Don Quixote de La Mancha," implies, the novel takes place in a real Spanish region situated south of Madrid. La Mancha is located in Castile, the area that represented dominant Christian Spain when *Don Quixote* was written, and also borders Andalusia, a southern region highly influenced by Islamic and Jewish traditions. As such, in Cervantes's hand, the landscapes of La Mancha can be seen to symbolize the multifarious ethnic identity of Spain itself. Furthermore the novel famously begins in a vague unspecified village, and although many real places are mentioned, they are not described in any detail. La Mancha for Don Quixote is not a place to stay, but a space in which to roam during his adventures, or "sallies." The descriptions given are not realistic, but symbolic and literary. For example, the caves and sierras where the Don carries out his self-imposed penance are drawn from the chivalric tradition, the beech trees against which shepherds lean as they sing and talk do not grow in La Mancha but in the pastoral poems that Cervantes parodies.

And while the real world has symbolic association for Cervantes, so does the imaginary. The Don is a character mired in delusion, driven mad by excessive reading of chivalric romances. In imitation of these legendary texts he sets out as a knight-errant seeking valor and adventure. His predicament not only satirizes the impracticality of lofty or extravagant ideals, but his delusions (most famously charging at windmills, mistaking them for giants) can be interpreted as reactions to the very real and traumatic technological

transformations that were being implemented in the Castilian landscape by the ruling Habsburgs. The windmills were not at that time a traditional feature of the Castilian landscape. On the contrary, they were monstrous new machines deployed on the windy Manchegan hills in order to drive the economy of the Habsburgs' global war. The trauma of windmills and what they represent is also powerfully and subtly expressed by the constant repetition of the word *molidos* (past participle of the verb *moler*, to grind), used to describe Don Quixote and Sancho's pitiful state almost every time they are beaten and battered—which they are frequently.

This powerful strategy of blurring the boundaries between the real and the imaginary enabled Cervantes to express his vision in times of censorship and oppression, when the truth could only circulate underground. Furthermore, his amazing capacity to turn fiction into reality and reality into fiction expanded the limits of literary expression, and showcased the highest powers of his imagination. For these reasons, among many others, *Don Quixote* is recognized as a masterpiece of literature and continues to inspire millions of writers and readers worldwide.

Honoré-Victorin Daumier, *Don Quixote and Sancho Panza*, c.1855. Daumier painted several works based on Cervantes's text. Here Don Quixote charges into the distance, while his squire Sancho Panza sits upon his donkey, drinking from a bottle.

WILLIAM SHAKESPEARE

THE TEMPEST (1611)

Shakespeare's final play centers upon an enchanted island inhabited by magician Prospero, his daughter Miranda, and their servants Ariel, a sprite, and the monstrous Caliban. The drama begins with a powerful storm and a shipwrecked party interrupts the isolated idyll.

First published as part of the "First Folio" by Edward Blount and Isaac Jaggard in 1623.

Statues of Ariel and Prospero stand outside the BBC Broadcasting House in London, symbolizing the magic of radio transmission.

The 1956 film *Forbidden Planet* is a science-fiction interpretation of *The Tempest*, in which Dr. Edward Morbius and his daughter Altaira are stranded on the distant planet, Altair IV.

The Tempest begins with a ship struggling on a stormy sea, its inhabitants fearful for their lives. The storm has been conjured by the powerful magician Prospero, who is marooned nearby on a desert island with his daughter, Miranda. Along with Prospero and Miranda, the island has two other inhabitants: Caliban, described as the son of a devil and a witch, and Ariel, a sprite whom Prospero has bound into his service.

Prospero's motive is revenge for his deposition and exile at the hands of his brother Antonio, who replaced him as Duke of Milan, and Alonso, King of Naples, who supported Antonio in his coup. He arranges for Alonso's son Ferdinand to be washed ashore, followed separately by Alonso himself and various crew and companions.

Although Shakespeare's (*c.*1564–1616) island is likely located somewhere in the Mediterranean, not too far from Milan and Naples, the idea of the "deserted" island derives from the discovery of the New World by Columbus in 1492, and in particular from the exploration of the Caribbean islands, which provided an entirely new and exotic location for adventure. Shakespeare was certainly deeply interested in the travelers' tales from the Caribbean. His description of the shipwreck contains ideas from an event of 1609 in which a ship, en route from England to Virginia, was thought lost in the Bermudas. In fact, all aboard eventually reached Virginia, after living easily for some months on their own "desert island."

To sixteenth- and seventeenth-century Europeans, the Caribbean was a land of contradictions. It was dangerous, in ways they had never encountered before, yet was fertile beyond anything they knew, and full of exotic novelties. There were other new and shocking dangers, such as hurricanes, which were first reported in English in 1555; sharks were also first mentioned around this time. (When Alonso thinks his son Ferdinand is dead, he wonders "what strange fish Hath made his meal on thee?") Similarly, early travelers did not know quite what to make of native populations, and the New World was feared most because of its supposedly fierce and unpredictable inhabitants, often seen as devils or devil-worshipers. Furthermore, there were shocking

reports of man-eating tribes. (The word "cannibal" is first recorded in English in 1553 and comes from the same root as "Carib," Shakespeare's own "Caliban" looks like another deliberate variation.)

Yet Shakespeare was also aware of accounts describing how European colonists were poor at fishing, and how they had to be helped by native peoples. And as such he plays with the notion of the "native" throughout the play. When Prospero first arrived on the island, Caliban showed the magician the freshwater springs, and later he offers to show the sailors where the berries are and how to catch fish. Prospero and Miranda seem, in return, not to believe Caliban is naturally wicked and to have some kind of "civilizing mission" in mind in teaching him how to talk.

The Tempest was Shakespeare's final play, and as in many of his other plays, he not only drew upon contemporary events, but also integrated older stories, history, and fantasy. The Classical gods Juno, Iris, and Ceres are referenced and a famous speech by Prospero invokes Ovid's *Metamorphoses* (*c.*8, page 22). Other fantastical elements are culled from medieval legend and English folklore. The shipwrecked lords, for example, exclaim that after seeing Prospero's powerful display of wizardry they can easily believe

Be not afeard. The isle is full of noises,
Sounds, and sweet airs, that give delight and hurt not.
Sometimes a thousand twangling instruments
Will hum about mine ears, and sometime voices
That, if I then had waked after long sleep
Will make me sleep again; and then in dreaming
The clouds methought would open and show riches
Ready to drop upon me, that when I waked
I cried to dream again. (III.ii.130–8)

in unicorns and phoenixes. Ariel functions like the mischievous spirits of English folktales—elves and boggarts and hobgoblins. They pinch Caliban, they lead the sailors into mires and bogs, they turn will-o'-the-wisp, and create fairy rings: All were likely more familiar to Shakespeare's first audience than Caribbean tales or medieval legends.

Caliban and Ariel in a pen-and-ink drawing by Arthur Rackham, 1899–1906.

The Tempest may not contain the first "desert island" setting in literature, but it demonstrates its enormous potential as a blank canvas for a freewheeling mix of imagery and imagination, free from the constraints of reality. A potent notion that has inspired a wealth of literature, from Daniel Defoe's *Robinson Crusoe* (1719), Jonathan Swift's *Gulliver's Travels* (1726, page 74), R. L. Stevenson's *Treasure Island* (1883, page 100), H. G. Wells's *The Island of Dr. Moreau* (1896), and even William Golding's *Lord of the Flies* (1954). In particular, J. M. Barrie's *Peter Pan* (1911), with its Lost Boys, pirates, Indians, fairies, and mermaids, all brought together in "Never-Never Land," is particularly indebted to *The Tempest.*

The continuing social importance of this world, as well as its literary brilliance, has led to many famous stage productions in modern times, but *The Tempest* has also been translated into various media beyond the stage. Scenes have been painted, by artists including Hogarth, Fuseli, and Millais; Ariel's songs have been given new music; more than forty operas have been composed on the basis of the play; among the poems inspired by it are Browning's "Caliban upon Setebos" (1864) and W. H. Auden's Freudian "The Sea and the Mirror" (1944); and its television and screen adaptations are numerous.

This vast legacy of influence is one clue to the enduring importance of *The Tempest.* By creating this "other" world, both familiar and alien, Shakespeare explored many of the most important problems that the nation faced at a period of exploration and discovery, and, prophetically, that it still faces today—race, sex, colonization, and the experience of "otherness."

CYRANO DE BERGERAC

A VOYAGE TO THE MOON (1657)

*Cyrano de Bergerac's fictional Moon, a paradise inhabited by natives,
five humans, and a Tree of Knowledge, challenged the orthodoxies of
contemporary astronomy and the Christian religion.*

Originally titled *L'Autre
Monde: ou les États et Empires
de la Lune (The Other World:
or the States and Empires of
the Moon)*, it was published
posthumously in 1657 by
Charles de Sercy.

A fictionalized account
of Cyrano's life was
presented in a tremendously
popular 1897 play entitled
Cyrano de Bergerac by
Edmond Rostand.

Cyrano de Bergerac (1619–55) was writing his *Voyage dans la Lune*, and
its sequel, *L'Histoire des États et Empires du Soleil* not long after Rome had
condemned the idea of a sun-centered universe as heretical, and one of his
purposes was clearly to support the arguments of Copernicus, Kepler, and
Galileo. The Moon and Sun are worlds like our own, and he knows, because
he has been there.

In this first-person science fiction, Cyrano's mode of transport blends
old and new. His first idea is to strap bottles of dew around himself, since
dew is sucked up by the Sun. This expedient only gets him as far as French-
speaking Canada however, and he eventually reaches the Moon by
rocket-assisted takeoff, coupled with the attractive power of the Moon on
the beef marrow that he has coated himself in to relieve the bruises from
previous efforts.

Cyrano's main innovation is as a comic satirist. On the Moon, everything is topsy-turvy—people put their hats on and sit down to show respect,
the worst punishment that can be inflicted is to be sentenced to die a natural death of old age, and the mark of a gentleman is not a sword but an erect
metal phallus hung from the belt. More fancifully, the Moon people, who are
eighteen feet long but walk on all fours, are separated by class in their very
means of communication—conversing in music if upper class, and by gesture if lower.

The intrepid explorer also discovers that while the moon's inhabitants
have an elaborate cuisine, they actually live off the aroma of cooking food.
They also have long noses, like Cyrano himself, which they can use as sun-
dials and their currency is poetry—a sonnet buying dinners for a week. Free
love is not only practiced, but compulsory.

However, although comedy was possibly his main aim, Cyrano also
deserves some reputation as a prophet, having foreseen the concept of the
audiobook, as well as something like germ theory, with his attempt at an
explanation of the nature of light. When he encounters an atheist, however,
orthodoxy reasserts itself, for the atheist and Cyrano are both snatched up by

a devil and carried off toward Hell. Cyrano luckily cries out "Jesu Maria!" at which the devil drops him back on Earth. His later *History of the Sun* is a similar mix of hits and misses.

Cyrano de Bergerac first attempts to rise into outer space with the aid of birds (left) and then by balloon.

Since writing his fantastical tales of space exploration, Cyrano de Bergerac's works have been often mentioned in accounts of imaginary moon voyages (of which there are many), and in histories of science fiction. He has inspired many since, but his main influence may well be on Swift's *Gulliver's Travels* (1726, page 74) in which Gulliver, finding himself stranded in an alien land, similarly combines observation with comic surprise.

MARGARET CAVENDISH, DUCHESS OF NEWCASTLE

THE DESCRIPTION OF A NEW WORLD, CALLED THE BLAZING-WORLD (1666)

A lavish fantasy and early form of science fiction that critiques seventeenth-century scientific theories while bounding between elaborately depicted parallel worlds.

First published along with *Observations upon Experimental Philosophy*, printed by Anne Maxwell, in 1666. A second edition appeared in 1668 (above).

By the time she published *The Blazing-World*, Cavendish was already well known as a poet (*Poems and Fancies*, 1653), playwright (*Playes and Orations of Divers Sorts*, 1662), and as an essayist and philosopher (*The Worlds Olio*, 1655; *Philosophical Letters*, 1664).

Poems and Fancies (1653) includes poems on the theory of multiple worlds, and on atomic theory.

In his famous diary, Samuel Pepys records that on May 30, 1667, Margaret Cavendish (1623–74) visited the Royal Society, an unusual invitation that was a testament to her status as a wealthy, titled woman with a keen interest in science. There was of course no question of her contributing her own research or even merely joining their discussions at that time (in fact, women would have to wait until 1945 to be elected Fellows). In 1667, the idea of a woman interested in exploring scientific ideas being taken seriously could only take place in the realm of fiction.

The Blazing-World is a narrative companion to Cavendish's *Observations upon Experimental Philosophy*, a more serious critique of the latest developments in science and technology. *Observations* challenges science's claims to understand all Nature, and is critical of new technologies developed to further scientific research. Her concern is less about extending the frontiers of science itself, but more the arrogance that accompanies scientific accomplishments. If we think we can know everything through science, then whatever cannot be proven scientifically could be deemed to have no value.

The Blazing-World begins with a young, unnamed woman, abducted aboard a ship by a merchant who desires her. They are shipwrecked in a storm, but she and a handful of the crew survive in a lifeboat. All the men succumb to the cold, leaving the woman entirely alone. After a series of encounters with Bear-men—intelligent beings who resemble bears—Fox-men, Bird-men, and Satyrs, she is brought to the Emperor by mermen with green skin. The Emperor, believing the woman to be divine, marries her. The woman, hereafter designated "the Empress," undertakes to learn all she can about her new home, and sets out to establish a number of learned societies. The bulk of the story consists of dialogues with these societies, as she seeks answers to questions about the laws of nature in the Blazing-World.

The world itself is a group of archipelagos within interconnected networks of rivers and oceans. There are numerous cities, each made out of a different kind of material, including "some not known in our world," but all built in the style of classical Rome. The Imperial Palace in the Imperial

city of Paradise is, like the city itself, made of gold and decorated with precious stones. The inhabitants are both humans and intelligent animals—each animal having its own specialized branch of learning. From the explanations given by various scientists of the learned societies, the Blazing-World either operates upon radically different laws of physics to our world, or the scientists are spectacularly incompetent, providing odd explanations for natural phenomena that were understood even in Cavendish's time.

After an extended survey of all learning, including conversations with spirits about supernatural knowledge, the Empress composes "a Cabbala"—a compendium of the entirety of the esoteric knowledge. She finds her amanuensis in Cavendish herself—as "The Duchess"—who is able to visit the Empress in "spirit form." The Duchess invites the Empress to leave her physical body and visit Welbeck, her own estate in Nottinghamshire, and the two become "dear Platonick friends."

In the brief, second part of the work, the Empress learns that her native country (the fictional Kingdom of Esfi) has come under attack. The Duchess persuades the Empress to muster the forces of the Blazing-World to aid in the fight. The Empress calls her architects and engineers—who happen to be giants—to build, with the Duchess's direction, submarines to transport the forces through the gap between the Blazing-World and ours. The Empress then manages to rally the forces of her own country to victory.

The Blazing-World is one of the very first works of science fiction, and undoubtedly the only example published by a woman in the seventeenth century. Cavendish's vision of interconnected other worlds has proven influential in the development of science fiction, but her vision of a woman who effortlessly rises to absolute power through the accumulation of knowledge has been more recently embraced by scholars of feminist literature. Virginia Woolf refers to Cavendish in *A Room of One's Own* (1929); more recently Siri Hustvedt uses the text (and its title) to illustrate her story of a woman painter taking on misogyny in the New York art establishment.

An engraving by Abraham van Diepenbeeck from 1655 presents the duchess beside the accoutrements of wisdom and learning, a quill and inkwell, while above cherubs crown her with a laurel wreath.

Frontispiece to *A Connecticut Yankee in King Arthur's Court* (1889), see page 108.

2 SCIENCE & ROMANTICISM

The Industrial Revolution coincided with the heights of Gothic fantasy producing scientific miracles and a terrible fear of the unknown.

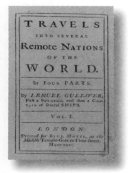

JONATHAN SWIFT

GULLIVER'S TRAVELS (1726)

This classic satire follows the adventures of Lemuel Gulliver among the miniature Lilliputians, the philosophizing Houyhnhnms, and the brutish Yahoos, and portrays a comic yet steely reflection of mankind.

First published in London by Benjamin Motte in 1726.

"Yahoo" has been accepted into the language as an insult meaning rude, unsophisticated, and uncouth. It was this definition that led Internet pioneers Jerry Yang and David Filo to adopt it as the name of their new search engine in 1994.

Opposite: Gulliver pinned to the ground by the Lilliputians, illustration from *Gulliver's Travels*, published by Nelson and Sons, 1860.

The Anglo-Irish essayist Jonathan Swift (1667–1745) is regarded today as the leading satirist in the English language, and his sardonic style is so ingrained that his name has become an adjective. The influence and import of his classic parody *Gulliver's Travels* is immeasurable and it has been continuously in print since its first publication.

The first two "travels" of Lemuel Gulliver are mirror images of each other. In the first the inhabitants of the island of Lilliput are very small, about six inches high. In Brobdingnag they are very large, about seventy feet high; Gulliver, having once been a giant, becomes like a doll. His third voyage takes him to the flying island of Laputa, the land beneath it (Balnibarbi), the necromancers' island of Glubbdubdrib, and the kingdom of Luggnagg, with its immortal but senile "struldbrugs." On his fourth voyage Gulliver is marooned on the land of the Houyhnhnms, intelligent horses, which is also inhabited by the Yahoos—a dirty, dangerous, and unteachable parody of humanity.

Throughout, Swift mingles marvels with satire, the latter eventually all but taking over. As a result, his first voyage has remained the best-known and the most popular for adaptations. Much of the account of the Lilliputians deals with the details of scale: How Gulliver is fed, how they try to control him, what feats he performs for the king and his court. Apart from scale, however, the land of the Lilliputians seems virtually identical with England. It has cows, sheep, horses, trees, and vegetation, all scaled down like the Lilliputians themselves, and a social system that parallels and parodies Swift's contemporary Britain.

Brobdingnag gives rise to similar, if inverse, effects, with Gulliver in serious danger from mastiff-sized rats, flies as big as birds, pet cats like lions, and dogs the size of elephants. Swift, moreover, seems to equate size with virtue. While the Lilliputian court is essentially ridiculous, providing in its faction-fighting a satirical image of British court-society, in Brobdingnag the satire comes from Gulliver's attempts to impress the Brobdingnagian king with his accounts of British power and skill. Even his account of gunpowder only makes the king contemptuous of the uses to which it is put.

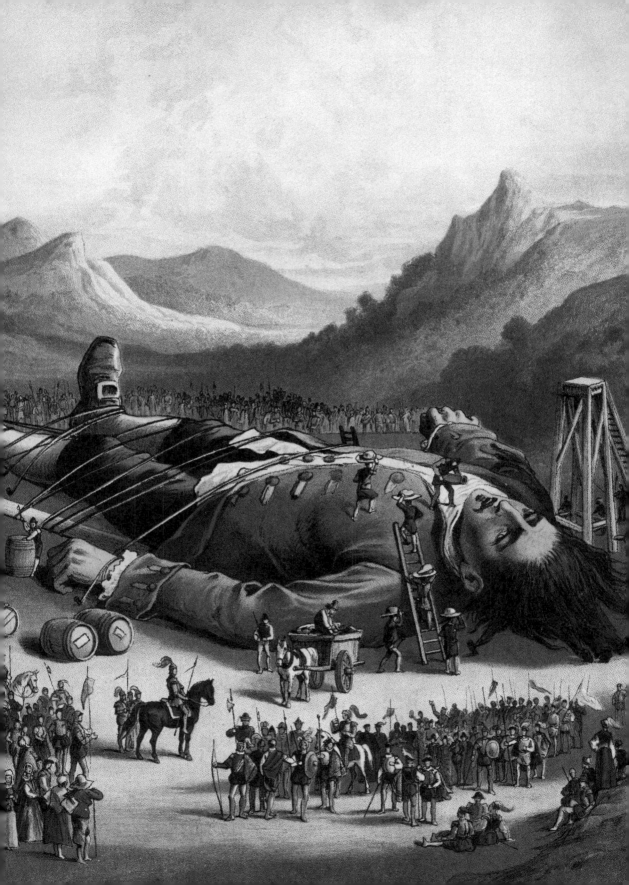

Stephen Baghot de la Bere,
*Gulliver and the
Houyhnhnms*, 1904.

[T]hey have no conception how a rational creature can be compelled, but only advised, or exhorted; because no person can disobey reason, without giving up his claim to being a rational creature.

Many have thought that in the third voyage Swift's satire goes well astray. The Laputians on their floating island, held aloft by a giant lodestone or magnet, respect only mathematics and music, and are totally impractical. Some are so absent-minded that they have to employ "flappers," who pat their ears and mouths gently to signify that it is time to listen or to speak. Their subjects on the island below are even worse, having begun to imitate the Laputians and set up an "Academy" for all kinds of ludicrous scientific experiments, distilling sunbeams from cucumbers, reconstituting dung into food, and inventing a universal language that would have no words, and communicate only by things. Swift was here satirizing the Royal Society, founded in 1660. One of its founders, John Wilkins, had indeed written an *Essay towards a Real Character and a Philosophical Language* (1668), and the Society's insistence on using objective language for describing experiments has since been accepted worldwide.

In the fourth voyage, finally, Swift's own misanthropy seems to have infected Gulliver. The Houyhnhnms (pronounced "Whinnn-im" in imitation of a horse's neigh) are polite, intelligent, virtuous, while the Yahoos are unspeakably vile. At the end, Gulliver, once again returned home, can hardly bear the company of his own species, including his wife, and sits talking to his horses for hours every day. Scholarship varies as to how seriously we should take his critiques of humanity.

Gulliver's Travels has given rise to several films and TV adaptations—including the animation *Laputa: Castle in the Sky* by acclaimed Japanese director Hayao Miyazaki—and Lilliputians appear in several comic books and novels.

Other Swiftian concepts reappear throughout science fiction. The animated American TV series *Land of the Giants* ran from 1968–70, which led to three novelizations by Murray Leinster. Laputa is remembered in James Blish's *Cities in Flight* tetralogy (1955–62), where a rogue city does what the Laputians sometimes threaten to do, and "makes the sky fall." The Houyhnhnms appear in John M. Myers' novel *Silverlock* (1949), and "struldbrugs" appear at the end of Frederik Pohl's *Drunkard's Walk* (1960), long-lived and senile as in *Gulliver's Travels*, but according to Pohl a secret society controlling human affairs.

LUDVIG HOLBERG

THE JOURNEY OF NIELS KLIM TO THE WORLD UNDERGROUND (1741)

Sometimes described as the first science-fiction novel, this subterranean adventure was the first to explore ideas of a hollow Earth.

The popularity of Holberg's satirical plays earned him the sobriquet the "Molière of the North."

Originally published in Latin (in Germany in 1741) as *Nicolai Klimii Iter Subterraneum*. The full English title is *The Journey of Niels Klim to the World Underground, with a new theory of the Earth and the History of the previously unknown Fifth Kingdom.*

Ludvig Holberg (1684–1754) is often referred to as the "father" of Danish and Norwegian literature—and his writing encompassed a wide range of fields. However he is best remembered for his satirical plays and for his creation of a "hollow Earth" in *The Journey of Niels Klim to the World Underground*.

The text recounts, as the title suggests, the adventures of one Niels Klim who, after his rope gives way while exploring a cave, falls to the center of Earth, where a solitary planet rotates around a subterranean sun. The first adventure is set in Potu, a utopian land inhabited by intelligent and mobile trees. Since Klim's legs allow him to move faster than the trees, he is commissioned to make a tour of the entire planet of Nazar and report back to the king. The planet is only about 600 miles in circumference, and his trip takes him two months instead of the two years it would take a tree. The narrative turns from utopia to satire as Klim visits the different provinces of Nazar. The descriptions of these countries—inhabited by different species of trees that speak the same language as the Potuans—are very brief, and most present satirical sketches of alternative societies. In Quamso everyone is happy, healthy, and bored; in Lalac, where there is no need to work, everyone is unhappy and sickly; in Kimal the citizens are wealthy, and spend their time worrying about thieves; and the "land of Liberty" is at war.

From the inner planet of Potu, Klim travels next to the underside of the Earth's crust, carried by a giant bird. His adventures begin in the kingdom of Martinia—a country of intelligent but capricious apes preoccupied with fashion. He makes a fortune by introducing wigs to the Martinians. From social satire the book now becomes fantasy as Klim is taken on a trading voyage to the Mezandorian islands, which lie across a vast sea and are inhabited by fabulous creatures, beginning with a country of jackdaws at war with their neighbors the thrushes, and a malodorous land of creatures who speak "*a posteriori,*" as well as a country of string basses who communicate by music.

After a shipwreck he finds himself in a remote country inhabited not by intelligent animals or trees, but by primitive humans, who, of all the creatures of the subterranean world, "alone were barbarous and uncivilized."

Klim sets out to redress the situation, intending that they "would recover that dominion which Nature has given to man over all other animals." Using his knowledge he manufactures gunpowder and conquers, one by one, all the countries of the firmament. Klim's many conquests lead him to see himself as the "Alexander of the Subterranean world," and he becomes a tyrant. When his subjects rebel, he is forced to flee; looking for shelter, he falls into the same hole through which he had previously fallen, thus returning to Norway.

Niels Klim is pulled from the water in a scene by Danish painter Nicolai Abraham Abildgaard.

Holberg's text is the first portrayal of a hollow Earth, but there is little evidence to suggest where this idea came from. As he is falling, Klim makes a reference to accounts of an interior realm, but without any details: "I fell to imagining that I was sunk into the subterranean world, and that the conjectures of those men are right who hold the Earth to be hollow, and that within the shell or outward crust there is another lesser globe, and another firmament adorned with lesser sun, stars, and planets." But who are "those men" and why did they hold Earth to be hollow? Some have pointed to the astronomer Edmond Halley's "concentric spheres" theory of the interior of the Earth (1692)—but Holberg's inner world is not a set of globes but a single planet circling an inner sun as well an inhabited inner crust—significant features of subsequent subterranean fictions, but not part of Halley's scheme. Like many other early utopias and satirical works, Holberg is indifferent to the physical details of the imaginary world. *Klim* was written at a time (1741) when the popular travel narratives of the sixteenth and seventeenth centuries had evolved into the imaginary voyages of the eighteenth century, allowing writers to visualize political and social alternatives while skirting the interdiction of speculation by passing it off as an authentic narrative.

The Water-Babies: A Fairy Tale for a Land Baby (1863)

A strange and powerful tale for children that combines imaginative exuberance, uplifting themes of redemption, and contemporary ideas about evolutionary theory and contemporary child labor.

First published in 1863 by Macmillan and Co., *The Water-Babies* echoes many other fairy tales in beginning with the words "Once upon a time . . ."

The book has been suggested as a trigger for the Chimney Sweepers Regulation Act of 1864.

Kingsley coined the term "cuddly," and it was first used in *The Water-Babies*.

The Water-Babies by Charles Kingsley (1819–75) might ostensibly be a fairy tale, but this most imaginative of Victorian fables is directed at thinking adults as much as children of the period.

The hero, Tom, is that stalwart of Victorian literature: a chimney sweep. He blunders down a chimney at Harthover House and finds himself in the bedroom of Ellie, a daughter of the family. Suddenly ashamed of himself, he realizes he is "dirty" and runs away. Obsessed with the idea that he must somehow become clean, Tom throws himself, suicidal, into a nearby stream. He does not drown, but is swept down to the ocean, washed clean, and morally and physically reborn in a series of fantastic adventures, involving, among others, his bullying master Grimes (who is finally dispatched on the Sisyphean task of sweeping Mount Etna) and the mysterious Mother Carey. He learns valuable life lessons from Mrs. Doasyouwouldbedoneby and less valuable lessons from Professor Ptthmllnsports. Finally Tom, who has undergone a literal "sea change," is united with Ellie and goes on to grow up "a great man of science," saved by the power of clean water.

Charles Kingsley was a clergyman, the leader of the so-called "Muscular Christianity" movement. He perceived the mission of a clergyman as confronting social problems. The social problem that most exercised him, to the point of obsession, was sanitation. If Kingsley pictured the devil it was not horns, tail, and cloven hoof, but filth. For Kingsley it was not the proverbial "cleanliness is next to godliness," but cleanliness *was* godliness. This obsession propels the narrative of this "not just for children" tale.

The origin of the story stems from the history of London. In 1854 the city had been ravaged by a cholera epidemic. These outbreaks happened every couple of years, and were regarded by Londoners as no more unusual than the coming of winter (which also killed thousands). The prevailing opinion thought the disease to be "miasmic," or spread by foul air. In 1854, however, a young doctor named John Snow traced the source of a recent outbreak, ascertaining that it was not, in fact, bad air but bad *water* that was responsible. Meanwhile, beneath the horse-manured and garbage-strewn streets of London, another revolution was taking place. The urban engineer Joseph Bazalgette was laying down the first effective sewage system since the Romans. Bazalgette's task was given added urgency by the famous "Great Stink" of the summer of 1858, which was so malodorous, and lethal, that it enforced the closure of Parliament. Bazalgette's network of subterranean sewers (replacing the old open canals, such as the one that gave Fleet Street its name) ensured it would never happen again.

According to one sardonic German historian, "the English think civilization is soap." Dickens certainly did. In 1850 he addressed the Metropolitan Sanitary Association: "I can honestly declare, that all the use I have made of my eyes—or nose [laughter] that all the information I have since been able to acquire through any of my senses, has strengthened me in the conviction that Searching Sanitary Reform must precede all other social remedies [cheers]. . . . Give me my first glimpse of Heaven through a little of its light and air—give me water, help me to be clean." He further prefaced *Martin Chuzzlewit* with the declaration: "I hope I have taken every available opportunity of showing the want of sanitary improvements in the neglected dwellings of the poor."

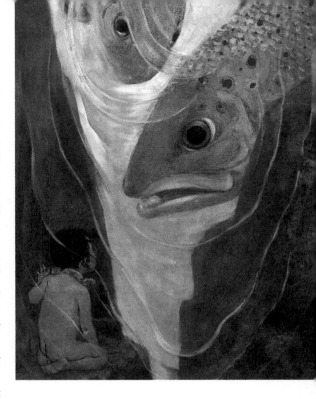

"'Oh, don't hurt me!' cried Tom. 'I only want to look at you; you are so handsome.'" Illustration by Jessie Wilcox-Smith, created for a 1916 edition.

Of all the persecutions of the Victorian child, chimney sweeping was the most vile. Oliver Twist narrowly escapes that fate: Had he remained in the brutal employment of Gamfield (who offers five pounds for ownership of the lad) Oliver, like many others, might well have succumbed to the cancer of the scrotum or pulmonary disease—two occupational hazards. Few sweeps made it to middle age, many did not even make it to adulthood.

Pure water had another centrally important value for the nineteenth century. It symbolized Christian salvation—by the primal rite of baptism. William Blake runs the ideas together in one of his "Songs of Innocence," "The Chimney Sweep." Blake's point is that death cleanses. But, more importantly, so did birth. Baptism was a huge event in Christian life in the nineteenth century. The baby (what with gowns, favors, christening mugs, and silver spoons) received almost as many gifts as a bride on her wedding day.

These two ideas—sanitary water supply and baptism—are fused in *The Water-Babies*. Reverend Kingsley believed, with all his soul, that social progress and fundamental religion were not contradictory. God wanted his creation to have water as pure as that in Eden. And, by God, Charles Kingsley would be at the head of those who fought for it.

LEWIS CARROLL (CHARLES LUTWIDGE DODGSON)

ALICE'S ADVENTURES IN WONDERLAND (1865)

A classic of nonsense fantasy and the curiosities it contains—a rabbit with a pocket watches, the Mad Hatter, the Cheshire Cat, and the tyrannical Queen of Hearts—it has enchanted readers, young and old, for more than 150 years.

First published by Macmillan and Co. in 1865.

A stickler for perfection, the book's original illustrator, John Tenniel, insisted the first edition of two thousand copies be pulped because his exquisite designs were imperfectly reproduced.

Opposite: "'But I don't want to go among mad people,' Alice remarked.
'Oh, you can't help that,' said the Cat: 'we're all mad here. I'm mad. You're mad.'
'How do you know I'm mad?' said Alice.
'You must be,' said the Cat, 'or you wouldn't have come here.'" Alice meets the grinning Cheshire Cat in an illustration after Tenniel.

Reverend Charles Lutwidge Dodgson was a mathematics don at Christ Church College in Oxford, and he famously wrote *Alice's Adventures in Wonderland* for a colleague's three little girls: Ina, Alice, and Edith Liddell, whom he used to take on outings on summer days to the river. He would entertain them by "telling them stories," and luckily for the Liddell girls, he was one of the greatest (if strangest) storytellers of all time.

A novelist friend of Dodgson, Henry Kingsley (brother of Charles, author of *The Water-Babies*, 1863, page 80), read the story and was of the opinion that Alice should be given to the world at large, urging Dodgson to have it published. The unworldly Dodgson first thought of Oxford University Press, however the house rejected the manuscript as not suitable for their learned list, and further it was intimated that it would do him no good academically to publish such a work under his own name.

Eventually Dodgson was persuaded to submit the work to Macmillan and Co., Kingsley's publisher, with illustrations by John Tenniel. Dodgson came up with a pen name that suited him and his witty tale, "Lewis Carroll." It was a pun, inevitably—and one that his colleagues at the high table at Christ Church College doubtless had a high time puzzling out (Lewis is etymologically linked, via Latin, to "Lutwidge"; Carroll, likewise, to "Charles").

The two "Alice books" (the successor to the bestselling adventures in "Wonderland" took the little girl *Through the Looking-Glass, and What Alice Found There*) are unusual among children's literature in appealing equally to adult readers. Ideally, clever adults, who are able to appreciate the depth of Carroll's intellectualism embedded in his writing.

The tale begins with Alice lolling under a tree in high summer and failing to read her book, when she sees a white rabbit rush by:

> There was nothing so *very* remarkable in that; nor did Alice think it so *very* much out of the way to hear the Rabbit say to itself, "Oh dear! Oh dear! I shall be late" (when she thought it over afterwards, it occurred to her that she ought to have wondered at this, but at the time it all seemed quite

Alice joins the Mad Hatter, the March Hare, and the Dormouse for tea in a hand-colored etching after Tenniel.

natural); but when the Rabbit actually *took a watch out of its waistcoat-pocket*, and looked at it, and then hurried on, Alice started to her feet, for it flashed across her mind that she had never before seen a rabbit with either a waistcoat-pocket, or a watch to take out of it, and burning with curiosity, she ran across the field after it, and fortunately was just in time to see it pop down a large rabbit-hole under the hedge.

In another moment down went Alice after it, never once considering how in the world she was to get out again.

We do not need the aid of Freud to work out that this little girl, eight years out of it, is "returning to the womb," finding herself in a mad world. Alice's way is blocked by locked doors, she eats and drinks substances that make her grow and shrink, she encounters mythical creatures like the Gryphon, extinct creatures like the Dodo, toothy, but smiling, creatures like the Cheshire Cat. She breaks in, uninvited, on the Mad Hatter's tea party and is finally sentenced to be beheaded by the irascible Queen of Hearts (a mother figure from hell).

As the queen's playing card entourage falls on her, with decapitation in mind, Alice wakes with dead leaves brushing her face. It was spring, and now is autumn. The little girl is growing up.

"Oh my ears and whiskers, how late it's getting!" The White Rabbit checks his pocket watch.

Opposite: Alice Pleasance Liddell (1852–1934) photographed as a "beggar maid" by Lewis Carroll.

Alice was beginning to get very tired of sitting by her sister on the bank and of having nothing to do: once or twice she had peeped into the book her sister was reading, but it had no pictures or conversations in it, "and what is the use of a book," thought Alice, "without pictures or conversations?"

JULES VERNE

TWENTY THOUSAND LEAGUES UNDER THE SEA (1870)

This classic tale of adventure by the "Father of Science Fiction" voyages through the realm of the imagination from the lost city of Atlantis to the South Pole.

Originally serialized from 1869 to 1870, *Twenty Thousand Leagues* was first published in book form by Pierre-Jules Hetzel in 1870. An edition with illustrations by Édouard Riou and the painter Alphonse de Neuville followed in 1871.

The novel is more explicitly scientific than many of Verne's other works, such as *Journey to the Center of the Earth* (1864), with the seemingly fantastical *Nautilus* based on the study of contemporary submarine designs.

Opposite: The view from the salon window aboard the *Nautilus,* engraving after Alphonse de Neuville (colored later).

The narrative of *Vingt mille lieues sous les mers* (*Twenty Thousand Leagues Under the Sea*), like those of all Verne's (1828–1905) major works, is no more than a row of pegs on which to hang wild flights of his distinctive imagination. Dip anywhere into the novel and there is page after page of vivid pictorialism—see, for example, the long descriptions of submarine "coral forests," the submerged ruins of Atlantis, the sunken galleons rotting in the Bay of Vigo. Verne was also a famously light-fingered writer. The novel's climax, detailing the attack by giant squid, is borrowed (with acknowledgment) from Victor Hugo's *Toilers of the Sea* (1866). The self-destruction of Captain Nemo and his craft in the great northern "maelstrom" is also borrowed, from Edgar Allen Poe's story "A Descent into the Maelstrom" (1841). However, one readily forgives these narrative larcenies, because there is so much in Verne's story that is hugely original.

Pierre Aronnax, a world-famous French marine biologist, narrates the story. On his way back from a North American expedition in March 1866, the U.S. government recruits him to help hunt down a mysterious giant, glowing creature. Aronnax sets out on the USS *Abraham Lincoln*, accompanied by his omni-competent, urbane manservant, Conseil, and a Canadian "king of harpooners," Ned Land, a character who seems to have walked off the pages of Herman Melville's *Moby Dick* (another source candidly plundered by Verne).

The *Abraham Lincoln* sights the mysterious, phosphorescent "cetacean," gives chase, and fires on the beast. It proves immune to artillery and turns on the ship, ramming it. Aronnax, Conseil, and Land tumble into the ocean. They cling to the sides of what turns out to be not a whale but an immense metallic submarine. The trio is taken aboard and the submarine *Nautilus* is revealed to be a miracle of modern technology—electrically propelled, air conditioned, and palatial in its amenities. The three captives are, however, informed that they can never leave. Ned Land takes this particularly badly and spends the whole novel plotting his escape from this "metal prison." Aronnax is delighted. For him it is not a prison but the world's finest laboratory. The body of the book details their 20,000-league, nine-month voyage

above and below the oceans. The heroes finally escape by being thrown clear of the maelstrom that sucks the craft and its crew to their destruction.

Aronnax controls the narrative, but it is Nemo, the captain of the *Nautilus*, who grips the reader's imagination. Verne wanted to make the captain a Polish aristocrat, bent on revenge against Russia for its brutal repression of the 1863 uprising. However, he was talked out of this by his publisher and instead Nemo was made enigmatic—a man of mystery whose name is Latin for "no one." We never learn what motivates him or where he comes from. He speaks five languages—none of which seem to be his native tongue despite his fluency in all of them. He is somber and gloom-ridden by nature, but omniscient on everything he talks about. His age is uncertain; his crew is drawn from the four corners of the earth. He is a walking question mark.

In the book's many film and television adaptations, Nemo is usually given comprehensible motives, but in all versions he is a man who has lost faith in humanity. In the 1954 film, Nemo was a former slave who had been subjected to inhuman treatment and now intends revenge—a Spartacus of the waves. Verne, more artfully, lets readers of the novel wonder, and stay wondering. Nemo is not a destroyer, but merely a self-willed exile from the human race and the lands it inhabits, the attraction of the seas being that no human resides there.

This anonymity is played with through hints and half-clues designed to tantalize rather than inform. The last image Aronnax has of his captor is of Nemo sobbing while gazing piteously at the picture of a woman and two children on his cabin wall, as the *Nautilus* is pulled down into the maw of the maelstrom. His wife? His mother? Aronnax will never know, nor shall we.

Twenty Thousand Leagues first appeared for French readers in installments in the *Magasin d'Education et de Recreation*, from March 1869 to June 1870. Verne's opening sentence is: "The year 1866 was marked by a bizarre development." The subsequent narrative takes the action forward to mid-1867. This is, for a novel, a strikingly contemporary setting. Moreover, the story references several significant current events. The name of the ship Aronnax embarks on, the *Abraham Lincoln*, is named for the sixteenth American president assassinated only two years earlier in 1865. There was nothing new about the idea of the submarine in 1869, but the first time submarines were used effectively in warfare was in the American Civil War by the Confederate Navy. They demonstrated the new crafts' immense military potential when the forty-foot *Hunley* (with an eight-man crew and a hand-operated propeller) sank the uss *Housatonic* off the coast of Charleston in 1864. Suddenly the world took note of this new kind of weapon, which would revolutionize warfare at sea.

These and innumerable other topicalities echo resonantly in the novel, and they relate to that feature in fiction, immediacy, which is specifically French rather than English or American. French popular novels tended to appear, as did *Twenty Thousand Leagues Under the Sea*, as what were called

The sea is everything. . . . It is an immense desert place where man is never lonely, for he senses the weaving of Creation on every hand. It is the physical embodiment of a supernatural existence. . . . For the sea is itself nothing but love and emotion. It is the Living Infinite, as one of your poets has said. Nature manifests herself in it, with her three kingdoms: mineral, vegetable, and animal. The ocean is the vast reservoir of Nature.

feuilletons—daily, weekly, or bi-weekly serials in newspapers. In Britain it was the monthly magazine and the hard-backed volume that were the principle vehicles for novels "of the day." The immediacy of the French practice goes back to the Revolution, fueled as it was by pamphlets and newspapers churned out by the hour by secret hand presses ("under the cloak" publications, as they were called). Verne's novel is likewise hot off the press.

With endless imagination and exhaustive detailing, Verne draws on contemporary discovery to expand into the new and unknown, putting forward technological, geographical, and dimensional concepts to create a world never before seen or imagined. Through this thorough and enthralling landscape, he meditates on the relationship of men with nature, with themselves, and with their freedom in the modern world.

Jules Verne may not be a great prose stylist—not even his warmest admirers make that claim—but his big ideas are unsurpassed in their daring and gripping nature. No more imaginative writer ever drew his pen across the page.

SAMUEL BUTLER

EREWHON (1872)

A provocative satire on the traditions of Victorian society, which also highlights a prescient comment on the rise of machines.

First published by Trübner and Co. in 1872.

Aldous Huxley acknowledged Butler's influence on *Brave New World* (1932, page 148) and George Orwell later praised Butler, noting that at the time of its publication *Erewhon* must have required an "imagination of a very high order to see that machinery could be dangerous as well as useful."

Samuel Butler's (1835–1920) great dystopian satire of Victorian society may be a little more obvious than some later imagined worlds, yet *Erewhon* is still as bracing as an ice-cold shower in showing the stupidity of viewing the British Empire—or indeed any modern society—as a righteous utopia.

Butler was one of the most eloquent skeptics of his age, among his propositions were a denunciation of Christ's resurrection, and the belief that the *Odyssey* must have been written by a woman. *Erewhon* was originally published anonymously but when it met with popular success Butler claimed it as his own, and it is now best remembered for his Darwinian-inspired discussions on what we would now describe as "artificial intelligence" and the evolution of the machine.

Erewhon, and the world it imagines, draws initially on Butler's own experience rearing sheep in New Zealand after his graduation from university. His narrator (later revealed to be called Higgs in Butler's inferior sequel, *Erewhon Revisited*, from 1901) is a young shepherd, who wonders if there is anything beyond the towering mountains that surround his farm. He embarks on a journey over perilous cliffs and a treacherous river to arrive at the unknown country of Erewhon. (Much like More's Utopia, Erewhon is a thinly veiled "nowhere" in anagram form.)

He first encounters a circle of "rude and barbaric" statues that elicit a terrible howl from the wind as it passes through them and cause him to collapse in fear. He is later awoken by girls tending goats who bring him to their elders. As a stranger Higgs is taken into custody, his watch removed and health assessed before being briefly imprisoned. Higgs observes that the practices and beliefs of the Erewhonians seem strangely topsy-turvy and in reverse to his own. Most intriguing is their response to the "crime" of becoming sick, in comparison to, one might assume, more voluntary transgressions:

> . . . if a man falls into ill health, or catches any disorder, or fails bodily in any way before he is seventy years old, he is tried before a jury of his countrymen, and if convicted is held up to public scorn. . . . But if a man forges

a check, or sets his house on fire, or robs with violence from the person, or does any other such things as are criminal in our own country, he is either taken to a hospital and most carefully tended at the public expense, or if he is in good circumstances, he lets it be known to all his friends that he is suffering from a severe fit of immorality . . .

Detail from Giovanni Bellini's, *Saint Jerome Reading in a Landscape*, as used to depict Butler's imaginary realm in a Penguin Classics edition of *Erewhon*.

This reversal is seen in many facets of daily life: Erewhonian youths attend Universities of Unreason, where nothing useful is taught; and any form of machinery is proscribed on the grounds that, if allowed to develop, the machines will take over society. The state religion is a worship of the goddess Ydgrun, another partial anagram making reference to "Mrs. Grundy," an off-stage character from Thomas Morton's play *Speed the Plough* (1798), who had, by Butler's time, become synonymous with censorious, "bluenosed" moralism.

Nosnibor—who is in the process of "recovering" from embezzling a widow and children out of all their money—takes Higgs under his wing after his release from prison, and the narrator falls in love with his daughter, Arowhena. He eventually escapes with her, and returns to the outside world by hot-air balloon. In Butler's 1901 sequel, *Erewhon Revisited*, a widowed Higgs returns to discover that following his mysterious disappearance into the sky he has become the center of a "Sunchild" cult. Human beings it seems, the skeptical Butler asserts, will believe anything.

RICHARD WAGNER

THE RING OF THE NIBELUNG
(1876)

This epic masterpiece of gods, heroes, and men is arguably the most extraordinary achievement in the history of opera.

Wagner worked on the libretto and music for the four operas for nearly thirty years, from 1848 to 1874.

King Ludwig II of Bavaria demanded previews of *The Rhinegold* (1869) and *The Valkyrie* (1870) before Wagner had completed the rest of the cycle. The first complete performance of the *Ring* was at the Bayreuth Festspielhaus (specifically built to Wagner's design) from 13 to 17 August 1876.

Opposite: Arthur Rackham depicts the Valkyrie Brünnhilde riding her faithful steed Grane into the funeral pyre of her lover Siegfried, in *Siegfried and the Twilight of the Gods* (1924).

There can be very few artists more explosively divisive than Richard Wagner (1813–83). The composer's own ideas about racial supremacy and, later, the appropriation of his music by the Nazis (Adolf Hitler would claim Wagner as one of his favorite composers) have cast a dark shadow over his work. Scholars still struggle with the question of whether it is possible, or even acceptable, to separate the music from the man. And yet Wagner created some of the most celebrated music in history, and his "Ride of the Valkyries" is arguably one of the most recognized musical themes ever written.

Wagner created both the music and the libretto (the text) for his operas, and his perception of their staged performance as a *Gesamtkunstwerk*— a "total work of art" combining drama, music, scenery and spectacle —revolutionized the art form. His creative vision was most fully realized in the epic four-opera cycle, "The Ring of the Nibelung" (or "Der Ring des Nibelungen" in its original German), a masterpiece that took him nearly thirty years to write.

The "Ring" is set in a world of Northern mythology that the composer adapted to suit his own vision. Many other writers, notably Tolkien, have found inspiration in these same sources, but Wagner's vision is original and distinctive. It is, to begin with, set on a consistently lofty plane. Wagner's main source, the Norse epic "The Saga of the Volsungs," is a story of great heroes, but they are human, and some are known to have actually existed. Wagner's world, by contrast, is dominated by figures from mythology: the gods, the giants, the dwarfs, the Valkyries (who carry off slain warriors from the battlefield to Valhalla, Wotan's home), and the Norns (female figures who control human destiny by spinning Fate). All of these beings are mentioned, if not in "The Saga of the Volsungs" then elsewhere in Old Norse literature, but Wagner expanded the roles of many of them and added others, notably the Rhinemaidens, who guard the Rhine's gold from which the titular magic ring is eventually forged.

As part of the *Gesamtkunstwerk,* Wagner's mythological libretto and complex characterization are accompanied by a wealth of detailed

stage directions (which must have been difficult to follow faithfully with only nineteenth-century technology). The opening scene of the first opera, *The Rhinegold* (*Das Rheingold*), for example, is set in swirling waters, with rocks, mist, and deep gorges, from which the dwarf Alberich (the "Nibelung" of the cycle's title) snatches the Rhinegold from the Rhinemaidens. The second scene is set outside the majestic hall of Valhalla, which the giants Fasolt and Fafner have just finished building for Wotan, chief of the gods. And so it goes on throughout the cycle, from the smoking forges of Nibelheim (where Alberich makes the magic ring), to cloud-strewn mountaintops and bird-filled forests. Wagner's capacity for epic world building knew no bounds. And yet curiously, unlike so many other world-creating artists, Wagner seems to have woven his intricate and detailed realm, with the specific intention of destroying it completely.

As *The Rhinegold* continues it is revealed that, in return for building Valhalla, Wotan has promised the giants the goddess Freia (his wife Fricka's sister) as payment. Since Freia possesses the Golden Apples that keep the gods immortal, this is clearly a dangerous gamble. It appears Freia is indeed lost until Wotan's clever and resourceful assistant Loge tells of Alberich's powerful ring. The giants agree that they will return the goddess if Wotan can present the ring to them by evening.

Wotan and Loge then trick Alberich into giving up the ring, and the furious dwarf places a deadly curse upon it. Wotan attempts to keep the ring, but eventually surrenders it to the giants, whereupon the curse takes its lethal effect and Fafner beats Fasolt to death as they quarrel over the ring.

The Valkyrie (*Die Walküre*) continues the epic story, explaining that Wotan is desperate to regain the ring before Alberich does, fearing disaster for the gods. The laws of the gods, however, prevent him from seizing it back by force. It has to be done by a hero who is free from these laws, whom Wotan tries to create by siring a son, Siegmund, with Erda, the embodiment of the Earth. Siegmund, however, falls in love with his own twin sister, Sieglinde, and Wotan's wife Fricka—guardian of propriety—insists that he must die. Wotan's daughter, the Valkyrie Brünnhilde, attempts to protect Siegmund, but Wotan shatters his son's sword and Siegmund is killed by Sieglinde's husband, Hunding. Brünnhilde manages to rescue the pregnant Sieglinde and the broken sword, though the Valkyrie is punished for her disobedience by being cast into a magic sleep.

The third opera, Siegfried, centers on the eponymous hero, child of Siegmund and Sieglinde, who grows up knowing no fear. Taught by Alberich's brother, Mime, Siegfried reforges his father's sword, kills Fafner with it and recaptures the ring. He goes on to waken the sleeping Brünnhilde, and instantly falls in love with her.

The final part of the cycle, *The Twilight of the Gods* (*Götterdämmerung*), begins with the three Norns weaving the rope of Destiny. Their song reveals that the gods' time will end and that Wotan will burn Valhalla.

Wotan's scheming is finally defeated in this last installment by Alberich's son Hagen. With a potion of oblivion he makes Siegfried forget his love for Brünnhilde, and sends him to her disguised as his half-brother Gunther. Siegfried takes back the ring and then hands Brünnhilde over to the real Gunther, but when Brünnhilde recognizes the ring, which she thought had been taken by Gunther, once again on Siegfried's finger, she realizes that she has been deceived and accuses Siegfried of raping her in Gunther's form. Hagen then murders Siegfried for the ring and also kills his brother.

The three Rhinemaidens from the first complete performance of Wagner's epic in 1876, played by Lilli Lehmann (Woglinde), Marie Lehmann (Wellgunde), and Minna Lammert (Flosshilde).

The ring is at last regained by Brünnhilde, who takes it with her into the funeral pyre. In the last spectacle the Rhinemaidens flood the pyre, seize the ring and drown Hagen, while in the background the gods and heroes in Valhalla are lost in flame.

Many questions arise from Wagner's complex plot. What happens in the end to Alberich? Why are the gods finally doomed along with Siegfried, when the ring is once again safe in the possession of the Rhinemaidens? The story is a fable of love and power, but the point of the fable remains an enigma. It has been interpreted as a critique of industrialization in modern society and, conversely, as an idealization of heroic force and individual energy.

Whatever Wagner's intention with the "The Ring of the Nibelung," its vast world has influenced all later attempts to portray apocalyptic themes in music, literature, art, and cinema. The most familiar being perhaps Francis Ford Coppola's *Apocalypse Now*, in which the "Ride of the Valkyries" is blasted from helicopter-mounted speakers as U.S. troops perform a bombing raid on a Vietnamese village.

ROBERT LOUIS STEVENSON

TREASURE ISLAND (1883)

One of the world's most enduring adventure stories, it is an engrossing and timeless tale of pirates, mutiny, buried treasure, and "x marks the spot."

Stevenson's story was serialized in *Young Folks* magazine in 1881, credited to "Captain George North." It was first published in book form by Cassell and Company, Ltd, in 1883, without the pseudonym (see above for the first U.S. edition, published by Roberts Brothers in 1884).

The original manuscript, like those of many of Stevenson's novels, is lost —his papers are famously scattered, having been auctioned by his family during World War I.

Opposite: Stevenson's treasure map resembles, according to the author, "a fat dragon standing up."

Take a poll of the greatest adventure stories ever written and the odds are that this rattling pirate tale will appear very high on the list. Robert Louis Stevenson (1850–94)—"Louis," as friends and family called him—was no longer a young man when he finally wrote what in later life he proclaimed to be "my first book." Stevenson and his new wife, Fanny, had returned from California to Louis's native Edinburgh for the summer of 1880. Fanny, previously married, brought to the marriage an eleven-year-old son, Lloyd. Back in his hometown Louis was reunited with an old comrade, W. E. Henley. The two men had earlier met in a hospital where Louis was being treated for his weak lungs and Henley had just had a leg amputated. Henley is today remembered for his poem, *Invictus*, with its rousing final lines: "I am the master of my fate/I am the captain of my soul." The character he inspired, however, has long been accepted into the collective memory.

As Stevenson admitted to Henley, after the publication of *Treasure Island*: "It was the sight of your maimed strength and masterfulness that begot [the novel's central villain] Long John Silver . . . the idea of the maimed man, ruling and dreaded by the sound, was entirely taken from you." Wooden legs were more usually associated in the nineteenth century, not with poets, but with sea-going men. At sea, if your leg was injured, in battle or even accidentally, immediate amputation was the surest remedy. Ships had no hospital facilities and cutting the damaged limb off at once and cauterizing the wound in boiling tar was the only protection against gangrene. Often the ship's cook performed the operation using kitchen knives. A piece of timber was strapped on after the wound had healed. If a hand was lost, one of the meat hooks in the ship's galley would serve as a replacement. (Captain Hook in *Peter Pan*, 1911, was directly inspired, as J. M. Barrie acknowledged, by Long John Silver.)

Doctors pronounced Edinburgh—known as "auld reekie" because of its smog-filled air—hazardous for Stevenson's health. Fanny and Louis did not have the funds to wander far and rented a cottage in Braemar in the Highlands. The weather was "absolutely and consistently vile" and the family was confined

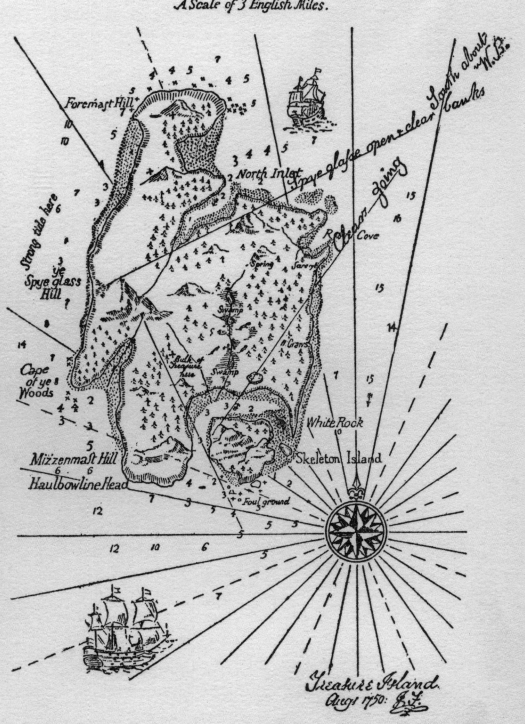

A Scale of 3 English Miles.

Foremast Hill

North Inlet

Spye glaſs open & clear to South about W.B.

Clear going

Strong tide here

ye Spye glaſs Hill

Rock Cove

Spring

Swamp

Cape of ye Woods

Bulk of Treasure here

Swamp

Graves

White Rock

Mizzenmast Hill

Haulbowline Head

Skeleton Island

Foul ground

Treasure Island.
Augt 1750. J.F.

Given by above J.F. & Mr. W Bones Maſter of ye Walrus
Savannah this twenty July 1754 W. B.

Facsimile of Chart; latitude and
longitude struck out by J. Hawkins

to the house. One day, in an effort to entertain Lloyd, Stevenson painted a map of an island.

> ... it was elaborately and (I thought) beautifully colored; the shape of it took my fancy beyond expression; it contained harbors that pleased me like sonnets ... as I paused on my map of "Treasure Island," the future character of the book began to appear there visibly among imaginary woods.... The next thing I knew I had some papers before me and was writing out a list of chapters.

The tale sprang from Stevenson's pen at the rate of a chapter every morning. Other more serious writing chores were suspended. At this stage it was entirely a domestic enterprise. Luckily, for literature and for Stevenson's career, a visitor, Dr. Alexander Hay Japp, was invited to listen to the ongoing tale. One should imagine Stevenson's thrilling, Scots-accented voice as the first paragraph was read out:

"'One more step, Mr. Hands,' said I, 'and I'll blow your brains out! Dead men don't bite, you know,' I added with a chuckle." Jim wrangles in the rigging with the pirate Israel Hands.

> I remember him as if it were yesterday, as he came plodding to the inn door, his sea-chest following behind him in a hand-barrow—a tall, strong, heavy, nut-brown man, his tarry pigtail falling over the shoulder of his soiled blue coat, his hands ragged and scarred, with black, broken nails, and the saber cut across one cheek, a dirty, livid white.

What Japp heard was the opening section of the story—that is, Billy Bones being tracked to the Admiral Benbow Inn by the Blind Pew; young Jim's discovering the map of the island where Captain Flint's treasure was buried; Squire Livesey and Dr. Trelawney joining forces with young Hawkins to mount an expedition on the good ship *Hispaniola*. Still to come were Long John Silver, the mutiny he leads aboard the *Hispaniola*, the marooned Ben Gunn, and the bloody fight to the death on the island. Eventually the heroes find the treasure and return home enriched beyond dreams. The villains get their just desserts—except for Silver, who escapes with his parrot and a pouch of doubloons. Stevenson, one guesses, may have foreseen a *Treasure Island II*, never written, about his amiable rogue.

As luck would have it, Japp was closely connected with the editor of the popular weekly comic, *Young Folks*. Based in London, the editor-proprietor was James Henderson, a fellow Scot. Why not, Japp suggested, publish the tale in *Young Folks*? It would make a welcome handful of "jingling guineas" for the author (who was, as it happened, in dire need of funds).

Stevenson completed the history of Jim Hawkins and *Treasure Island* was duly serialized, earning its author a little under £50, and Stevenson went on to make a small fortune from subsequent reprints. *Treasure Island* also heralded the arrival of a major new talent in British fiction. The story that had begun as a domestic entertainment, recited by the fireside to while away tedious days and nights, became a classic. One cannot imagine English fiction without it.

Astonishingly, given its later popularity, *Treasure Island* was not a great success in *Young Folks*. Arguably Stevenson's story was too complex, psychologically, for the paper's juvenile readership. And perhaps, more significantly, *Treasure Island* was rather too disturbing for young readers. The murder of Tom Redruth, for example, goes well beyond the routinely spilled gore relished by Victorian children. Silver has failed to recruit the Squire's loyal man to the mutineers' cause. It is Tom's death sentence. On witnessing the brutal homicide, described gruesomely, Jim faints. And the reader, whether adult or child, also finds it hard to restrain a shudder—not least at the thought of Silver surviving, unpunished for this callous crime, and rewarded with ill-gotten gold, to crack further spines that may happen to raise his ire. Whatever happened to the poetic justice that is the stock in trade of children's fiction?

Treasure Island is a richly complex work of imagination. And where did the novel's imagined world begin? With a wooden leg, bad weather, and the chance visit of a stranger.

"Down went Pew with a cry that rang high into the night." The pirate Blind Pew is run down by tax collectors on horseback.

It was Silver's voice, and before I had heard a dozen words, I would not have shown myself for all the world. I lay there, trembling and listening, in the extreme of fear and curiosity, for, in those dozen words, I understood that the lives of all the honest men aboard depended on me alone.

"A SQUARE" (EDWIN A. ABBOTT)

FLATLAND: A ROMANCE OF MANY DIMENSIONS (1884)

This short classic of science fiction describes the mathematical journeys of A. Square through the varied dimensions of Spaceland, Lineland, and Pointland.

First published by Seeley and Co. in 1884.

Abbott was best known in his own lifetime as an educator, and theological and linguistic scholar; he authored a number of textbooks, theological treatises, and even a biography of the philosopher Francis Bacon.

The story was adapted into an animated film in 2007, with the voices of Martin Sheen and Kristen Bell.

Mathematicians write interesting novels (such as Lewis Carroll's *Alice's Adventures in Wonderland*, 1865, for example, page 82). *Flatland's* author, Edwin A. Abbott (1838–1926), was a schoolteacher, a philologist, a theologian, and the possessor of one of the more playfully inquiring minds of his incurably inquiring age. In *Flatland*, he produced the prototype of the allegorical science-fiction story.

The novel—if it can be called such (it reads, at times, like an extended intellectual joke)—imagines a two-dimensional (that is, flat) universe. The narrator is "A Square," a geometric everyman. The narrative takes the form of an extended meditation on life and social mores in his single-plane universe, and sets out the fate of those who question or transgress its boundaries. Addressing his readers privileged to live in "space," Square explains:

> Imagine a sheet of paper on which straight Lines, Triangles, Squares, Pentagons, Hexagons, and other figures, instead of remaining fixed in their places, move freely about, on or in the surface, but without the power of rising above or sinking below it, very much like shadows—only hard with luminous edges—and you will then have a pretty correct notion of my country and countrymen.

The first half of the book, especially, focuses on the rigid and hierarchical social structure of Flatland, and gives the book its reputation as a satire of Victorian social norms. Classes in Flatland are determined by the number of angles a character possesses, with many-sided polygons constituting a kind of aristocracy and isosceles triangles a working class, while regular quadrilaterals, like the narrator, are solidly middle class. Social mobility is limited and possible only for men (sons acquire additional angles with each generation), while women, who are lines only, are unable to improve their station. In addition, women, who might be mistaken for "points" when seen head-on, are required to use separate doors and shout aloud when moving around Flatland, in order to avoid accidentally stabbing their countrymen.

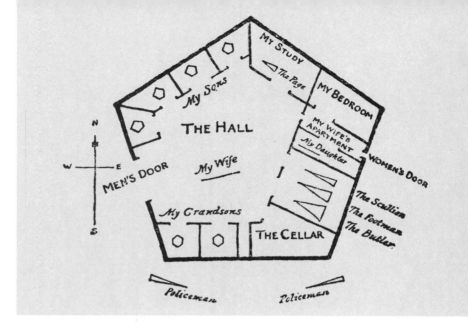

The image shows a map of A. Square's house. Labels on the map include: MY STUDY, The Page, MY BEDROOM, My Sons, MY WIFE'S APARTMENT, My Daughter, THE HALL, WOMEN'S DOOR, MEN'S DOOR, My Wife, The Scullion, The Footman, The Butler, My Grandsons, THE CELLAR, Policeman, Policeman. A compass rose shows N, E, W, S.

While it might seem anachronistic or heavy-handed to attribute "feminist" consciousness to Abbott, he does seem to acknowledge his satirical intentions in the preface to a revised edition of the book, arguing that: "(until very recent times) the destinies of Women and of the masses of mankind have seldom been deemed worthy of mention and never of careful consideration."

In the year 1999, as a new millennium dawns, Square dreams of an even less dimensional world—Lineland —where existence is unilinear (does a line have four sides, like a quadrilateral? It does if you draw it with a pencil, it doesn't in geometry. Let your mind wrestle with that).

Like the hero of H. G. Wells's story "The Country of the Blind" (1904), Square is unable to persuade the king of Lineland that there may be worlds other than that over which he is sovereign. Mathematicians, of course, are used to people not understanding what they are talking about. Square is himself bewildered by a spherical visitor from three-dimensional Spaceland (that is, our world). Are there yet other worlds with different geometries? Pointland, where all existence is confined to a single dot, is alluded to, but Sphere himself, in his turn, refuses to countenance the possibility of fourth, fifth, or higher dimensions beyond his, and our, own (though these are now a commonplace of modern physics and mathematics). Announcing his discoveries to his fellow Flatlanders, Square finds himself imprisoned for heresy. He has, so to speak, stepped over the line. Abbott's tale is dedicated, as he declares, to "the enlargement of the imagination." Many readers will find his imagined worlds brain-stretchers, indeed, but none the less entertaining for that.

The first cover featured a map of A. Square's house, with a wider door for the polygon males and a narrow shaft for the female lines.

EDWARD BELLAMY

LOOKING BACKWARD:
2000–1887 (1888)

The most influential nineteenth-century "utopia" and a book with a political vision that inspired a network of "Bellamy Clubs" and, ultimately, a political party.

First published by Ticknor and Co. in 1888.

By 1900, *Looking Backward* was the third best-selling book of all time in the U.S, behind *Uncle Tom's Cabin* (1852) and *Ben-Hur: A Tale of the Christ* (1880).

Bellamy's "sleep and time travel" idea was picked up by fellow socialist H. G. Wells in *The Sleeper Awakes* (1910). Wells added the ingenious wrinkle that, after sleeping for one hundred years, the sleeper awakes to discover his savings account has swelled to make him the richest man in the world.

In Edward Bellamy's (1850–98) story, Julian West, a well-bred Bostonian, is a blessed man. He has great wealth, high intellect, and, in Edith Bartlett, a beautiful fiancée. There are two flies in Julian's ointment. One is his vague unease regarding the huge, unfair divisions between rich and poor in 1887. The other is an "insomnia," worse even than Macbeth's. Julian is a happy man, yes, but a worried man.

Street noise is particularly troublesome to Julian. He constructs a secret, soundproof room under his house, known only to his servant, where, after being mesmerized by a friend (in the 1880s, "mesmerization," or hypnosis, was all the rage,) Julian hopes to fall into a deep slumber. It is not to be. So successful is the mesmerization that Julian wakes on September 10, 2000—113 years into the future. He discovers that a fire destroyed his house soon after he fell asleep and killed the servant who alone knew his master's location. No one could discover what had happened to Julian West and, after all this time, no one cares.

Bellamy was very excited about what he called "the rate of change" in his world, and appended a postscript on the subject to his fable. His vision of the future was, however, rather too accelerated; *Looking Backward*'s "Year 2000" is very different from that we actually experienced (the fate of many utopias—was 1984 at all like Orwell's *Nineteen Eighty-Four*?)

Bellamy's 2000 is literally "millennial," the perfect world at the end of time. Julian discovers a perfect society, which has solved the problems of industrialization by abolishing laissez-faire capitalism in favor of socialism (though Bellamy was careful to avoid this word, freighted with negative associations for his readership). Wealth is equally distributed and private property abolished. Everyone receives a college education and lifelong care from a benevolent state. Work is light and rewarding and the retirement age is forty-five—life expectancy is now much higher and social ills including crime, corruption, and poverty have vanished.

Unable to return to his "present" (mesmerism offers no return tickets— only H. G. Wells's time machine could do that, see page 110) Julian is happy

The effect of change in surroundings is like that of lapse of time in making the past seem remote.

Vol. 2.   DECEMBER, 1889.   No. 1.

"THE NATIONALIZATION OF INDUSTRY AND THE PROMOTION OF THE BROTHERHOOD OF HUMANITY."—*Constitution of the Nationalist Club, Boston, Mass.*

THE

NATIONALIST

THIS EDITION ___ 35,000.

PUBLISHED BY

THE NATIONALIST EDUCATIONAL ASSOCIATION,

No. 77 BOYLSTON STREET, BOSTON, MASS.

Copyright, 1889, by Nationalist Educational Association. Entered at the Boston Post-Office as second-class matter

PRICE $1.00 A YEAR.   SINGLE NUMBERS 10 CENTS.

to be transported permanently into the future and, in fact, has a truly nightmarish moment when he thinks that this voyage to 2000 is all a fantasy. He falls in love with Edith Leete, the great-grand-daughter of his first and former love, Edith Bartlett, and Bellamy ends the story with the following, uplifting declaration:

> All thoughtful men agree that the present aspect of society is portentous of great changes. The only question is, whether they will be for the better or the worse. Those who believe in man's essential noble-ness lean to the former view, those who believe in his essential baseness to the latter. For my part, I hold to the former opinion. *Looking Backward* was written in the belief that the Golden Age lies before us and not behind us, and is not far away.

Cover for *The Nationalist,* an American socialist magazine established by followers of Bellamy's utopian ideas, from December 1889.

Bellamy's book itself had a fairly immediate impact, becoming a national best-seller in the year after its initial release. It has stayed in print continually since first publication and spawned a huge number of sequels, as well as literary "responses" (not consistently positive), including William Morris's utopian *News From Nowhere* (1890). In the immediate aftermath of its release, hundreds of "Nationalist" (or "Bellamy") clubs sprang up across the U.S.— forums in which the novel's ideas, and their potential for realization, were earnestly discussed. Bellamy joined the increasingly politicized movement in the early 1890s and even ran his own, short-lived magazine, *The New Nation* (previously *The Nationalist*), to disseminate the group's ideas. Financial difficulties and the increasing popularity of the People's Party (which itself later merged with the Democratic party) saw the Nationalist movement wane in the mid-1890s, but Bellamy's book—which he had, at one point, described as a "literary fantasy, a fairy tale"—had already made its mark.

MARK TWAIN (SAMUEL LANGHORNE CLEMENS)

A CONNECTICUT YANKEE IN KING ARTHUR'S COURT (1889)

This satirical story imagines a very different Camelot as nineteenth-century American citizen Hank Morgan is transported to medieval England following a blow to the head.

Originally titled *A Yankee in King Arthur's Court*, the book was first published by Charles L. Webster and Co. in 1889.

Twain was inspired to write *A Connecticut Yankee* after acquiring a copy of Thomas Malory's tale of chivalrous knights *Le Morte d'Arthur* (1485, page 44).

"I am not an American. I am *the* American," is a pronouncement often misattributed to celebrated writer and humorist Mark Twain (he was, in fact, quoting his friend Frank Fuller), and it is easy to see why, since, among American writers, he has the firmest grasp of the national voice. But what, this most American of American writers wondered, was it to be American?

The core question, as Twain saw it, was the new country's (America) relationship with the old country (England). There was conflict as well as inheritance in the American mix. It was this contradiction that Twain set his imagination to probe in his major work of fiction, *A Connecticut Yankee in King Arthur's Court* (1889).

As the nineteenth century drew to a close, a number of writers became fascinated by the idea of time travel as a fictional device, but most, such as H. G. Wells, were happier with travel into the future than into the past. After all, if you alter the past, how can you preserve the present you have just left? Twain rode roughshod over the possible paradoxes. *A Connecticut Yankee* opens with Twain meeting a stranger who has an amazing tale to tell. Hank Morgan has returned from Camelot—King Arthur's court. This was the place where the ideals of British nobility, gentlemanliness, and chivalry had been formed. It was the starting point of English civilization.

Hank is bashed on the head with a crowbar and finds himself transported from 1879 Hartford, Connecticut, to a field just outside Camelot, England, in 528. Our hero's first reaction, on being told by a passer-by where he has landed, is despair: "I felt a mournful sinking at the heart, and muttered: 'I shall never see my friends again—never, never again. They will not be born for more than thirteen hundred years yet.'" Despair gives way to terror when a passing knight picks on him for a bit of lance-practice.

Hank is a true American, however. He introduces himself and takes a tour of that England and is both amused and disgusted by what he sees. Merlin turns out to be fake—no more skillful than a third-rate circus magician—and England is riddled with a corrupt class system. To a freeborn Connecticut Yankee it is confusing and horrifying. Hank takes charge. What

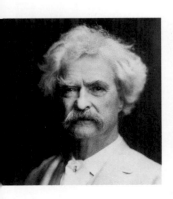

You can't depend on
your eyes when your
imagination is out of focus.

An illustration from the first edition by Daniel Carter Beard, showing Sir Launcelot riding a penny farthing.

the sixth century needs, he perceives, is some good old (that's to say "new") American know-how. Technology, industry, factories, steam power, telephones, bicycles, guns. In no time at all, wheels have replaced hooves. In no time at all he is the most important man in the country, more important indeed than the king. He assumes a title—Sir Boss.

The plot, thereafter, becomes complicated. Hank marries and has a baby. He sets up (secretly) a military training institution, based on West Point. His men are trained in modern warfare, with modern weaponry. They are few in number but formidable. Civil War breaks out and Hank's tiny force defeats the Church's attempted coup with electric fences and machine guns, but at the moment of his triumph, Hank is wounded. Merlin, in disguise, poisons him.

How should we read this world? Twain's American contemporaries saw the tale as a wholly patriotic fable—its satire on the filth, servitude, and superstition of "old England" made their new country shine all the brighter. Twain himself seems partly to have supported this view. But, like all great works of imagination, *A Connecticut Yankee* can be read more than one way. The tale does not fit Twain's own too-neat description of a moral lesson benevolently given by an American teacher to the English people. Hank represents progress—but it is the progress of blood, iron, and mass murder. In his passages of Gatling guns spitting death at the unarmed opponents, Twain is surely thinking of the American Civil War. Extraordinarily, with that strange foresight that great artists have, Twain seems to have been vouchsafed a vision of the carnage to come in 1914. It's terrible—but funny too—and very Twain.

H. G. WELLS

THE TIME MACHINE (1895)

Popularizing the concept of machinery as a means of time travel, Wells's enduring fantasy depicts a distant future populated by frail, simple humanoids and dark, twisted cannibals.

First published in 1895 in serial form in *The New Review*. The eleventh chapter, which appeared in the serial, was cut from the novel, published later the same year by William Heinemann.

Wells wrote several other important works of science fiction, including *The Island of Doctor Moreau* (1896), *The Invisible Man* (1897), and *The War of the Worlds* (1897).

Opposite: Poster advertising the 1960 MGM film adaptation, produced and directed by George Pal.

Who is the Shakespeare of imaginative fiction? For many it's a debate between H. G. Wells and Jules Verne. Yet, the hallmark Vernian and Wellsian narratives are different. The Frenchman's specialism was the *voyage imaginaire*—spectacular tourism into the unexplored—conducting his travelers 20,000 leagues under the sea (see page 88), to the center of and around Earth (in a timetable-defying eighty days), and even to the moon. Wells's preferred style was what he called "scientific romances"—works of the imagination plausibly anchored in the most recent discoveries of science. Imagination, for Wells, went hand in hand with authentication, and his eye for the fictional possibilities in scientific advancements was uncanny. *The Invisible Man* was produced barely months after Wilhelm Roentgen demonstrated the power of the X-ray to see through flesh, *The War of the Worlds* took off from W. H. Pickering's observations of suspiciously active "canals" on the surface of Mars, and *The War in the Air* followed two years after the Wright Brothers' first successful flight at Kitty Hawk.

Where did this brilliantly imaginative popularizer of the latest science come from? H. G. Wells sprang from a generation and class liberated from traditional servitudes by the 1870 Universal Education Act. His father was a professional cricketer who, after injury, turned small—and unsuccessful—shopkeeper. The family broke up when Wells was thirteen, and his mother went to work in a large country house, where he was allowed the run of the library. On leaving school, the young Wells served an apprenticeship in a draper's "emporium," which he loathed (the experience is immortalized in his comedy *Kipps*).

Sharp as a tack, at eighteen he won a government scholarship to the Normal School of Science where he was heavily influenced by T. H. Huxley, the evolutionary advocate known as "Darwin's Bulldog." *The Origin of Species* (published seven years before Wells was born) became the young author's bible, and his belief in its infallibility would be unshaken until his death. Huxley had introduced into the creed the notion of "survival of the fittest"—something ensured by eternal

struggle within and between the species. It, too, became an article of faith for the young man.

Wells did not excel in his classes. He was too preoccupied with writing in the student journal: notably on an early version of *The Time Machine*—a short story called "The Chronic Argonauts." Had he worked on his lessons, Wells might have become a middlingly successful scientist. But his genius lay in absorbing new scientific discoveries and imaginatively repackaging them for the unscientific masses. What form should that package take? Wells was initially unsure. *The Time Machine* began as a series of rather plodding explanatory essays. But he soon realized that audiences prefer stories to lectures. Thus his career, and its hundred books, began.

The Time Machine was Wells's first published scientific romance, and was more *voyage imaginaire* than even Verne could have devised. He wrote the story in the chance of finding a market for it. Completed at a low point in his early life, Wells remembers—in *Experiment in Autobiography*—working on it late one summer night by an open window in a meager lodgings in Kent, England, while a disagreeable landlady grumbled at him in the darkness outside because of the excessive use of her lamp.

The Time Machine opens with a vivid paragraph, designed to hook the casually skimming reader of the magazine *The New Review* in which it was first serialized:

> The Time Traveler (for so it will be convenient to speak of him) was expounding a recondite matter to us. His grey eyes shone and twinkled, and his usually pale face was flushed and animated. The fire burned brightly, and the soft radiance of the incandescent lights in the lilies of silver caught the bubbles that flashed and passed in our glasses.

In "The Chronic Argonauts" the traveler was given a name: Dr. Nebogipfel (it translates from German as "foggy mountain peak"). In this later incantation, rendering the traveler and his audience anonymous at their regular Thursday evening gatherings was a fine touch. His identity must, of course, be kept secret to preserve the secrecy of the time machine.

To his friends (an all-male company, of course) the traveler explains two things. First, the nature of the fourth dimension; second, the fact that he has invented a time machine to navigate it. His audience is gathered to witness his first experimental voyage, from which he will return the following Thursday. He duly returns and reports on his three journeys into the future.

The first is to the year 802,701. He discovers that evolution has gone into reverse—human kind has devolved into two contrary species: the effete Eloi, who spend their lives in a kind of Garden of Eden, doing nothing but play; and the cannibalistic Morlocks, slaving in a subterranean factory world, emerging only at night, to feast on their captors.

The Eloi live their pretty and pointless lives under a gigantic decayed Sphinx, recalling Shelley's sonnet "Ozymandias" and the fall of civilization. The Eloi are themselves versions of the late-nineteenth-century decadents, notably Oscar Wilde and his followers. After battling the Morlocks the traveler makes two further trips forward, witnessing the heat-death of the solar system in the sun's dying days, with nothing living in it but fungus and sinister crablike things. With this, he takes off again, never to return.

Time travel had been a favorite motif of imaginative literature long before Wells's chronic fantasies. The weak point in the scenario, however, was how you actually got into the future, or the past. A popular technique was that of Bunyan, in *The Pilgrim's Progress*:

> As I walk'd through the wilderness of this world, I lighted on a certain place where was a Den, and I laid me down in that place to sleep; and as I slept, I dreamed a Dream.

Two imaginative works that influenced *The Time Machine* use this device: Edward Bellamy's *Looking Backward* (1889, page 106) and William Morris's *News from Nowhere* (1890). Both have protagonists who fall asleep and, like Washington Irving's Rip van Winkle, mysteriously wake up in the far future. But is it the real future, or a dream future? Morris and Bellamy were proto-socialists, and congenial to young Wells, but there was something fundamentally lame in the dream-vision gimmick. While another early title for his story was "The Time Traveller," Wells finally settled on *The Time Machine*—for him, the mechanics of the story were all-important.

But what, precisely, is the machine? Wells does not give a detailed description, other than it has a saddle and a triangular frame, and some mysterious crystals propelling it. Clearly, it is a version of the bicycle—the machine that liberated the late-Victorian slaving masses, cooped up in the urban centers of late industrial England (the next novel Wells wrote, *The Wheels of Chance* [1896] was on just this theme.) A bicycle capable of whizzing along the fourth dimension is implausible. But Wells's bejeweled roadster makes the point that, if we ever do cross the time-barrier, technology will get us there.

One direct inspiration for *The Time Machine* was an article by Simon Newcomb published in *Nature* in 1894, which the traveler mentions in his initial exposition to his friends. Newcomb, one of the country's leading mathematicians, argued that, "as a perfectly legitimate exercise of thought" we should admit the possibility of objects existing in a fourth dimension—time. Wells undertook just such an exercise.

The other scientific validation of his story for Wells was a lecture by his mentor T. H. Huxley in 1894, who made the supremely pessimistic point that, "our globe has been in a state of fusion, and, like the sun, is gradually cooling down . . . the time will come when evolution will mean an adaptation to universal winter, and all forms of life will die out . . . if for millions of years our globe has taken the upward road, yet some time the summit will be reached and the downward road will be commenced." Mathematical speculation and cosmic gloom aside, *The Time Machine* is a fun adventure and reads as freshly today as it did in 1895.

Class conflict was another topic. Was society in the 1890s polarizing rather than coming together? Would the working class, like the Morlocks— the exploited "many" as Shelley called them—revenge themselves at some point in the future on the privileged "few"? How should a socialist deal with that? Was there a solution? (The formation of the Independent Labor Party, a couple of years before was one; and one of which Wells approved.)

However, one of the problems of scientific romance is that the basic science can be demonstrably wrong. Wells's fellow novelist Israel Zangwill pointed out that the traveler, hurtling forward through time, would pass the date of his own death. Moreover, over the millennia, the steel frame of the time machine would rust. All that would arrive in 802,701 would be some bones, metal fragments, and a few dulled crystals.

The science, which seemed plausible in 1895, is now not so. Humankind currently lives in an interglacial period, between ice ages. In ten thousand years or so, the elliptical orbit of the earth will bring with it another ice age—Wells saw a continuous climatic line from 1895 to 802,701, with no intervening ice ages. Nor will the sun gradually cool, as Huxley predicted, like some gigantic radiator. When its nuclear fuel is used up, it will explode into a vast fireball, not ending cosmically frozen, but fried.

Wells also avoids the biggest paradox of all. The time machine has a reverse gear. What if the traveler went into the past, met himself—or his ancestors—and changed both his and the planet's future history? Over the seven years he wrote his story, Wells toyed with a trip to the past, and actually drafted a chapter in which his traveler returns to the Pleistocene period. In the end, he decided to keep his story simple. Simple, and wonderfully imaginative, the novel has never been out of print since its first publication in 1895, and who knows, it may still be in print—and enjoyed —in 802,701.

Rod Taylor in the 1960 film
adaptation directed by
George Pal.

L. FRANK BAUM

THE WONDERFUL WIZARD
OF OZ (1900)

*Named "America's greatest and best-loved homegrown fairy tale" by
the Library of Congress, the ageless morality tale of Dorothy, Toto, the
Scarecrow, the Tin Woodman, and the Cowardly Lion continues to
captivate readers young and old.*

First published by George M.
Hill Company in 1900.

Baum recalled taking the
name for his magical
kingdom from a filing
cabinet in which his papers
"O–Z" were stored.

On finishing the work, Baum
knew instinctively that he
had created something
remarkable. After writing
the last page he had his
pencil framed and placed
over his desk under the
inscription: "With this pencil
I wrote the manuscript of
'The Emerald City.'"

Opposite: Dorothy meets
the Cowardly Lion, drawn
for the first edition by
W. W. Denslow.

L. Frank Baum (1856–1919; the L. stands for Lyman) was born in New York
State, the son of a merchant enriched by the oil business. Baum went into
journalism and published his first book for children in 1897. Thereafter,
writing for the children's market was his principal activity and, in 1900,
together with the illustrator W. W. Denslow (1856–1915), he produced *The
Wonderful Wizard of Oz* (first entitled "The Emerald City"). Baum later span
off a series of "Oz" sequels and was one of the first generation of American
writers to adapt his work for the screen, moving himself and his family to
Hollywood to do so.

Now more people have seen *The Wizard of Oz* than have read it. MGM's
epoch-making film of 1939 (the eighth movie to be based on the story), however, is fairly faithful to what Baum wrote and Denslow pictured. The book
was conceived and published during one of the recurrent depressions in
American commercial life, and one of the points that Baum makes in his 1900
preface is that his story is "modernized"—set in the uncomfortable present.
This realism at the heart of the fantasy is something that makes it an innovative "fairy story."

The narrative opens on an impoverished farm, in a bleak landscape of the
"great Kansas prairies." An orphan, Dorothy is cared for by her Uncle Henry
and Auntie Em. The description of Dorothy's home is of a humble, dusty
place, setting up a stark comparison to the glittering world she is to discover:

> There were four walls, a floor, and a roof, which made one room; and this
> room contained a rusty looking cookstove, a cupboard for the dishes, a
> table, three or four chairs, and the beds. . . . There was no garret at all, and
> no cellar—except a small hole dug in the ground, called a cyclone cellar,
> where the family could go in case one of those great whirlwinds arose . . .

And sure enough, a cyclone does come. It carries away the rackety old
house, Dorothy and her faithful dog Toto inside, transporting it to the land of
the dwarfish Munchkins in the republic of Oz. From there Dorothy and Toto

" You ought to be ashamed of yourself ! "

Dorothy, the Tin Woodman, the Scarecrow, and the Cowardly Lion make their approach to the Emerald City in MGM's legendary 1939 film.

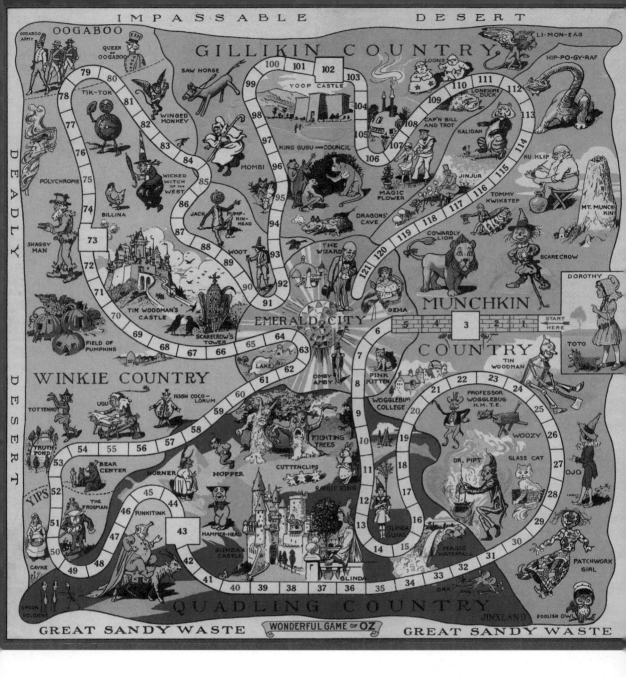

"That proves you are unusual," returned the Scarecrow; "and I am convinced that the only people worthy of consideration in this world are the unusual ones. For the common folks are like the leaves of a tree, and live and die unnoticed."

set off along the yellow brick road for the Emerald City, where, she understands, she will find a wizard who can help her get home to Kansas. On the way she meets up with her famous three companions: a Scarecrow, a Tin-Woodman, and a (Cowardly) Lion.

After various adventures along the way, the quartet arrives at the magnificent city and is ushered into the chamber of the Great Wizard. Quickly though, they discover the him to be a fraud and a "humbug," fed up with his pretenses and dreaming of his previous life as a circus clown. The Emerald City, too, is nothing but an illusion produced by the green spectacles worn by everyone who visits. The moral is clear. Help yourself—the traditional American remedy of self-improvement, which Dorothy and her companions eventually manage with some aid from the Good Witch of the South. And too, by her own efforts, Dorothy gets back to Kansas, realizing that however poor it is, she loves her humble home.

Over the last half-century, in which *The Wonderful Wizard of Oz* has become one of the best-known fairy stories in the world, scholars have got to work on it. No longer it is a text for children of all ages, but evidence for the inquisitive social scientist and historian. Baum, as has been said, was writing a period of severe economic depression and he had been very impressed, in 1894, by a hunger march on the White House by "Coxey's Army," named after the political organizer, Jacob Coxey. The unemployed, in their hundreds and sometimes thousands, marched across America to the capitol. Eventually their demonstration was broken up in Washington and the leaders arrested on charges of "trespassing on the White House lawn."

As such, some have interpreted the phony Wizard of Oz as representing the all-talk-and-no-action President of America, William McKinley. And, on their epic march up the yellow brick road (taken to be an allusion to the gold standard, which Coxey and other populists wanted to get rid of) Dorothy, the farm girl, represents the decent working classes; the Scarecrow represents the rural poor; and the Tin Man represents the toiling masses in the factories. The Lion is harder to fit in, although various "cowardly" leaders of the people have been proposed.

It's intriguing stuff—but not, in the end, particularly nourishing. While many things can be read into this much-loved tale of the real and unreal, the dream and nightmare, in the end it is incidental—albeit one that adds to the charm of this perennially fascinating work of imagination.

Opposite: "The Wonderful Game of Oz," a spin-off board game featuring all the lands and characters, which was manufactured by Parker Brothers in 1921.

3 GOLDEN AGE OF FANTASY

The early twentieth century saw a wealth of imaginary realms, from pulp space fantasies to chilling visions of a dystopian future, while the unprecedented violence of the World Wars was to alter fiction forever.

"The fairies have their tiffs with the birds."
Illustration by Arthur Rackham from *Peter Pan in Kensington Gardens* (1910), see page 124.

J. M. BARRIE

PETER PAN IN KENSINGTON GARDENS (1906)

A London park becomes an after-dark wonderland, the realm of fairies, talking birds, walking trees, and a little boy who can never grow up.

First published by Hodder and Stoughton in 1906.

Kensington Gardens were once the private gardens of Kensington Palace, but are today combined with Hyde Park as one of the Royal Parks of London.

J. M. Barrie wrote a number of works featuring Peter Pan: *The Little White Bird* (1902), *Peter Pan, or The Boy Who Wouldn't Grow Up* (a play from 1904), *When Wendy Grew Up* (a short play from 1908), and *Peter and Wendy* (1911), which was reprinted as *Peter Pan and Wendy*, and now usually published as simply *Peter Pan*.

Not all great stories arrive fully formed—it is in the nature of the legendary to accrue incident and resonance as time passes. So it is with Peter Pan, and the first book to bear the name of the boy who never grows up does not tell the story twenty-first century readers might expect. There is no Wendy, Neverland, Captain Hook, no pirates, crocodile, Lost Boys, or Tinker Bell. There are fairies, for *Peter Pan in Kensington Gardens* is in essence a fairy story, one that turns a region of London into an after-hours wonderland.

Peter Pan in Kensington Gardens was published in 1906, by which time the character of Peter Pan was famous, being at the heart of J. M. Barrie's (1860–1937) box-office record-setting 1904 play *Peter Pan, or The Boy Who Wouldn't Grow Up*. It was through the play that the story of Peter Pan developed its most familiar form. It was there that Hook, Wendy, and the rest were introduced. So then, when two years later *Peter Pan in Kensington Gardens* was published, readers might have expected a version of the play in novel form, or perhaps a sequel to the play. Instead, it was something akin to what would now be called an "origin story." The book was not even newly written, but had first appeared as Chapters 13–18 of Barrie's 1902 novel, *The Little White Bird*. A book extracted from a book, *Peter Pan in Kensington Gardens* is more a thematically linked series of stories and incidents than a novel.

The Little White Bird was written for adults. It is set mostly in turn-of-the-century London, around Kensington Gardens (the first U.S. edition was published with an additional subtitle—*or Adventures in Kensington Gardens*), and is narrated by a middle-aged, ex-army officer, Captain W__. The book tells the story of the captain's friendship with six-year-old David and how the Captain brought the boy's parents together. In a touch that now seems pre-postmodern, Captain W__ refers to his own writing of the text, at the end finishing the manuscript and giving the book to David's mother.

Peter Pan in Kensington Gardens begins with a Grand Tour of the Gardens, and while this does what it promises, introducing the famous landmarks—the Broad Walk, the Round Pond, the Serpentine—by the second paragraph the text has taken to whimsy. A lady sits by one of the garden's

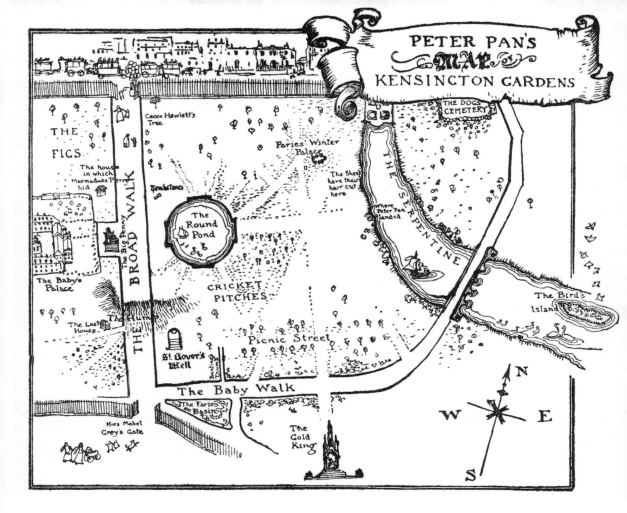

The following text labels appear on the map:

PETER PAN'S
MAP
KENSINGTON GARDENS

THE FICS

THE DOGS CEMETERY

Cecco Hewlett's Tree

The house in which Marmaduke Perry hid

Fairies' Winter Palace

Tombstones

The Sheep have their hair cut here

THE SERPENTINE

The Big Penny

THE BROAD WALK

The Round Pond

Where Peter Pan landed

The Baby's Palace

The Bird's Island

The Last House

THE STUMP

CRICKET PITCHES

St. Govor's Well

Picnic Street

The Baby Walk

Miss Mabel Grey's Gate

The Fairies Basin

The Gold King

N
W E
S

gates selling balloons. She must hold onto the railings always, for if she lets go "the balloons would lift her up, and she would be flown away." So far in this very middle-class world in which nurses and nannies take babies for "an airing in a perambulator," and where older children sail stick boats, she has held her position more successfully than her predecessor.

Strangely, even in the 1902 text, when Peter Pan is first mentioned, it is as if the reader already knows who he is. Writing about the notion that at night drowned stars appear in the Serpentine, Barrie first mentions his hero with the words: "If so, Peter Pan sees them when he is sailing across the lake..." Before he is properly introduced, it is established that Peter Pan has been famous for generations, that he was as legendary then as he is to us now: "if you ask your grandmother whether she knew about Peter Pan when she was a girl, she also says, 'Why, of course I did.'"

In Peter's world, before children were babies they were birds, and Peter escapes at seven-days old from becoming fully human by flying out his nursery window and back to Kensington Gardens. He will never be any older, no matter how long he lives. After frightening every fairy he meets, Peter

"Peter Pan's Kensington Gardens," a map from *Peter Pan in Kensington Gardens* by the illustrator of the original edition, Arthur Rackham.

"Autumn Fairies" by Arthur Rackham, from *Peter Pan in Kensington Gardens*.

consults with the birds, and flies to the island in the Serpentine. There is a touch of Christian allegory—the reason birds can fly and we can't is simply that they have perfect faith, and to have faith is to have wings—which rests oddly with the tale's essentially pantheist heart: Peter is a much sanitized image of the Greek god Pan.

On the island Peter meets Solomon Caw, depicted in Arthur Rackham's first edition illustrations as a crow. The Bible mentions by name only three children of the historical Solomon, but a man who had 700 wives and 300 concubines might be assumed to have had far more. Barrie allots his avian Solomon the task of dispatching a multitude of young birds out into the world to turn into human babies. It is also Solomon who makes Peter realize that he has lost his faith, and so will never be able to fly again. Trapped on the island, Peter makes a reed pipe and eventually the birds build him a boat in the form of a gigantic thrush's nest, which he uses to sail back into Kensington Gardens.

He sleeps by day on the island but plays by night, not entirely successfully, with whatever he finds in the gardens: a hoop, a pail, a balloon, even a perambulator "near the entrance to the Fairy Queen's Winter Palace." Peter comes to know the fairies well, and plays his pipe for their balls and dances. They grant him two wishes, both of which he uses to fly home. The first time he sees his mother sleeping, he almost stays. On the second occasion he resolves to stay, but finds the windows barred, "his mother sleeping peacefully with her arm around another little boy."

As much as Peter can never grow up, nor can he ever go home, and so he makes his world with the fairies. We are told that ". . . there are fairies wherever there are children. Long ago children were forbidden the Gardens, and at that time there was not a fairy in the place. . . ." Barrie makes his fairy society a parody of the everyday world, with every rank from postman to princess represented. And while his fairies are mostly harmless, "they never do anything useful."

From ambulatory, sentient trees, which prefigure the Ents of *The Lord of the Rings*, to a fairy world in which love is determined by a doctor's observations of physiological reaction, *Peter Pan in Kensington Gardens* fuses fancy and satire with rich yet restricted imagination. The vision would only become unfettered when Peter took to the stage.

The book ends in darkness, with the warning that it is not safe to stay in Kensington Gardens once the gates are locked for the night. That sometimes children perish of the "cold and dark" because Peter, riding on his goat, arrives too late to save them. In which case he digs a grave and "erects a little tombstone." Peter, not entirely responsible at his tender age, has been too late several times.

Opposite: Bronze statue of Peter Pan, "the boy who never grew up," in Kensington Gardens, Hyde Park, London. J. M. Barrie commissioned Sir George Frampton to make the statue in 1902, and it was erected in Kensington Gardens in 1912.

THE LOST WORLD (1912)

Professor Challenger embarks on a suspense-filled search for prehistoric creatures in the wilds of the Amazon, but his troop soon finds itself marooned among dinosaurs and the savage ape-people.

First published by Hodder and Stoughton in 1912.

Doyle was not the first to employ dinosaurs in fiction; writers James De Mille, Jules Lermina, and Frank Mackenzie Savile had all published adventure tales featuring the creatures after the first scientific descriptions of the "megalosaurus," were published in 1824.

Doyle was inspired by the Regent's Park Zoo in London, an offshoot of the nearby Zoological Society that is terrorized by the presentation of the pterodactyl in the book.

By 1912, Arthur Conan Doyle (1859–1930) was a hugely successful author, but he felt hampered by the vast popularity of his great detective, Sherlock Holmes, and wanted to try something new. *The Lost World* is the first, and most enduringly popular, of Doyle's "Professor Challenger" series in which the popular Victorian author aimed "to do for the boy's book what Sherlock Holmes did for the detective tale."

The fantasy draws on the author's own fascination with dinosaurs (iguanodon footprints had been discovered in Crowborough, Sussex, near the author's home in 1909) as well as the contemporary real-life expeditions of archaeologist and explorer Colonel Percival Harrison Fawcett. Doyle was also highly influenced by the prehistoric realms created in Jules Verne's *Journey to the Center of the Earth* (1864), but with its introduction of the extinct giants, *The Lost World* sets the standard for all future man-meets-monster adventures.

Doyle's narrator is a brash, young journalist, Edward "Ed" Malone of the *Daily Gazette*. Ed's Scottish editor, McArdle, sends him out to get a story on an eccentric professor who thinks he has discovered a secret valley containing prehistoric monsters. This is none other than Professor Challenger—a man notorious for physically assaulting newspaper reporters.

At a meeting of the Zoological Society, Challenger and his great opponent, the skeptical Professor Summerlee, agree to mount a scientific expedition to the Amazon and the secret valley in its remotest region. They take with them a professional explorer, the cool-headed Sir John Roxton ("the essence of the English country gentleman, the keen, alert, open-air lover of dogs and of horses"). Malone goes along too, to write the expedition up as a scoop for his paper.

The explorers travel up the great river (an area not well explored at this time)—experiencing adventures all the way—until they discover the "lost world." They take photographs of dinosaurs and fight a pitched battle against the "Ape-men." On their return home, they present their findings to the Zoological Society, which refuses to believe them, until they present some very compelling evidence:

[He] drew off the top of the case, which formed a sliding lid. . . . An instant later, with a scratching, rattling sound, a most horrible and loathsome creature appeared from below and perched itself upon the side of the case. . . . The face of the creature was like the wildest gargoyle that the imagination of a mad medieval builder could have conceived. It was malicious, horrible, with two small red eyes as bright as points of burning coal. Its long, savage mouth, which was held half-open, was full of a double row of shark-like teeth.

Still from *The Lost World* (1925), a silent film directed by Harry O. Hoyt, which featured pioneering stop-motion special effects by Willis O'Brien, animator of the original King Kong. Doyle himself supported the film, and supposedly even used a test reel to convince an audience that dinosaurs were real in 1922.

The novel retains some unpleasant descriptions of non-European ethnicity, ideas typical of Doyle's age, which can be interpreted as being uncomfortably linked to the evolution of species that is a central theme of the novel. However, while some passages of *The Lost World* undeniably stoop to racial stereotypes by today's standards, Doyle was also an active human-rights campaigner in his day, and his book *The Crime of the Congo* (1909) exposed the merciless enforced labor inflicted on indigenous people in the Congo Free State.

EDGAR RICE BURROUGHS

AT THE EARTH'S CORE (1914)

Prehistoric men and beasts are discovered in the subterranean world of "Pellucidar," buried within Earth's hollow interior in a pulp classic from the creator of Tarzan and John Carter.

At the Earth's Core was the first of Burroughs's six novels, the Pellucidar series, and was first published as a four-part serial in the *All-Story* weekly in April 1914. It was first published in book form (above) by A. C. McClurg and Co. in 1922.

Edgar Rice Burroughs used the pseudonym "Norman Bean" to protect his reputation at the start of his writing career.

Following the attacks on Pearl Harbor during World War II, Burroughs, by this time sixty years old, became a war correspondent.

At the Earth's Core is the first volume in what was to become a classic pulp science-fiction series from Edgar Rice Burroughs (1875–1950), based on the subterranean world of "Pellucidar." Burroughs was born in Chicago in 1875 and, after being discharged from the armed forces on health grounds, took on a number of low-wage jobs throughout the 1900s to support his family. He read numerous pulp-fiction magazines and decided to try his hand at writing. His brand of science-fiction adventure story found success at the *All-Story Magazine* and allowed him to write full time, creating, in 1912, Tarzan of the Apes, the character who would make his fortune. It was his Pellucidar series, however, that pushed the boundaries of the literary imagined realm.

At the Earth's Core sees the series' hero, David Innes, a mine owner, traveling to the Sahara accompanied by Abner Perry, the inventor of a mechanical device—the "Prospector"—used for boring deep underground. By means of their machine, the young men have discovered that the earth is actually hollow—concentrically within its sphere there is another smaller sphere, or world, called Pellucidar, lodged some five hundred miles beneath the earth's crust. Pellucidar has its own miniature sun, cosmos, and geography, which are all elaborated upon in detail in subsequent installments of the series. The description of the adventurers arrival is typical Burrovian kitsch:

> Together we stepped out to stand in silent contemplation of a landscape at once weird and beautiful. Before us a low and level shore stretched down to a silent sea. As far as the eye could reach the surface of the water was dotted with countless tiny isles—some of towering, barren, granitic rock—others resplendent in gorgeous trappings of tropical vegetation, myriad starred with the magnificent splendor of vivid blooms.

The local population, tyrannized by the all-female avian reptile Mahars who keep Pellucidarian humans for food and slavery, and the romantic involvement between Innes and Dian the Beautiful (who is attempting to escape the hated clutches of Jubal the Ugly) are all covered in this initial

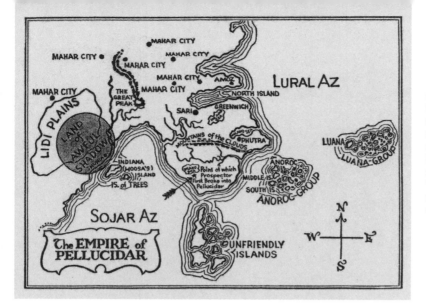

Burroughs's map of the Pellucidar Empire, which accompanied the second story in the series, *Pellucidar* (1915), and plots the many Mahar (all-female avian reptiles) cities as well as the "Land of Awful Shadow," a region in darkness as a result of a perpetual eclipse.

incarnation, but it is cut off inconclusively. However, in the next in the series, *Pellucidar* (1915), Innes is able to trail a long telegraph wire behind the Prospector through which he relays his subsequent adventures back to the surface of Earth, and Burroughs's millions of readers.

Bizarre as it now seems, the "hollow Earth" theory was seriously pondered by geologists of the early nineteenth century, and still held the status of folkloric belief when Burroughs was writing. The leading proponent of hollow-Earthism, John Cleves Symmes Jr. (1779–1829) urged the U.S. government to sponsor a voyage of exploration to the center of the earth via what he fantasized as "the North Pole Hole" and plant the Stars and Stripes at the earth's core. It would, as modern geology informs us, need to be made of asbestos given the fiery temperatures there.

Novelists had too long fantasized about a world under our feet (see Ludvig Holberg's, *The Journey of Niels Klim*, 1741, page 78). Edward Bulwer Lytton broke the earth's crust, so to speak, with his early science-fiction novel, *The Coming Race* (1870). It documents the journey of an American engineer, who penetrates to the center of the earth, discovering a race (dominated by superwomen) who have identified a new, hugely powerful energy source— "vril." (A beef essence manufacturer was quick to capitalize on the popularity of Lytton's novel with *Bovril*—"the vril of the bull, bull being "bos" in Latin). Likewise, Jules Verne's *voyage imaginaire*, *A Journey to the Center of the Earth* (1864), played with the same idea, even before Lytton and Burroughs. It, by contrast, imagined a prehistoric subterranean world, but all of these fables were inspired by the advance of geology (principally for mining) in the nineteenth century—a century fueled by coal.

The profligacy and popularity of these novels are testimony to our never-ending fascination with what may lie beneath our feet—as wonderful as anything that may one day be found in the stars.

HERLAND (1915)

Gilman's utopian novel presents an idealized world populated entirely by women, resulting in a society free from war and organized as a gigantic family.

Herland was only first published in book form in 1979 by Pantheon Books (see above).

A sequel to *Herland*, called *With Her in Ourland* (1916) describes Van and Ellador's return to Herland, after Ellador is horrified by what she finds in "Ourland."

Gilman was photographed (below) by Frances Benjamin Johnston, a pioneering American female photographer and photojournalist.

The country of Herland, like Arthur Conan Doyle's eponymous Lost World (1912, page 130), which was published three years earlier, is situated on an inaccessible plateau surrounded by jungle. Created by the American writer, editor, and feminist activist Charlotte Perkins Gilman (1860–1935), it is a utopia of calm, tolerance, and plenty, but its main distinguishing feature is its population. This fantastic land is peopled entirely by women, who reproduce asexually, and have never come into contact with men—that is, until the arrival of three male explorers. By contrasting life in Herland with the descriptions the three men offer of the world they have left behind, Gilman demonstrates the falsity of contemporary male assumptions about the intelligence, competence, and, written as it was in 1915 when the campaign for women's rights was at its peak, the political capacity of women. It would be another five years before the 19th Amendment to the U.S. Constitution gave American women the right to vote; in Britain, women over thirty were given the vote in 1918.

The women the explorers meet when they are captured after landing in Herland are "calm, grave, wise, wholly unafraid, evidently assured, and determined," and without any of the supposedly "feminine" characteristics the explorers expect to find. They have short hair and no interest in fine clothes or decoration, and although they are horrified at displays of violence, they show no fear and assert their will over the intruders through sheer force of numbers (aided when necessary by deftly applied doses of chloroform).

Wars and natural disasters had wiped out all the men in the country two thousand years earlier, and the modern population was descended from one woman who miraculously became pregnant and gave birth to five daughters. The community the explorers find is organized as a single gigantic family, with property owned in common. Political authority is exercised on the basis of experience, wisdom, and respect. The women are vegetarian, and are dismayed by the waste and profligacy of the world their guests describe.

Herland was originally published in serial form in *Forerunner*, a magazine edited and written by Gilman, who was a leading campaigner for the

equality of women, particularly within marriage. In 1898 she had argued in her book *Women and Economics* that women needed full financial independence as well as voting rights, and her 1903 study *The Home—Its Work and Influence* had drawn attention to the oppression that women suffered by being confined to the domestic sphere.

Charlotte Perkins Gilman addressing members of the Federation of Women's Clubs, 1916.

In *Herland*, these injustices no longer exist, and the narrator, Van, one of the three explorers, becomes completely converted to the feminist philosophy of the country. His colleague Jeff also accepts the superiority of life there, although his response is tinged with an idealistic chivalry that seems to ignore the athleticism, strength, and endurance of the women he meets. However, Terry, the third explorer, is unable to accept the idea that women are as capable of ruling themselves as men.

The attitude toward sex is a major point of difference between the population of Herland and the three explorers. The women argue that the only value of sexual intercourse lies in procreation and the passing on of desirable personal characteristics to strengthen the community, while the men believe that pleasure and the expression of love are important as well. All three men marry Herland women, encouraged by the population, who believe that involving men in their community can only improve their society, but Terry, seeing himself as a "masterful" man, provokes a crisis by attempting to force himself on his unwilling wife.

Gilman, whose life was blighted by severe bouts of depression, killed herself in 1935 after a diagnosis of terminal breast cancer. It was another forty-four years before *Herland* first appeared in book form (1979), but with its quiet and insistent irony it has now established itself as an early and influential feminist view of a peaceful and tolerant world.

TALES OF SNUGGLEPOT AND CUDDLEPIE: THEIR ADVENTURES WONDERFUL (1918)

A children's fantasy set in a miniature world inhabited by the "gumnut babies" who embody the Australian native flora.

First published by Angus and Robertson in 1918.

Snugglepot and Cuddlepie was among the first generation of major illustrated children's books that were locally inspired and culture-specific to Australia and published in competition with the overseas book trade.

This book has remained in print ever since 1918 and was adapted into a ballet and a musical.

May Gibbs established a cast of bushland characters who have become central elements in Australian folklore.

The Australian bush—a wonderland or the site of unimaginable terror? Certainly, from the earliest days of white settlement, terror was the prevailing opinion. The fear of being lost in the bush, where lurking horrors from both European folklore and Aboriginal legend became wildly intertwined, haunted real life as well as the country's evolving literature. The lure of Australia's utterly novel landscape became a fatal attraction as convicts and then free settlers became lost and perished. And the epitome of the Australian image of a devouring landscape was international news with the ill-fated end to the Burke and Wills Expedition in 1861.

Nineteenth-century adventure stories set in the bush were replete with such scenarios from writers including Henry Kingsley, Marcus Clarke, and Henry Lawson. And as late as 1911 a popular London publication entitled *Life in the Australian Backblocks* warned: "The mother . . . knows the horrors that wait the bushed youngster. So she tells them that . . . in yonder scrub, there is a 'bogy-man.'"

Only five years later, however, this threatening wonderland was to be completely inverted into a place of enchantment and fantasy.

Although May Gibbs (1877–1969) was born in England, her earliest Australian experiences as a four-year-old child who emigrated to that country with her family in 1881 became fundamental to the creation of her gumnut world. In both text and illustration her children's books established a completely original image of native flora and fauna. This enriched the country's pictorial vocabulary and made Gibbs a household name across Australia.

After sailing to London three times between 1900 and 1909 to study art, Gibbs returned to Australia in 1913 on the eve of World War I. She then settled in Sydney, a highly sensible move considering that it housed the offices of the leading publishers and magazines of the day. A wartime demand for patriotic and nationalistic images helped inspire the creation of her miniature world that mirrored the human world beyond the confines and protection of the bush. Appearing on magazine covers, in syndicated comic strips, and on a range of ephemera, her gumnut babies soon conquered the nation.

Color frontispiece by Gibbs showing the gumnut babies in the "The Gum Blossom Ballet."

As a professional illustrator trained in London schools such as the Chelsea Polytechnic and Blackburn's, she began a series of five small booklets somewhat reminiscent of Beatrix Potter. The emerging appreciation of nature education, outdoor recreation, and even conservation in Australia fostered an unprecedented demand for her work and her first full-length children's book, *Snugglepot and Cuddlepie*, added new names to the literary pantheon:

> Cuddlepie [lived] side by side with Snugglepot.... One day a wise old kookaburra came to the neighborhood.... He said... "I have seen Humans!... They can scratch one stick upon another and, lo, there will be a Bush Fire."... "I want to see a Human," said Snugglepot. "In the distance," said Cuddlepie.

Contemporary reviews all across the British Empire were fulsome in their praise. The publisher could rightfully boast that the book was "a link which binds together the children of the Empire." They maintained that Australia was "in every line and picture" in which Gibbs's "bears, kangaroos, possums, and kookaburras have all the human virtues and weaknesses." Like other twentieth-century creators of wonderlands such as Mervyn Peake (page 170), Gibbs added her own visual dimension to her texts that greatly solidified her creation in the public imagination.

Since Gibbs's death, her book has inspired a ballet, a musical, and a series of postage stamps. The cottage she created as her home and studio looking over Sydney Harbour was saved from developers and has become as iconic to visitors as Beatrix Potter's Hilltop Farm.

YEVGENY ZAMYATIN

WE (1924)

Set in a futuristic, authoritarian dystopia, We *follows D-503, an engineer, who lives, perpetually observed by spies and secret police, in the vast glass conurbation of OneState, where individuality has almost all but been eradicated.*

First published in New York, in English, by E. P. Dutton in 1924.

The Russian title of the novel, *Мы*, means "We" in English but is, of course, also the English singular version of the word "ours"—nicely appropriate for a novel about an individual's rebellion against the collective.

In 1921, *We* was the first work banned by Goskomizdat, the State Committee for Publishing, which functioned as the Soviet censorship bureau. Before being exiled to Paris in the 1930s, Zamyatin saw the world he predicted in 1920 coming true around him, as Stalin seized power in the USSR.

Zamyatin's dystopian novel *We* was written in 1920, but considered so incendiary the Soviet Union blocked its publication until the glasnost year of 1988. However, an unauthorized unofficial English language translation appeared in New York in 1924. *We* is set in a futuristic world called "OneState" in which every aspect of life is controlled by a secret police, the Bureau of Guardians. Citizens have numbers rather than names, and live in transparent apartments so they can be observed at all times. The plot concerns a mathematician and engineer, D-503, who is helping to build a spacecraft called the *Integral*, designed to export OneState's regime to other planets. He keeps a journal in which he expresses his increasing doubts about the supposedly utopian world in which he lives.

If the world of *We* seems familiar, it is because Zamyatin established many conventions of classic dystopian fiction. Indeed, the novel was a direct inspiration for Orwell's *Nineteen Eighty-Four* (1949, page 178), Aldous Huxley's *Brave New World* (1932, page 148), and Ursula K. Le Guin's *The Dispossessed* (1974). OneState is presided over by the dictatorial "Benefactor," citizens are surveilled at all times, and every hour of life is mapped out by a schedule known as "the Table." Everybody dresses in light-blue overalls, eats the same synthetic food, and exercises at the same time. OneState is surrounded by a vast, "Green Wall," allegedly built to keep the wilds of nature out, although we later learn that earlier a global war had killed all but 0.2 percent of the population, and the world outside the wall is a ruined landscape. Within OneState friendships, relationships, and breeding are rigorously controlled, and all sexual contact is limited to state-approved partners. It is, perhaps, the only flaw in Zamyatin's dystopian imagination that the transparent walls of apartments are occluded only when people have sex. It seems unlikely that OneState would respect its citizen's privacy at such a time.

We is written in a series of short sections or "records." Their tone contrasts the chilly, regulated world against the often rich and moving thoughts and emotions of D-503: happy and optimistic in the beginning, and increasingly despairing as it goes on. And this contrast is also echoed in the landscape of

the novel: Inside the Green Wall everything is systematically ordered, with clarity and precision. (Even some aspects of mathematics are not allowed since they are too chaotic: For example, D-503 mediates on such forbidden quantities as the square root of minus 1.) Everything imprecise is banished, including human passions such as those D-503 experiences in an illegal affair with the sprightly female I-330, who does such illogical things as smoke cigarettes, drink alcohol, and flirt.

This world might strike a reader as implausibly schematic and simplified, but Zamyatin makes it work by making schematization the very logic of the society he portrays. It helps that his prose is vivid, colorful, and evocative, and that the human dilemma of D-503 is so engagingly rendered. As such, *We* remains one of the most prophetic and powerful dystopias ever written.

Futuristic Buildings and City (detail) by Anton Brzezinski, used to illustrate the front cover of a recent Penguin Classics edition. Brzezinski (b.1946) is known to many as "Polish Picasso," and has had a rich career in creating classic science-fiction covers.

FRANZ KAFKA

THE CASTLE (1926)

Kafka's unfinished and ambiguous story of one man's struggle to comprehend the absurdist, labyrinthine world in which he finds himself reflects complex truths about the nature of existence.

Kafka died before finishing the novel, and it is questionable whether he intended to finish it if he had survived tuberculosis. The book was published posthumously by Kurt Wolff in 1926, having been edited by Kafka's friend, Max Brod.

The first few chapters of the Kafka's handwritten manuscript were written in the first person and were later changed to a third-person narrator.

The Castle was the last of Kafka's three great novels, following *The Metamorphosis* (1915) and *The Trial* (1925).

Opposite: K in front of the Castle, illustration by Sam Caldwell.

The Castle, in any traditional narrative sense, goes nowhere. In the same traditional sense it is plotless. Franz Kafka (1883–1924) never finished writing it. The story breaks off mid-sentence and one could argue that, like the fallen-down "ruins," with which romantics liked to ornament their estates, the incompleteness of *The Castle* is its reason for being. A statement is being made by its refusal to give a statement.

K.—a land surveyor—arrives at a village, somewhere in Middle Europe. His mission is to call on the Count who lives in the fog-shrouded Castle that looms, ominously, over the village. The young man has arrived at dusk and he finds himself unwelcome. Peasants glare at him and fall silent. What mystery, one wonders, awaits the visitor? What world have we entered?

Kafka wrote *The Castle* in 1922, two years before his death and three years after the Austro-Hungarian Empire fell apart with the end of World War I. The period is indisputably "modern"—there are telephones and electric lights in the village. But where, if anywhere, is the 1914–18 cataclysm? Has it happened? Is it about to happen? Or are we in a universe where it never happens? There is no echo of the carnage to be heard in *The Castle*. Kafka has imagined the biggest event of the century out of existence.

Everything shivers with enigma. K. is a name, but no name. It is twilight—that nothing time between day and night. K. is on a bridge, suspended in the space between the outside world and the village. Fog, darkness, and snow shroud the Castle. Is there anything in front of him but emptiness? And is there anything behind him? Where has K. come from? We learn in the first chapter that he has traveled for a long time from far away. What country are we in? Most of the village inhabitants have German names, but in chaotic breakdown of the Austro-Hungarian Empire in which Kafka was writing, leaves geography uncertain.

K., fatefully, crosses the bridge. At the Bridge Inn, the innkeeper grudgingly allows K. a straw mattress on the taproom floor. It stinks of beer and peasant sweat and rats run over his feet, and he is almost immediately roused

from his fitful rest by an emissary from the Castle who roughly asks what he is doing in the domain of "Count Westwest." Does he have the necessary "permit"? A flustered K. declares himself to be a "land surveyor," "sent for by the Count." Is he making it up?

Initially, the Castle's representative, denounces K. as an impostor. Then, following a phone call, he radically changes his tune. The stranger, he now accepts, is what he claims he is. An emboldened K. goes on to say that his assistants and equipment "are coming tomorrow by carriage." In fact, two assistants do turn up on foot the next day, but from the Castle. They know nothing about surveying (or anything else) and have no "instruments." Bizarrely, K. claims to know them, identifying them as his "old assistants"—yet he does not know their names, which, with preposterous high-handedness, he conjoins as "Arthur." To add further confusion, a comically inept messenger named Barnabas, is charged with arranging K.'s communications with the Castle. He does not.

The main obstacle between K. and the Castle is apparently Klamm, the Count's man-in-the-village. Klamm never speaks to anyone on business, and hastens from the room when any official matters are mentioned. He is a cartoon bureaucrat, stout, suited, with a pince-nez, and smoking a Virginia cigar. Critics have noted that Klamm bears a striking similarity to photographs of Kafka's father, Hermann. K., denied access to the man himself, now seduces Klamm's current mistress, the barmaid Frieda.

Kafka was familiar with the work of Sigmund Freud and it is tempting to interpret these events and others in the novel in a Freudian reading. However, in a more romantic narrative one might call it love at first sight. After one look at K., Frieda surrenders herself to him, sealing the arrangement with a passionate coupling in the beer puddles under the counter in the taproom. Thereafter she refers to herself as his fiancée. K. informs the landlady that he intends to marry Frieda. However, the first chapter obliquely noted that K. already has a wife and child.

The "authorities" in the Castle decide they do not require the services of a surveyor and reappoint K., in a surreal move, as a temporary school janitor. Remuneration, of an indeterminate amount, he is informed, will be forthcoming at some indefinite future point. Perhaps. K. sees it as a victory, but he promptly loses the job after robbing the school woodshed in order to keep him and Frieda warm at night.

The first half of The Castle is a quixotic quest. In its second half, it modulates into a conversation novel. Having lost the faithless Frieda to one of his assistants, K. becomes closely involved with Barnabas's sisters, Amalia and Olga. The daughters of a once-thriving shoemaker have fallen on hard times. Amalia made the mistake of declining to surrender her body to a lecherous bureaucrat and the family were duly reduced to penury. As restitution, Olga—a woman of impeccable morality—surrenders her body twice a week to the "insatiable" Castle riffraff. She suffers this heroically, in a religious spirit of self-sacrifice.

> . . . K. kept feeling that he had lost himself, or was further away in a strange land than anyone had ever been before, a distant country where even the air was unlike the air at home . . .

The novel drifts to its end in an anticlimactic welter of talk and paralytic inaction. Finally it has not even to the energy to finish a sentence.

What should we make of the bewildering—at times horrific—"imagined world" that Kafka presents in *The Castle*? In fact, one must note, he did not intend to present it at all. His deathbed instruction to his closest friend, Max Brod, was that all his manuscripts (virtually the whole of what we now have as his oeuvre) should be burned after his death, unread.

"Death" is the operative word here. *The Castle* is Kafka's terminal work— he was dying of incurable tuberculosis as he wrote it. What does a great author "imagine" when standing on the threshold between this world and the next?

Kafka confided to Brod in September 1922—following his return to Prague—that he would never finish the "Castle novel." Nevertheless, he also confided a possible ending. Were he to finish the book, it would end with the death of K. and simultaneous permission from the Castle to reside, but not legally, in the village. He is to be the perennial outsider.

However, looking at the novel through a veneer of death is only one of the many ways to interpret the text. Kafka was virtually unknown in the English-speaking world, until the first translations began to appear in the 1930s. For a couple of decades he was regarded as a wildly experimental writer, of interest only to the avant-garde. This changed with the rise of popular interest in French existentialism during the late 1940s and 1950s, which addressed the idea that "absurdity," and ultimately meaninglessness, may be what the universe means after all. The existential philosopher Albert Camus, pictured it as the labor of Sisyphus: forever rolling a rock up a hill, only for it to roll back again. "A first sign of the beginning of understanding," declared Camus, bleakly, "is the wish to die." And, if you are Kafka, burn everything you have labored to create in life.

Many of the "imagined worlds" described in literary wonderlands are warm, comfortable places, to which one can escape from the cold realities of everyday existence. *The Castle* imagines an even colder world than that in which most of us live but one that, as Sartre uncomfortably reminds us, is more real.

THE CTHULHU MYTHOS
(1928–37)

The lore and legend of Lovecraft's "Great Old One" broke new ground in the realm of fantasy fiction, and the terrifying entity of Cthulhu has influenced generations of horror writers.

Stephen King has paid tribute to Lovecraft as the most important influence on his own early writing, and named him as the greatest horror writer of the twentieth century.

Author Michel Houellebecq has described Lovecraft's stories as "an open slice of howling fear."

Contemporary readers have also struggled with Lovecraft's views and the overt racism in some of his work. In 2015, the World Fantasy Awards announced that it would be remodeling its award trophy (which was previously in the form of a bust of Lovecraft).

Few writers have made humanity as insignificant and powerless as the American Howard Phillips Lovecraft (1890–1937) in his horror stories of the Cthulhu Mythos. He wrote thirteen of these stories in all, which appeared between 1928 and 1941, mostly in the influential *Weird Tales* and other magazines. The last story in the sequence, *The Case of Charles Dexter Ward*, was published posthumously.

The most influential, *The Call of Cthulhu*, appeared in 1928 and established Lovecraft's conception of a vast and malevolent universe dominated by the Great Old Ones, amoral elemental deities who survived the almost inconceivably remote past—Lovecraft used the term "vigintillions of years," a vigintillion being one with sixty-three zeros (a billion, billion, billion, billion, billion, billion, billion).

These monstrous and mysterious powers have been apparently dead for all that time but will one day—"when the stars are right"—awaken and ravage the earth, and occasionally encounter incautious humans. Cthulhu himself, high priest to the Old Ones, has been hidden in the sunken city of R'lyeh, and bursts out when explorers open a huge carved door into a rocky cavern on a remote and uncharted island in the South Pacific.

Earth is an infinitesimally tiny part of Lovecraft's universe, but his descriptions of those specific parts in which his "Great Old Ones" appear establish an atmosphere of mysterious horror. Whether a remote island in the South Pacific, the relatively familiar landscape of the eastern United States, or the wastes of the Antarctic, these places are suffused with an air of menace:

> Great barren peaks of mystery loomed up constantly against the west as the low northern sun of noon or the still lower horizon-grazing southern sun of midnight poured its hazy reddish rays over the white snow, bluish ice and water lanes, and black bits of exposed granite slope. Through the desolate summits swept ranging, intermittent gusts of the terrible Antarctic wind; whose cadences sometimes held vague suggestions of a wild and half-sentient musical piping, with notes extending over a wide range, and

which for some subconscious mnemonic reason seemed to me disquieting and even dimly terrible. (*At the Mountains of Madness*, 1936)

A different sort of foreboding is experienced by travelers in *The Dunwich Horror* (1929):

> The planted fields appear singularly few and barren; while the sparsely scattered houses wear a surprisingly uniform aspect of age, squalor, and dilapidation.

> Without knowing why, one hesitates to ask directions from the gnarled solitary figures spied now and then on crumbling doorsteps or on the sloping, rock-strewn meadows. Those figures are so silent and furtive that one feels somehow confronted by forbidden things, with which it would be better to have nothing to do.

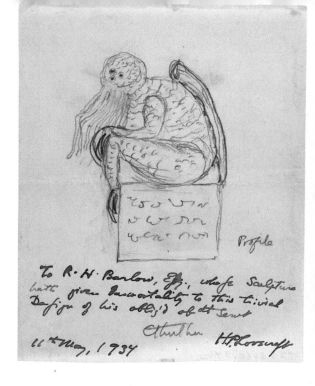

Lovecraft's own sketch of Cthulhu, drawn on a letter to fellow writer and friend, R. H. Barlow (1934).

That phrase "without knowing why" sums up the nameless, indefinable horror of Lovecraft's work. The immense scale of the imaginary environment he created—a universe rather than simply a world—and the nightmarish, terrifying vagueness of the powers wielded by its gods, have influenced fantasy and horror writers ever since.

When *The Call of Cthulhu* was published, Lovecraft had already written three other stories using various aspects of what became known as his "Cthulhu Mythos." He never intended to create a coherent vision of an imaginary world, but rather a loose and occasionally inconsistent framework of places, names, and fearsome godlike creatures—what he referred to as his "pseudomythology"—to serve as a background for his stories.

Many of the stories are set in the idyllic Massachusetts settlement of Arkham, a fictional town as is the equally fictional Miskatonic University, which holds an unrivaled collection of occult books. The books provide a gateway through which academics and adventurers can come into contact with the awesome powers of Lovecraft's more sinister creation, usually with fatal and devastating results. In *The Dunwich Horror*, for instance, an attempt to steal the Necronomicon—a secret grimoire or book of ancient magic that gives access to the Great Old Ones—leads to the death of the would-be thief and the eruption of a mysterious and invisible presence that devours local people and destroys their property.

The gods who hold the ultimate power in Lovecraft's world have an aura of implacable evil, but are rarely presented in any physical detail. Although hideous sculptures are described at the start of *The Call of Cthulhu* depicting a monster with "an octopus-like head whose face was a mass of feelers, a scaly, rubbery-looking body, prodigious claws on hind and fore feet, and long, narrow wings behind," the creature itself is revealed only as "The Thing that cannot be described," with witnesses remembering just a few vague details of green, sticky, writhing slime.

Lovecraft was born in 1890 in Providence, Rhode Island, where, following the death of his father when he was eight, he was raised by his mother, maternal grandfather, and two aunts. From his childhood he suffered from terrifying nightmares, which could have been the inspiration for some of his later fiction. As a small boy, he would also listen, enthralled, to tales of Gothic horror told by his grandfather.

As he grew up, there was a growing awareness among writers and the reading public in Europe and America of the terrifying malign potential of the scientific advances that were being made—H. G. Wells's *The War of the Worlds* appeared when Lovecraft was eight, and *The Gods of Pegana*, by the Anglo-Irish writer Lord Dunsany, when he was in his mid-teens. Exploration, whether in Lord Dunsany's fantasy world of Pegana or in the Antarctic in Lovecraft's *At the Mountains of Madness* (1936) might uncover unexpected horrors. In *The Call of Cthulhu*, Lovecraft wrote:

> We live on a placid island of ignorance in the midst of black seas of infinity, and it was not meant that we should voyage far. The sciences, each straining in its own direction, have hitherto harmed us little; but some day the piecing together of dissociated knowledge will open up such terrifying vistas of reality, and of our frightful position therein, that we shall either go mad from the revelation or flee from the light into the peace and safety of a new dark age.

This idea of forbidden and dangerous knowledge is a constant theme throughout the stories.

Lovecraft maintained very close relations by letter with other horror writers of his day, including Clark Ashton Smith, Robert Bloch, who wrote *Psycho*, and Robert E. Howard, the author of the Conan the Barbarian stories (1932–36, page 154). The group became known as the Lovecraft Circle, and characters, settings, and other elements of Lovecraft's stories appeared occasionally in their works, with his consent. It was his publisher, August Derleth, who coined the phrase "the Cthulhu Mythos" to popularize the stories when he published a collection in 1939, two years after Lovecraft's death.

The Mythos endures and is added to in books, magazines, video games, and even in popular music. However Lovecraft has also been the subject of controversy as contemporary readers have drawn attention to the recurring racism that is evidenced in much of his work.

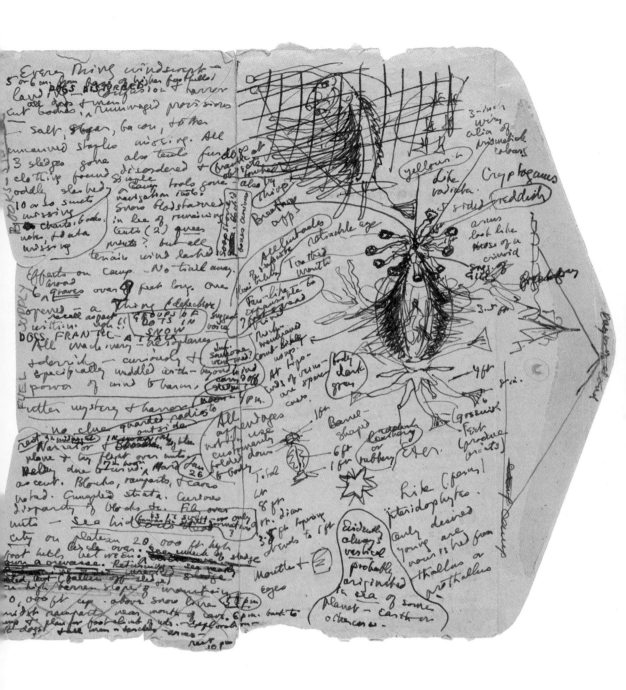

ALDOUS HUXLEY

BRAVE NEW WORLD (1932)

Huxley's enduring masterpiece of a future world continues to shine a somber light on the possibilities of genetic engineering and the loss of the individual in contemporary society.

First published by Chatto and Windus in 1932.

The novel is set in the year 2540, 632 years after the launch of the Model T Ford. The revered memory of the industrialist Henry Ford gives the World State the nearest thing it has to a god—"Our Ford."

Opposite: The Gammas, Deltas, and Epsilons, the lower of the five ranked castes of Brave Alpha carry out the manual labor. Illustration by Finn Dean.

When George Orwell published *Nineteen Eighty-Four* in 1949 (page 174), he set his bleak and brutal vision of a totalitarian world less than four decades in the future, but Aldous Huxley (1894–1963) looked more than six hundred years ahead for the setting of *Brave New World*. Even so, its world remains rooted firmly in the 1930s—its main characters have the names of leading industrialists and political figures of Huxley's day, and the hypnotism, the selective breeding, and the production-line lifestyle of the World State all reflect aspects of the world as Huxley knew it.

Where Orwell, writing so soon after the horrors of Nazism and Soviet Russia, famously saw the future as "a boot stamping on a human face—for ever," Huxley presented in *Brave New World* a gentler, more insidious nightmare. There is no doubting the repressive power of the state—but though there are riot police to be called out in times of trouble, they wield nothing more brutal than feel-good drugs, anesthetic gas, and gentle words. There is no freedom of thought, but it seems hardly anybody wants it; there is no political opposition to the Resident Controller, and practically everybody accepts the status quo.

When *Brave New World* was published in 1932, the moving assembly lines of car manufacturer Henry Ford had been bringing cheap cars to the masses for twenty years or so, and in the memorable scenes in the Central London Hatchery with which the novel opens, Huxley applied this mass-production technology to human reproduction. The characters in the novel have no mothers, no fathers, no family: They, like the thousands of embryos moving sedately along the production line, were cloned and grown in bottles to fulfill their predestined roles as ruling Alphas or subservient Betas, Gammas, Deltas, and Epsilons.

Today, with Nazism behind us, it is easy to see the brutal implications of the "science" of eugenics, or selective breeding—"the self-direction of human evolution," as it was described at the Second International Eugenics Conference in 1921—but in the early 1930s it had many influential adherents. H. G. Wells, George Bernard Shaw, and John Maynard Keynes were all

known as supporters. So too was Huxley—but *Brave New World* presents a somber vision of what relying on the theories of the eugenicists might bring.

Thinking for oneself, passion, or originality are not only deviant and sinful in the World State, but generally inconceivable: Besides being created specifically for their role in society, the inhabitants, from Alpha-pluses to Epsilon-minus semi-morons, are subject to constant indoctrination and psychological manipulation to keep them malleable. Every aspect of their life is ordered by the central power—in this case, the mysterious ten Controllers.

In return, they live in a society of casual sex and hypnotic and mind-altering drugs, which are regularly distributed as a form of relaxation and escape. It is a world of absolute totalitarianism and unbridled hedonism, in which the traditional morality of Huxley's day is turned on its head: Monogamy is frowned upon, the family seen as an antiquated tool of repression, and the idea of motherhood considered obscene. Illness, pain, and even aging have been abolished, although sexism has apparently survived the six centuries—women, who seem to play no part in the administration of the World State, are patted dismissively on their bottoms by their bosses, and valued exclusively for the "pneumatic" qualities of their "firm and sunburnt flesh." Some changes, apparently, were inconceivable for an educated man like Huxley in the early 1930s.

Huxley was born in 1894 into an impeccably middle-class family, the son of a schoolmaster—but he was an intellectual aristocrat with an impressive pedigree. His grandfather was T. H. Huxley, nicknamed "Darwin's bulldog" for his combative defense of the theory of evolution. T. H. Huxley championed the teaching of science in schools, and the works of his great-uncle the poet and critic Matthew Arnold, who famously believed that culture existed "to make all men live in an atmosphere of sweetness and light."

Huxley, though, developed other ideas as he moved easily from Eton to Oxford. He loathed mass culture, and he believed that education should be the prerogative of those who could profit from it, by which he meant people like him. "Universal education has created an immense class of what I may call the New Stupid," he declared dismissively. That view is clearly relevant to Huxley's vision of a world that is organized as a bizarre updating of the Hindu caste system. His grandfather had suggested that utopias could never be achieved by humans, only by insects, and it is significant that the masses in *Brave New World* are frequently described as locusts, aphids, ants, and maggots.

Huxley's conception of the World State was influenced radically by his personal experiences in the U.S.—where he shuddered at the self-conscious glitz and glamour of the film industry in California—and in the streets and factories of industrial England at the start of the Depression. The American experiment with Prohibition, just drawing to its messy close, was reflected in impractical proposals for banning soma, the drug that keeps Huxley's masses in a state of catatonic content, while the talking pictures, "movies," were reproduced as the "feelies," in which the audience shares not only

the sights and sounds, but the smells and sensations of the characters on the screen.

The title of Huxley's novel comes from Miranda's expression of naive admiration in Shakespeare's *The Tempest* (1611, page 64), when she meets the shipwrecked courtiers wandering Prospero's island: "Oh brave new world, that hath such people in't!" Huxley, of course, is being heavily ironic in applying that line to the World State, but if the society he described was deeply flawed, he saw no hope for humanity either in the Romantic myth of the noble savage. His friend the novelist D. H. Lawrence had written passionately about the instinctive energy and vitality of the Mexican Indians in *The Plumed Serpent* and elsewhere—but Huxley presented a different, bleaker picture. The "savage" tribes living in *Brave New World's* New Mexico reservation are without the constraints of the inhabitants of the World State, but their freedom is marked by brutality and squalor. It is only on a few remote islands that life sounds even remotely ideal. They are places where "all the people...who've got independent ideas of their own" are exiled.

In his 1946 foreword to *Brave New World*, Huxley described this lack of a positive vision of the future in the novel as a mistake. "Today, I feel no wish to demonstrate that sanity is impossible," he wrote. But much of the continuing power of the book derives from the implication that there is no escape from a world that, with, its cultured brutality, its genetic manipulation, its psychological brainwashing, and its dozy drug-and-sex culture, lies only just beyond the limits of our own experience. He said in his foreword, "Then, I projected it six hundred years into the future: today, it seems quite possible that the horror may be upon us within a single century." More than sixty years later, it is an uncomfortable thought.

Bernard Marx brings back John, the "Savage," from a reservation outside World State. John becomes a society "hit," but while touring factories and schools he becomes increasingly disturbed by what he sees. Illustration by Finn Dean.

ROBERT E. HOWARD

CONAN THE BARBARIAN
(1932–36)

The enduring hero of sword and sorcery has transcended his pulp-fiction roots and been the subject of multiple film, television, video game, and comic-book adaptations.

Conan first appeared in *Weird Tales* magazine in December 1932 (above) in the story "The Phoenix on the Sword" in which an older Conan attempts to rule the kingdom of Aquilonia and must foil an assignation plot by the "Rebel Four."

Howard was a friend of horrormaster H. P. Lovecraft (see page 144). The two authors corresponded frequently and made references to each others' works in their own writing.

In 1982 the film adaptation Conan the Barbarian brought bodybuilder and future governor of California, Arnold Schwarzenegger, his big-screen break.

To tell his stories of Conan, the wandering barbarian thief, outlaw, and mercenary from the far north, the Texan writer Robert E. Howard (1906–36) traveled thousands of years back to a time before any of the known great civilizations.

Howard had already written stories set in the distant past—his first published work in the pulp magazine *Weird Tales*, "Spear and Fang," deals with a prehistoric battle between Cro-Magnon and Neanderthal cavemen—but for his new character, he devised an entirely imaginary age of history. The stories were set in the Hyborean Age, "between the years when the oceans drank Atlantis and the gleaming cities, and the years of the rise of the sons of Aryas"—between, that is, the mythical destruction of Atlantis and the emergence of the Indo-European races.

The fantasy world setting of Conan's adventures is one of magic and sorcery, of beautiful maidens and venomous monsters, and of strange, malevolent gods and miraculous interventions, very loosely based on an adapted version of Europe and North America. The Cimmerians, for instance, of whom Conan is one, have similarities with the Celtic people; far to the east is the Kingdom of Khitai, which corresponds to China; the historical Picts appear as wild savages on the fringes of civilization; and Shem is recognizable as the area that we know as Mesopotamia, Arabia, Syria, and Palestine.

In fact, the settings of the twenty-one Conan tales vary from an Arabian Nights vision of the Middle East in "The Slithering Shadow" to an Arthurian romance-style picture of knights "in richly wrought plate armor, colored plumes waving above their burnished sallets." One of Howard's main themes is the corrupting and debilitating effect of civilization. There is no serious attempt to describe any social structure, beyond the power of various kings, counts, high priests, and wizards: Conan's world is mythical and psychological rather than political.

There are several aspects of that frequently violent psychology that are troubling to a modern reader. For example, the theories of eugenics and racial purity, which were popular at the time, echo throughout Howard's

Hither came Conan, the Cimmerian, black-haired, sullen-eyed, sword in hand, a thief, a reaver, a slayer, with gigantic melancholies and gigantic mirth, to tread the jeweled thrones of the Earth under his sandaled feet.
—"The Phoenix on the Sword"

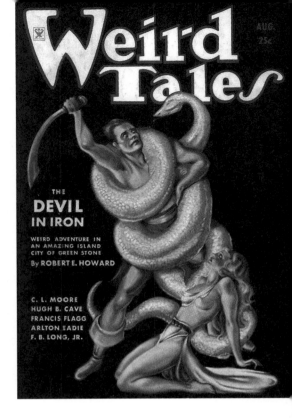

imagined history. Conan himself, in disguise in a sleazy thieves' kitchen, is described as having "broad, heavy shoulders, [a] massive chest, lean waist, and heavy arms. His skin was brown from outland suns, his eyes blue and smoldering; a shock of tousled black hair crowned his broad forehead." For all the black hair, the mighty swordsman and man of action would not have been out of place as one of Hitler's Übermenschen.

Women play a supporting role in many of the stories, generally wearing clothes that coyly do little to conceal their "sleek limbs and ivory breasts," and occasionally whipped until they scream and writhe. Conan himself, generally a silent and terrifying man of action, occasionally grumbles like a 1930s old man about how long they take beautifying themselves.

Howard's own life was short and very ordinary. As a boy, in and around the town of Cross Plains, Texas, he idolized his sick and ailing mother and immersed himself in comics and pulp fiction. He was chronically shy and melancholy by disposition, and poured out reams of fiction and poetry through his adolescence, before his first story was accepted when he was eighteen. He lived with his parents all his life, although by the time he was twenty-five, his short stories were bringing him a growing reputation. Conan enjoyed spectacular success.

In 1936, however, his mother fell into a coma caused by her tuberculosis, and her nurse said she was unlikely to recover. Howard walked out to his car and shot himself in the head, dying a day before her. Conan, however, has survived not just in Howard's stories but also in comic books, television programs, video games, and films. Many of them bear little resemblance to Howard's original creation, but the "noble savage" idea of a barbarian standing alone against the corruption of civilization, continues to exert a powerful attraction.

Conan appears on the cover of *Weird Tales* in August 1934 wrestling a giant serpent summoned by a recently resurrected mythical demon. Although "The Devil in Iron" is not considered one of the better early Conan stories, this cover depicts Conan as the archetypal warrior defeating a monster to save a scantily clad beauty and promises "weird adventure in an amazing island city of Green Stone."

VLADIMIR BARTOL

ALAMUT (1938)

A story set in the mystical world of an eleventh-century cult leader serves as an allegory of Mussolini's twentieth-century fascist state.

Originally published in 1938 in Slovenian, the first English edition was translated by Michael Biggins and published in 2004 by Scala House Press (their most recent edition is shown above).

Following the attacks of September 11, 2001, more than 20,000 copies were sold of a new Slovenian edition, and the book was translated into nineteen languages.

A regular refrain from the novel is "Nothing is an absolute reality, all is permitted."

Vladimir Bartol (1903–67), the Slovenian writer and intellectual who died in Ljubljana with most of his work out of print, could easily have slipped away without making a lasting mark in his own field—let alone in one yet to be invented. Instead, his novel *Alamut* is arguably the most internationally popular work ever to come out of Slovenia and is the inspiration for the video-game series, *Assassin's Creed*.

At first glance, the subject matter of *Alamut* appears as unlikely for Bartol as its twenty-first-century spin-off. First published in 1938 (although not translated into English until 2004), the novel is set in an eleventh-century Persian fortress, where sectarian leader Hasan ibn Sabbah, or Sayyiduna, has devised an ingenious and disturbing strategy for incentivizing his troops (or "*fedayeen*") to fight to the death: recreating paradise on earth.

Writing about such a challenging and alien subject required Bartol to prepare extensively. His inspiration for the tale is found in *The Travels of Marco Polo* (*c*.1300), which includes a story about a powerful Persian warlord who uses hashish and a secret garden of women to fool young men into thinking he has the power to transport them to paradise and back, and he spent ten years researching and structuring his book. He then retreated for nine months to the mountain town of Kamnik to write it, while the Anschluss proceeded just thirty miles away and Mussolini's Fascists persecuted the Slovenian population of his birthplace, Trieste.

The result is a rich and engrossing evocation of a terrifying world. In Sayyiduna's hands, the remote mountain fort of Alamut becomes a crucible in which to conduct "an experiment in altering human nature" based on the motto that underpins his brand of Ismailism (a religious sect with roots in Islam): "Nothing is an absolute reality; everything is permitted." As his enemies advance to lay siege to his stronghold, the dangerously charismatic despot delves deeper into the desires and psychology of the youths under his control, steeling them to display fearlessness in the face of inevitable defeat.

Bartol's greatest achievement is that he makes Alamut almost as alluring as it is sinister. Seen through the eyes of two newcomers, young harem recruit

Halima and prospective fighter ibn Tahir, the fort is a place of mystery and delight, where misgivings flower into fear and disillusionment. Wandering Alamut's passages and secret places with Halima and ibn Tahir, peeling back layer after layer of Sayyiduna's horrific vision, we are at once charmed and appalled. As with the best action-packed computer games, the book makes us feel we are unable to look away even as we gasp.

Unsurprisingly, the world of *Alamut* is often read as an allegory for the evils of Fascism. The parallels with real-world events don't stop there, however: subsequent generations have found that many experiences resonate in its pages, among them life under Josip Broz Tito's oppressive regime in Yugoslavia and the events of the Balkan war. Many twenty-first-century readers also see reflections of the radicalization of young jihadis in the novel.

Yet the eclecticism of the story's resonances and applications serve as a reminder that what Bartol criticizes is not a particular ideology but the human readiness to believe and follow compelling leaders unquestioningly. As Sayyiduna himself explains, the key to his power lies in his realization that "people wanted fairy tales and fabrications and they were fond of the blindness they blundered through." Knowing this enables him to control and manipulate his subjects as deftly as avatars in the virtual gaming worlds that were invented decades after Bartol committed this mesmerizing and terrible world to the page.

Hasan ibn Sabbah or Sayyiduna, leader of a secretive eleventh-century cult from the Levant, demonstrates his authority by ordering one of his assassins to kill himself.

JORGE LUIS BORGES

TLÖN, UQBAR, ORBIS TERTIUS
(1941)

A short story incorporating many of Borges's philosophical preoccupations, which details the creation of an alternate world and its infiltration of our own.

First published in Argentine journal *Sur* in 1940, the story appears in collection *The Garden of Forking Paths* (later *Ficciones*), first published by Editorial Sur in 1941.

Borges was born into a wealthy Argentine family in Buenos Aires and his love of literature was established at a young age when he came across his father's library.

Under the dictatorship of Juan Perón during World War II, Borges was dismissed from his post at the Buenos Aires library for showing support for the Allies.

"The composition of vast books is a laborious and impoverishing extravagance. A better course of procedure is to pretend that these books already exist, and then to offer a résumé, a commentary," writes Jorge Luis Borges (1899–1986) in the brief prologue to *Ficciones*, the 1941 volume of short stories that begins with "Tlön, Uqbar, Orbis Tertius." Characteristically, Borges's self-deprecation masks considerable ambition: "Tlön" proposes just such a commentary, but the essayistic, even academic, veneer of the story distracts readers while Borges constructs the most extraordinarily compact of literary wonderlands. "Tlön" is a scant twenty pages that remake the world.

Borges turned to fiction only shortly before his fortieth birthday, to affirm his mental faculties in the wake of a head injury. With "Tlön," his second story after the accident, Borges manages to blend the "epic destiny" he yearned for, on the model of the many military heroes among his forebears, with the bookishness and frailty that marked him from earliest youth. In a long autobiographical reminiscence published in *The New Yorker* in 1970, Borges observes that, "if I were asked to name the chief event in my life, I should say my father's library." One way to understand "Tlön" is as a singularly successful attempt to make a library into an event.

From the start, the story blurs the lines between the literary and the literal, the figurative and real-life figures. It is dotted with the names of Borges's contemporaries, scaffolded on his ability to reference obscure philosophical tomes with breezy assurance—and free with its attribution of made-up quotations to both. Borges describes himself dining with his frequent collaborator Adolfo Bioy Casares, who recalls a statement made by a heresiarch of Uqbar: "mirrors and copulation are abominable, since they both multiply the numbers of man." Intrigued, Borges asks for his source; Bioy points him toward the *Anglo-American Cyclopedia*, a "literal but delinquent" reprint of the 1902 *Encyclopedia Britannica*. Borges's edition makes no mention of Uqbar, but Bioy's own copy includes four pages on Uqbar tucked into the end of Volume XLVI. The article is vague on Uqbar's whereabouts, and largely uninspiring, but piques Borges's interest with its observation that Uqbar's literature uniformly shuns realism in favor of fantasy and takes place entirely within the imaginary regions of Mlejnas and Tlön.

Most of the remainder of the story elaborates on the fantastic, aided by Borges's discovery two years later of an entire volume of the *First Encyclopedia of Tlön*. It is "something to be reckoned with," Borges writes, not "a brief description of a false country," but "a substantial fragment of the complete history of an unknown planet, with its architecture and its playing cards, its mythological terrors and the sound of its dialects, its emperors and its oceans, its minerals, its birds, and its fishes, its algebra and its fire, its theological and metaphysical arguments." Not only the philosophical disputes, but all the rest of Tlön too, depends on Berkeleyan idealism, which holds that the physical universe does not exist other than as a projection of our minds.

Under the guise of encyclopedic pedantry, Borges plays out numerous implications of such a stance—impugning ideas of causality and of time itself, subordinating all scientific disciplines to psychology, teasing out the scandalous "doctrine of materialism," and, most tellingly, exploring several visions of literature that might emerge from this conceptual confluence. All books are treated as the work of one "timeless and anonymous" author, pieces of fiction contain every permutation of a single plot, poetry eschews nominatives in favor of massive agglomerations of adjectives or verbs. "There are famous poems," Borges notes, "made up of one enormous word, a word which in truth forms a poetic *object*, the creation of the writer." At length, Borges reveals that "centuries and centuries of idealism have not failed to influence reality" in Tlön, that real objects, too, may be produced by desire or expectation. Lost items have long been rediscovered by more than one person at once; archaeologists have arrived at the methodical production of ancient artifacts, rendering the past "no less malleable or obedient than the future."

This unexpectedly concrete development sets up the story's final pivots: from past to future, from fantasy to reality, and from poetry to prose and back again. In time, Borges learns that Bishop Berkeley himself took part in an early-seventeenth-century secret society dedicated to inventing an imaginary country. The work demands generations, and two centuries later gains the financial backing of a pugilistic American atheist millionaire who bequeaths the society his fortune on the condition that it accord itself to American audacity and create an entire planet. Members receive the complete forty-volume *First Encyclopedia of Tlön* in 1914. Then, Borges writes, "about 1942, events began to speed up"—the fabulist qualities of the literature of an imaginary country itself situated in the literature of an imaginary country start to impinge on the real.

Borges dates the bulk of his story to 1940, reflecting the actual moment of its composition, but he appends a postscript fictitiously dated 1947, narrating Tlön's conquest of the realist precincts he has carefully woven through the rest of the tale. The specific contours of this wonderland then become more clear: that it will not lie quiescent down a rabbit-hole or over a rainbow, and that "literary" is not in this case a contingent modifier but an absolutely

essential one. This is a wonderland predicated on *poiesis*—the origin of our word "poetry"—in its root sense in Greek: to make. Just as Tlön's poets fashion "poetic objects" out of enormous compound words, so too does Tlön finally insinuate its brand of poetry into the prosaic precincts of our own world. Borges is present when a compass encircled by Tlönian lettering emerges from a French packing crate in Buenos Aires, and again some months later when a dead man in rural Uruguay turns out to be in possession of a small but impossibly heavy cone made of a metal that "does not exist in this world"—an "image of divinity in certain religions of Tlön."

And then the world submits to Tlön, at first in decidedly literary terms: "manuals, anthologies, summaries, literal versions, authorized reprints, and pirated editions of the Master Work of Man poured and continue to pour out into the world." Its languages and its "harmonious history" supplant ours, its "transparent tigers" and "towers of blood" fill the popular magazines and "captivate" humanity. Borges likens this overwhelming embrace of the "minute and vast evidence of an ordered planet" to the widespread appeal enjoyed by "any symmetrical system whatsoever which gave the appearance of order—dialectical materialism, anti-Semitism, Nazism"—in the 1930s. We can read the quiet resignation of the Borges character at the close, then, working on a Spanish translation of Sir Thomas Browne he does not hope to publish, as a counterpoint to the more aggressive stance taken by Borges as author, protesting the conquests being made by actual totalitarian states even as he was writing. But we should remember, on the other hand, that Borges was indoctrinated in philosophical idealism at his father's knee and always remained fascinated by it, that many of Tlön's outré literary practices reflect conceits animating Borges's writing all along the decades. It seems no accident, then, that his narrated self is immediately caught up by Bioy Casares' initial maxim, with its fusion of appearance (mirrors) and reality (copulation), or that a veritable paroxysm of delight attends his initial discovery of a volume of the *Encyclopedia*. If "Tlön" implicitly critiques real-world imperialism, it celebrates a more literary imperiousness with considerable fervor.

Within the story but also beyond it, Borges makes poetic sensibility and conviction into an engine for real-world change, both narrating and subtly effecting a shift from the Enlightenment project of the Encyclopedists—to distill and record the whole of human knowledge—to the yet more radical undertaking of writing the world afresh.

AUSTIN TAPPAN WRIGHT

ISLANDIA (1942)

The story of the adventures of John Lang, a Harvard graduate who secures the position of first American consul to the utopian territory of Islandia. Rich in detail and brilliantly conceived, Wright's creation of the Karain continent is rivaled only by Tolkien's Middle-earth.

First published by Farrar and Rinehart, Inc., in 1942.

Even though Wright's sister and widow edited the text down after he died prematurely in a traffic accident in 1931, it still exceeds 900 pages.

Despite receiving little critical attention, Austin Tappan Wright's (1883–1931) *Islandia*, published posthumously, has become a cult classic and was praised by Ursula K. Le Guin for being the only utopian work that directly addressed the issues of Westernization and "progress."

The novel takes place in the first years of the twentieth century when imperialism was at its peak; the maps that accompany the text—designed by Wright's geographer brother John Kirtland Wright—show Islandia as bordered by a German protectorate as well as French and British colonies. The novel is unusually detailed in its topographical descriptions. John Lang first learns of the territory through an Islandian friend at Harvard and, after learning the local language, his uncle—a prosperous businessman who sees Islandia as a potential market for American goods—negotiates him a position in the consulate. Lang's arrival dramatizes the main issue of the novel: whether Islandia should open its doors to overseas trade or preserve its independence on the edge of empire. As spelled out explicitly, the country's predicament resembles that of Japan in the 1850s, which suggests Islandian independence will not last long.

Islandia appeals to Lang for being rather old-fashioned and only lightly industrialized. His travels, mostly on horseback or by boat, around the country, are leisurely paced in contrast to the tempo of American life. In the first half, Lang is gradually learning Islandian society and an essential first step is to process his perceptions of the landscape. On approaching a farm: "the narrow road was rutted in places and with grassy patches, not in regular ridges as at home where wheeled traffic is so much, but in patches here and there, soft under the horses' feet. And quite unexpectedly we came upon three of the Islandian gray deer, with their short antlers and round bodies and long colt-like legs." The reader is encouraged to pay attention to small differences from America and we are constantly invited to infer the better quality of life lying behind his descriptions.

Islandian society still possesses feudal elements, yet it displays greater gender equality than Lang is used to. He is initially impressed by the peaceful

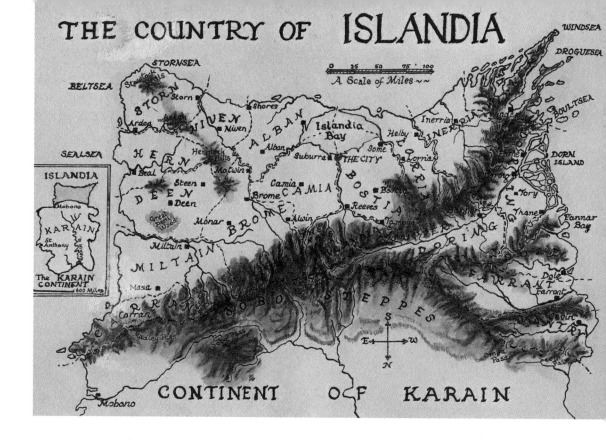

THE COUNTRY OF ISLANDIA

CONTINENT OF KARAIN

John Kirtland Wright's
(brother of the author) map
of Islandia recreated in color
by Edward Relph.

appearance of the country and also by the simplicity of dress worn by the locals. The latter greatly reduces social ritual and eases Lang's encounters with the new society. The most striking event comes when the Islandian council debates a proposal to open the country to foreign trade. Two parties have formed, the more utopian one resisting this incursion of external values, while the other camp insists that they move with the times. The council vote goes against change. This does not mean that change per se is blocked because, of course, Lang's own narrative can be read as an example of external influence.

Lang's account is divided into three phases, each revolving around a romance, but in every case the romance plot is used as a medium for cultural debate and comparison. Initially he sets his sights on the sister of a Harvard friend but that fails when she admits to the pull of family obligations. Lang's second love is for a weaver, who consummates their relationship but argues against marriage. At that point Lang returns to America, which he sees through estranged eyes, and he finally persuades an American woman to travel with him to Islandia, marry, and set up a household there. Virtually the last words of the novel are when Lang declares to his wife "we are Islandians," but this conclusion only comes after many heated arguments over the attractions of Islandian culture.

ANTOINE DE SAINT-EXUPÉRY

THE LITTLE PRINCE (1943)

A loving lament for a friend who fell to Earth, shared the desert, guilelessly offered parables of human truth, and died in order to return to his celestial home.

First published by Reynal and Hitchcock, Inc., in 1943.

Le Petit Prince is the second most widely translated book (after *Pinocchio*, 1883) and the third highest-selling single work of fiction ever (after *A Tale of Two Cities*, 1859, and *The Hobbit*, 1937).

The B612 Foundation, an NGO conducting research to defend Earth against asteroid collision, is named for the tiny home "planet" of Saint-Exupéry's Little Prince. A real asteroid has been named B612 to honor *The Little Prince* and another (Asteroid 2578) was renamed Saint-Exupéry.

The Little Prince (published first in French as *Le Petit Prince*) is a bittersweet palimpsest that has entranced generations, deploying multiple layers of meaning to acknowledge gently the hard truths of life, leaving adults sad but hopeful, yearning for the child from the stars and his laughter. It is the best-known work of the French writer, poet, and aviator Antoine de Saint-Exupéry (1900–44) and remains one of the most-translated books ever, a modern classic suggesting that the simplest things in life are the most important.

In writing *The Little Prince*, Saint-Exupéry drew on his own experiences as a pilot (he had qualified as one in 1922), including a period serving in North Africa. In 1944 during World War II he attempted a reconnaissance mission over France and never returned. In 2004 the wreckage of his plane was recovered, although the exact cause of the crash remains unknown.

The story begins with one of Saint-Exupéry's watercolors, an image copied from a "true" jungle book the narrator read at age six. A boa constrictor coils around a "wild beast" whose eyes bulge as the snake's mouth gapes to consume him. As a child, the narrator explains, he attempted to recreate the image; resulting in something "grown-ups" took for a hat, but which the six-year-old clearly saw as a snake digesting an elephant. On the next page, the narrator reprints the mundane, gray scale, explanatory cutaway view of the snake with a small, dismayed elephant standing inside it. In this simple depiction of mortality Saint-Exupéry demonstrates the clash of potential meaning—which children see directly—and mundane interpretation, which blinds adults to seeing the potential. Within the narrative, however, this clash is productive: *The Little Prince* chides grown-ups, but enriches them, too.

The narrator, now an adult, has grown up to become a pilot who has crashed in a barren desert with no signs of civilization. While he struggles to fix his plane, a young boy with golden hair and a scarf appears as if from nowhere. Over the next eight days the Little Prince tells the narrator vivid tales of his home on a faraway asteroid, his adventures on other planets, and how he fell to Earth. These tales are parabolic and present culturally symbolic themes. The Little Prince tells the narrator, for example, of a man on a tiny

Je crois qu'il profita, pour son évasion, d'une migration
d'oiseaux sauvages.

ANTOINE DE SAINT-EXUPÉRY

Le Petit Prince

Avec dessins par l'auteur

REYNAL & HITCHCOCK · NEW YORK

planet who forgot to tend to his bushes. Three of the seeds should have been plucked when they began to sprout, because they were "bad." Instead, they grew to be powerful baobabs that he could not cut down, trees that sucked the life out of his planet and shattered it. "Children," the narrator writes, recounting this story, "Watch out for baobabs!" (We must learn for ourselves, of course, what are the baobabs in our own lives.)

This boy who fell to Earth is not an avatar of Jesus. His views, story, and effect are, however, consonant with the Christian thread in Western culture: "Unless you change and become like little children, you will never enter the kingdom of heaven" (Matthew 18:3). Furthermore, as Jesus told his doubting disciple Thomas, "Because you have seen me, you have believed; blessed are those who have not seen and yet have believed" (John 20:29), the Little Prince tells the pilot, "The important thing is what can't be seen. . . ." The Little Prince does not die for his friend, however. He dies to get back to his rose, which he loves because he has tended her. Still, his home asteroid, B-612, bears the number 4 (symbolic in the Bible of Earthly completeness) multiplied by 153 (the number of miraculous fish—or souls—that Peter nets in obeying the risen Jesus [John 21:11]).

The last image of the book shows a desert landscape with only a star. The narrator asks us to let him know if we ever see this landscape, and under that star, a child. "Don't let me go on being so sad: Send word immediately that he's come back."

Title page from the first edition illustrated by Saint-Exupéry.

The "grown-ups" mistook the first drawing for a hat, whereas a six-year-old clearly understands it is a snake digesting an elephant.

TOVE JANSSON

THE MOOMINS AND THE GREAT FLOOD (1945)

Jansson's much-loved tales of Moomin trolls taught generations of children the importance of kindness and good manners, even amid chaotic adventure.

First published by Schildts in 1945.

In addition to the nine Moomin novels, Jansson wrote a regular comic strip featuring the Moomins. The strip was eventually taken over by her brother Lars.

Jansson also wrote novels and short stories for adults. Several of these include characters who write children's books or cartoons. One heroine of the novel *The True Deceiver* is a rich but misanthropic writer struggling to maintain control of her Moominlike creations in the face of the relentless forces of marketing and merchandising.

Tove Jansson (1914–2001), inventor of the Moomin trolls, is a Scandinavian institution, and her strange, gentle, unfailingly polite little creatures have delighted millions around the world. Jansson originally came up with the Moomins, or something very like them, in her childhood, and continued developing them when she became a professional artist and illustrator. They first appear in her adult work in political cartoons she drew for the satirical magazine *Garm*.

The first of the Moomin books published, *The Moomins and the Great Flood* (really a short story of about sixty pages), is not "officially" part of the Moomin series. It can, however, be seen as proof of concept for the ensuing series (and the enormous franchise that they later became). The world described in the book is one in flux. The Moomins travel from forest to swamp to cliffside cave to beach, before finally being swept away by the titular flood. (They even spend the night in a candy meadow with rivers of chocolate and jam, perhaps inspiring Roald Dahl's *Charlie and the Chocolate Factory*.) The book ends with the family reuniting, and with Moominpapa announcing he has found the perfect valley for them to build a house to live in, which serves as the setting for all future Moomin books.

And yet the world of this book (published in 1945, English translation 2012) is a great deal more civilized than we might expect. When the Moomins part from friends, Moominmama promises: "We'll send you both a letter and tell you what happened." Even in the midst of this wilderness, it seems, one can still rely on the mail. And after the flood, the various displaced creatures sit together around campfires, sharing their surviving utensils and making each other warm drinks, as good neighbors should. Manners, and neighborly behavior, are central to these books and their world, which for all its fantastic qualities, is rooted in the Finnish landscape and Swedish culture in which Tove Jansson grew up. There is something reminiscent of Tolkien's hobbits and the Shire in the world of the Moomins (Jansson illustrated the first Swedish translation of *The Hobbit*, published in 1947). The Moomins are earthy, eager for both diversion and comfort, and keen to have everything in

Their tulip was glowing again, it had opened all its petals and in the midst of them stood a girl with bright blue hair that reached all the way down to her feet.

its right place. The world they construct for themselves reflects these preoccupations: the Moomins' house is cozy and full of all the odds and ends that one needs to feel fully at ease. Moominmama, meanwhile, never sets out on an excursion without a full meal, complete with cutlery and a butter dish, and a purse full of whatever she and her children might need to be well and happy.

The change of the seasons determines the shape and nature of the Moomin world. A later novel, *Finn Family Moomintroll* (1948, English translation 1950) takes place over a long summer, and features such quintessentially Scandinavian summer excursions as a boat trip to the islands and a night under the stars. In *Moominland Midwinter* (1957), Moomintroll wakes up unexpectedly during his hibernation, and finds the world altered and frighteningly foreign. Too-Ticky, who he finds living in the family's beach house (thus transforming it, too, into something unfamiliar), explains: "There are such a lot of things that have no place in summer and autumn and spring. Everything that's a little shy and a little rum. Some kinds of night animals and people that don't fit in with others and that nobody really believes in. They keep out of the way all the year. And then when everything's quiet and white and the nights are long and most people are asleep—then they appear." In *Moominvalley in November* (1971, English translation 1971), the family are absent, and their friends' and neighbors' anxiety over this, their feeling that the world does not make sense without this welcoming family at its center, is expressed through the gloomy, rainy weather of the Finnish autumn. The world of the Moomins is simultaneously fantastic and familiar, cozy and frightening, eternal and ever-changing—a tension that explains why this series of books has resonated so powerfully with generations of children who are just starting to discover their own world.

Tove Jansson's "Map of Moomin Valley," also detailing the two floors of the Moomin family house.

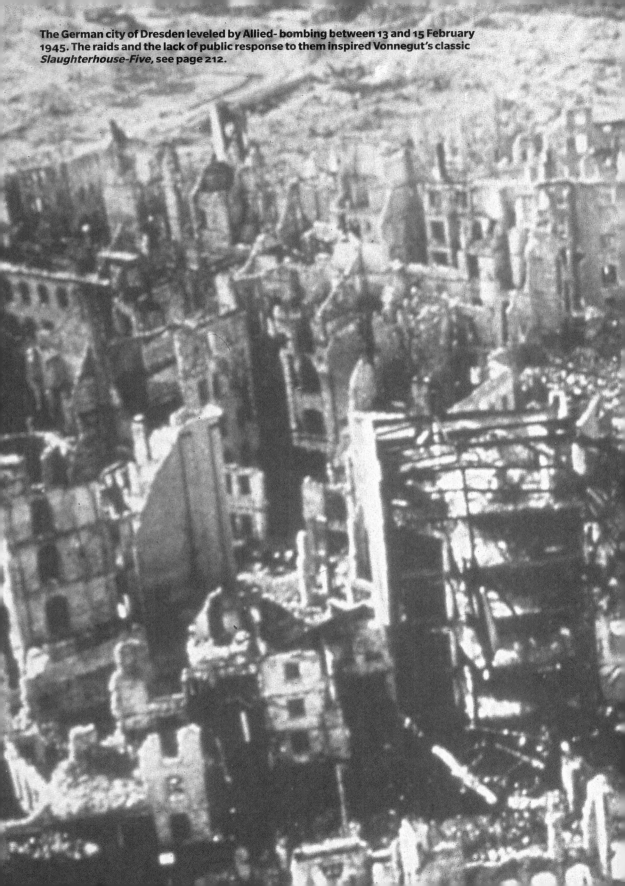

The German city of Dresden leveled by Allied- bombing between 13 and 15 February 1945. The raids and the lack of public response to them inspired Vonnegut's classic *Slaughterhouse-Five*, see page 212.

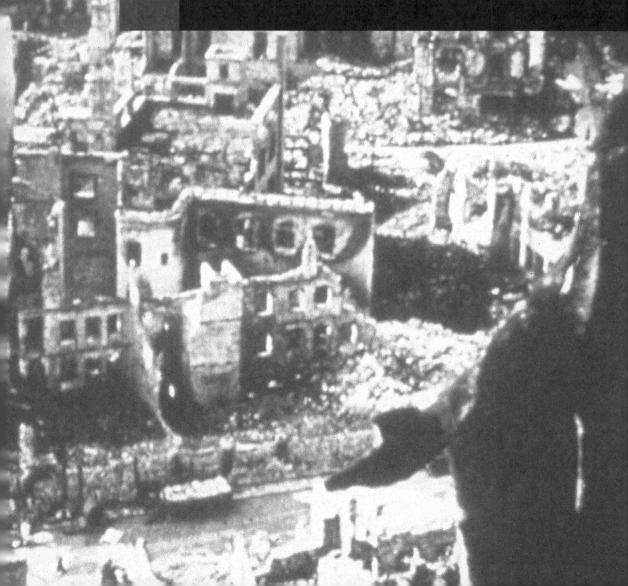

1946–1980

4 NEW WORLD ORDER

The legacy of World War II and ensuing Cold War tensions shell-shocked a generation of writers, each seeking to find a voice for the unspeakable. Feminist and postmodern writing also sought to redress tired tropes dogging the genre.

GORMENGHAST (1946–59)

Peake's enduring gothic tales of the vast and crumbling Gormenghast castle and its curious inhabitants explore a dark world of age-old rituals, treachery, manipulation, and murder.

Titus Groan (1946), *Gormenghast* (1950), and *Titus Alone* (1959) are the three core novels of Peake's trilogy (all published by Eyre and Spottiswoode), and Peake was making plans for a fourth, *Titus Awakes,* when he became too ill to write, around 1960.

Peake studied at the Royal Academy, London, and developed a reputation as a painter and illustrator during the prewar years. As well as his own works he provided illustrations for *Alice's Adventures in Wonderland, The Rime of the Ancient Mariner, The Strange Case of Dr. Jekyll and Mr. Hyde,* and the Grimms' fairy tales.

The fantasy world of Gormenghast Castle is as hard to pin down as a nightmare. Mervyn Peake's (1911–68) trilogy, written during and after World War II, describes the life of Titus Groan, heir to the ancient Earldom of Gormenghast. Parts of the story echo the unimaginable horrors Peake experienced at the end of the war, when he worked as an artist in the newly liberated Bergen-Belsen concentration camp. There is, for instance, the pitiless savagery with which some of the characters are murdered; the blind, unthinking obedience to rules and traditions that beset the castle; and the cold-hearted evil of Steerpike, who tries to seize control.

But it is impossible to make detailed comparisons, still less to see Gormenghast Castle and its massive Tower of Flints against a background of twentieth-century Europe and the Nazis. The Gothic towers of the rambling castle where Titus Groan is born—more a city than a single home, with miles of twisting, shadowy streets running through it and secret, dilapidated areas where no one ever goes—seem to place it in medieval times, as do the ancient rites read from dusty old volumes and the banquets set with gold plate and crimson goblets. Some of the characters, such as Irma Prunesquallor, with her spectacles, her hair pulled into a bun, her flower-trimmed veil, and her neurotic obsessions, could be caricatures from the 1920s. In the third book, *Titus Alone* (1959), Titus journeys away from the castle among cars, skyscrapers, and televisions.

Gormenghast is in a world of its own, isolated both in space and time. Nothing that happens can definitely be said to be supernatural, but an aura of magic hangs over the story. A strange tree grows horizontally out of the castle wall, its trunk so massive that Titus's two aunts, Cora and Clarice, can set a table there to have tea. The Countess of Groan, with her eerie warning, "There is evil in the castle," seems to have a mysterious premonition of the disasters to come and, by the end, she speaks with almost supernatural knowledge as she warns the departing Titus, "There is nowhere else. You will only tread a circle.... Everything comes to Gormenghast."

These ambiguities run throughout. Some characters, such as the Professors, are comic Dickensian figures, while Steerpike is painted with chilling psychological realism, with a terrifying, almost psychotic lack of empathy or remorse.

Unlike novels such as *Brave New World* (1932, page 148), *Nineteen Eighty-Four* (1949, page 174), or *Herland* (1915, page 134), *Gormenghast* presents no political warning or ideal. Rather, the literary influences on Peake's imagination are the comic vision of Dickens, the zany nonsense world of *Alice's Adventures in Wonderland* (1865, page 82), and the adventurous challenges of R. L. Stevenson's *Treasure Island* (1883, page 100). *Gormenghast* stands alone. Its world is neither magical nor realistic, neither wholly comic nor wholly tragic, neither utopia nor dystopia. Perhaps it is this shifting focus and the misty, nightmarish quality that has made *Gormenghast* so consistently popular since its publication.

The first impression of Gormenghast Castle is its sheer size, with its massive, ivy-covered walls looming over the mud huts of the Outer Dwellers huddled below. The Tower of Flints dominates everything "like a mutilated finger from among the fists of knuckled masonry and pointed blasphemously at heaven," and the sheer Outer Wall, like a gray cliff, encloses several square miles of open ground and countless other towers, wings, and passageways. The whole complex is so extensive that most of the people who live inside never venture out.

A page from Peake's original manuscript for *Gormenghast* showing his illustrations of Steerpike and Fuchsia Groan.

The Castle stands at the foot of the craggy Gormenghast Mountain, with the virtually impenetrable Twisted Woods and Gormenghast River at its foot. On its other three sides, marshland, quicksand, and swamps stretch into the distance. This is the waterlogged, inhospitable setting for the great flood, the waters of which rise to the highest floors of the castle and nearly destroy it.

Within the castle walls, the world looks resolutely backward. Much of the fabric of the buildings is falling down, held together only by the ivy that covers it. More importantly, this atmosphere of decay extends to the people who inhabit the buildings. The ancestors of the Earl of Groan have ruled Gormenghast since time immemorial, but now the sole function of the family is to fulfill the endless, detailed, and apparently ridiculous rituals and traditions recorded in old ledgers, interpreted by the Earl's Master of Ritual. Titus, whose birth was recounted in *Titus Groan*, is reintroduced at the start of *Gormenghast* as "suckled on shadows; weaned, as it were, on webs of ritual." This is the world, overwhelmed by the past, from which he wants to escape, and over which the evil Steerpike is determined to rule.

Titus Groan, Gormenghast, and *Titus Alone* have been described by the novelist Anthony Burgess as some of the most important works of the imagination to come out of the modern age. The books present a coherent fantasy world with its own bizarre rules and assumptions, but beneath the surface can be seen several aspects of Peake's own life. His father was a Christian missionary, and Peake was born in Kuling, in China's Kiang-hsi Province, spending most of his childhood in Tianjin, southeast of Beijing. Some see echoes of Imperial China in the rituals and customs of Gormenghast Castle and the Groan family, and the precipitous landscapes of Peake's birthplace, where fortified Chinese towns cling to the steep mountain slopes, are reflected in the descriptions of the castle's setting.

Furthermore, Peake spent several years before and after World War II living on the island of Sark, in the Channel Islands, from where he took some of the place-names in Gormenghast, such as the Coupée, Silvermines, Gory, and Little Sark. However, probably the most significant period of his life was the time he spent drawing in the Nazi concentration camp at Bergen-Belsen in 1945. He wrote several moving and tortured poems, and the horrific sights and experiences of Belsen clearly left a dark and ineradicable impression on his imagination.

Like an earlier fantasy novel, Kenneth Grahame's *The Wind in the Willows, Gormenghast* demonstrates its author's anxiety about the growing demand for social equality in the first half of the twentieth century. The rule of the Groan family may be overbearing, hidebound, self-obsessed, and crippled by its stultifying sense of duty to tradition for its own sake, but the aspiring new meritocracy represented by Steerpike presents a chilling alternative. In one memorable scene, Steerpike slowly pulls the legs off a beetle, murmuring to himself as he does so, "Equality is the great thing—equality is everything."

The three books that tell the Gormenghast story are not a true trilogy, since they were originally planned as part of a longer series intended to follow Titus throughout his life. But, by the mid-1950s, with two books completed and work on the third in hand, Peake was beginning to show early signs of Parkinson's disease. He was increasingly incapacitated both physically and mentally over the next few years, and he died in 1968, at age fifty-seven, after several years in a nursing home.

A rare view of Gormenghast Castle over Titus's shoulder in a sketch by Peake.

Apart from *Titus Groan, Gormenghast,* and *Titus Alone*—and the illustrations that established him as an artist—Peake also produced a series of highly regarded portraits and wrote several volumes of poetry and a number of other novels for children and adults, including the darkly humorous *Mr. Pye* (1953). Many of his books, including the *Gormenghast* novels, have been adapted for radio and television, and a fourth book in the series, *Titus Awakes*, was posthumously published in 2011 by Peake's widow Maeve, to mark the centenary of his birth.

Ultimately, the world of Gormenghast defies classification—unique, fascinating, enthralling, beguiling, and occasionally horrifying. It is a place of dreams, fantasies, and nightmares drawn from experience.

GEORGE ORWELL (ERIC ARTHUR BLAIR)

Nineteen Eighty-Four
(1949)

One of the great dystopias of the twentieth century, Orwell's bleak vision of a totalitarian near-future has spawned many imitators and its instantly recognizable ideas and terms have entered into the public consciousness.

First published by Secker and Warburg in 1949.

Nineteen Eighty-Four frequently appears in polls as one of the greatest books of the twentieth century, and its fame is so great that a 2013 edition appeared with the author's name and the book's title entirely redacted, and yet was still immediately recognizable.

Opposite: Children play beneath the ever-watchful eyes of "Big Brother" on the set of Michael Anderson's film *1984* (Columbia, 1956).

To twenty-first-century readers, the imagined world of *Nineteen Eighty-Four* can seem over-the-top (though the surveillance state of Oceania might seem quaint by today's standards of satellite imagery and drones). In the late 1940s, however, George Orwell's (1903–50) depictions were legitimate extrapolations of very recent history, pushing contemporary trends to their grotesque ends. In 1949, it was not yet five years since the death of Adolf Hitler. Stalin still lived and ruled with a monstrous despotism that had killed millions in intentional famines, party purges ("the Great Terror"), and war crimes. The term "socialist" had been appropriated by Hitler's "National Socialist German Workers' Party" and "the Union of Soviet Socialist Republics". Hope for a benevolent Russian revolution had been betrayed. Nazism, Communism, and World War II had demonstrated shocking human capacities for producing and accepting outrageous propaganda, fanatical commitment to orthodoxy, blatant rewriting of history, cynical side-switching, bureaucratic time-serving and tyranny, torture, mass enslavement, mass murder, and lust for power. Orwell's bleak vision of the future was within legitimate limits of satiric exaggeration.

Nineteen Eighty-Four centers on a triangular relationship between protagonist Winston Smith, his lover Julia, and O'Brien, an older male official of the ruling elite. The story is set in a near-future dystopia—although now in our past—where the major characters compete for our attention with the world of the story and its embedded satirical targets. Perhaps unfairly to *Nineteen Eighty-Four* as novel, it is the world of Orwell's imagined 1984 that has determined *Nineteen Eighty-Four*'s continuing influence, and made "Orwellian" part of English political vocabulary.

The central setting is "London, chief city of Airstrip One," a province of the superpower Oceania (comprising North and South America, the United Kingdom, southern Africa, and Australasia). What was once the United Kingdom is now simply the airstrip nearest to Oceania's two, alternately opposing and allied, superstates of Eurasia and Eastasia. Eurasia encompasses the rest of Europe and Russia, while the boundaries of Eastasia are less

defined but include modern-day China, Japan, Taiwan, and Korea. Orwell's fictional divisions are a reflection of actual and forecast geopolitical alignments after World War II.

Nineteen Eighty-Four is set against the backdrop of a global nuclear and civil war that raged during the 1950s. London is barely rebuilt and is still regularly hit by "rocket bombs." Most people outside the ruling ministries are dirty, poor, and malnourished. Oceanian society is divided into a broad-based, three-tiered pyramid, with the Party Leader, Big Brother, at the apex (although it is not known if Big Brother is dead, or even existed). Around six million members of the Inner Party (known as "the brain of the State" and accounting for fewer than two percent of the population) are just below him, and below them the Outer Party (comprised of minor functionaries such as Smith). Below that come "the dumb masses . . . 'the proles,'" about eighty-five percent of the population.

Smith meets Julia at his workplace—the Ministry of Truth (a perversely named institution designed to edit and revise all existent texts to appear in support of the ruling Party)—and, on realizing their shared rejection of Big Brother, they begin an affair. Together they make contact with O'Brien in an effort to join the "Brotherhood" in resistance against the Party. Smith and Julia are eventually arrested by the Thought Police, the Party's security services, and taken to the Ministry of Love—a place of torture designed specifically to destroy independent human and humane relationships.

Nineteen Eighty-Four largely plays out in small, cramped spaces: Smith's squalid apartment, ministry offices, and the tiny room over a shop in a "prole" neighborhood where Winston and Julia carry on their love affair. These confined environs are later echoed in the cells and interrogation rooms of the Ministry of Love, and climax in "Room 101" (the ultimate torture chamber containing a prisoner's own worst nightmare, fear, or phobia). The pervading claustrophobia is only briefly punctuated by a countryside scene in which Winston and Julia make love for the first time and Winston's dreams glimpses of the "Golden Country" of his past.

Winston and Julia's room over the shop, with its apparently safe enclosure and love-bed, is also evocative of the past world surviving, tenuously, among the proles: a world of private loyalties, emotionally charged sexuality, and simple decency. The room contains an old paperweight—"a little chunk of history" the Party overlooked, a "message from a hundred years ago"—a richly symbolic and fragile object that elegantly speaks volumes when contrasted with the massive pyramids of the Ministries. Lying in the bed with Julia in their room, Winston observes: "The paperweight was the room he was in, and the coral was Julia's life and his own, fixed in a sort of eternity at the heart of the crystal." On another occasion, Winston thinks that a dream he has just had "occurred inside the glass paperweight," that its essence was in "a gesture of the arm made by his mother, and made again thirty years later by the Jewish woman he had seen on the news film [an event recorded

It was almost normal for people over thirty to be frightened of their own children. And with good reason, for hardly a week passed in which *The Times* did not carry a paragraph describing how some eavesdropping little sneak—"child hero" was the phrase generally used—had overheard some compromising remark and denounced its parents to the Thought Police.

at the beginning of his diary], trying to shelter the small boy from the bullets, before the helicopters blew them both to pieces."

The fragile paperweight correlates with Winston and Julia's love, apparently safe enclosure, and with the world of the past; the pyramids correlate with hierarchy, bureaucracy on a monumental scale, and crushing totalitarian power. Centrally, the paperweight correlates with a past in which people could be "governed by private loyalties" and value "individual relationships," a world where "a completely helpless gesture, an embrace . . . could have value in itself."

In *Nineteen Eighty-Four,* Oceania, Eurasia, and Eastasia are all totalitarian states related to one another in cynical alliance or through hatred and warfare (although Julia is astute enough—more astute than Winston—to speculate that the war itself may be phony, with Oceania bombing its own people). The only hope in the novel is the faint one of the proles' remaining human, and Winston and Julia's time of love and loyalty, a "helpless gesture," perhaps, but one with value.

Orwell's aim with *Nineteen Eighty-Four* was to highlight the totalitarian horrors of the first half of the twentieth century and thereby help to avoid their repetition. And he has arguably achieved his aim, as evidenced by the fact that so many of the ideas within the novel—"Big Brother is watching you," "newspeak," "doublethink," "thoughtcrime," "reality control"—have entered into common usage and remain as a warning.

THE CHRONICLES OF NARNIA
(1950–56)

"Always winter and never Christmas; think of that!" C. S. Lewis's enchanted realm beyond the wardrobe and its cast of magical inhabitants have captivated readers of all ages for decades.

The Chronicles of Narnia were written over two years while their author nursed a dying (and querulous) old lady, coped with a binge-drinking brother, and continued the work of an Oxford don specializing in medieval and Renaissance literature. The books were originally published by Geoffrey Bles and The Bodley Head, the latter publishing the final two books of the series.

As a youth, Lewis discovered Norse mythology, which impressed him as ineffably severe, melancholy, and beautiful. This infatuation with what he called "Northerness" provided common ground in his early acquaintance with J. R. R. Tolkien; as fledgling dons at Oxford in the 1920s.

Born to a middle-class Anglo-Irish family in Belfast, Clive Staples Lewis (known to his friends and family as Jack), described himself as "a product of long corridors, empty sunlit rooms, upstairs indoor silences, attics explored in solitude, distant noises of gurgling cisterns and pipes, and the noise of wind under the tiles. Also, of endless books." His mother died when he was nine and, although he remained close to his older brother Warren for the rest of his life, his relationship with his father was difficult. With Warren, he invented an imaginary realm the boys called Boxen, populated by animals who wore clothes and discussed politics, transport, and industry. Lewis himself dismissed it as "almost astonishingly prosaic."

The works of Beatrix Potter and E. Nesbit made the most powerful impressions on him as a small boy, and the narration and sibling relationships of the *Chronicles* show how strongly Nesbit shaped his notion of what children's fiction should be. The irony and relatively sophisticated social comedy that both Nesbit and Lewis employ (for example, in the diary of the awful Eustace Scrub in *The Voyage of the Dawn Treader*, 1952) derive from the nineteenth-century British novel—Austen and Trollope—the sort of books Lewis loved.

The critic William Empson called Lewis "the best read man of his generation, one who read everything and remembered everything he read." This was chiefly because he read for pleasure. Although he could be narrow-minded and intolerant, Lewis's literary criticism (rather unjustly overshadowed by his popular theological writings) shows him to be a magnanimous and sympathetic reader, always willing to meet an author halfway and forever mounting defenses for Latin allegorists that no one else bothered even to know about, let alone read. (He drew the line, however, at modernism, an aesthetic movement that the conservative Lewis regarded with knee-jerk hostility.) When his oldest friend reproached him for writing letters entirely about books, Lewis replied, "I leave to others all the sordid and uninteresting worries about so-called practical life, and share with you those joys and experiences which make that life desirable...but seriously, what can you

have been thinking about when you said "only" books, music, etc., just as if these weren't the real things!"

The medieval literature Lewis loved and that underpinned his own work was essentially syncretic—a fusion of pagan, folkloric, and Christian elements. It's a deliberately patchwork aesthetic that seeks to collect and harmonize rather than to unify and homogenize, on the principle that all the things of this world testify to the infinitely varied goodness of God. So, likewise, the talking animals, Northern European dwarves, classical fauns, and Arthurian knights of Narnia all happily coexist under the banner of the lion god, Aslan. The underlying thinking is platonic—or, rather, neoplatonic: All these seemingly incompatible elements are not lies that contradict the truth and each other, but rather the many shadows that human beings have invented to conjure the one great reality we can never encounter directly in this life.

The closest model for Narnia is the Faerie Land of Edmund Spenser (see page 54), the sixteenth-century English poet whose work was Lewis's academic specialty. Like Faerie Land, and the Celtic notion of the underground kingdom of the Tuatha Dé Danann (which Lewis heard about as a boy from his Irish nurse), Narnia is a separate world that nevertheless

The four Pevensie children (Susan, Peter, Lucy, and Edmund) discover the snow-covered land of Narnia in a scene from *The Chronicles of Narnia: The Lion, the Witch and the Wardrobe* (2005) directed by Andrew Adamson and co-produced by Walden Media and Walt Disney Pictures.

Mr. Tumnus is the first creature Lucy Pevensie meets in Narnia, when she comes across the faun carrying his umbrella and packages through a snowy wood in an early passage of *The Lion, the Witch, and the Wardrobe* (1950). Tumnus also appears in *The Horse and His Boy (1954)* and *The Last Battle* (1956).

intersects with our world at certain places and times, permitting the traffic of people between the two. The four Pevensie children enter Narnia through an enchanted wardrobe in *The Lion, the Witch, and the Wardrobe*, to find the land suffering under the tyrannous reign of the White Witch, who has cursed it to be "always winter and never Christmas." The siblings are enlisted by Aslan to defeat the witch, but first the lion god must sacrifice his own life to pay for the treachery of Edmund Pevensie, then be triumphantly resurrected.

In each of the other six Chronicles (with the exception of *A Horse and His Boy*), children from our world are brought over to save Narnia or Narnians. Yet, notably, surprisingly little of the action takes place in Narnia itself and, when it does, it is a Narnia gone wrong: frozen by the White Witch; its magical nature suppressed by the Telemarines in *Prince Caspian*; or sliding into corruption in the final Chronicle, *The Last Battle*. The quintessential Narnia—best captured in the fireside tales of Mr. Tumnus in *The Lion, the Witch, and the Wardrobe*—is almost always seen from a distance, either in space or time, or else savored in brief snatches before the children are back to this world. This ideal Narnia is a never-ending round of pastoral revelry:

> . . . he told about the midnight dances and how the Nymphs who lived in
> the wells and the Dryads who lived in the trees came out to dance with the

fauns; about long hunting parties after the milk white stag who could give you wishes if you caught him; about feasting and treasure seeking with the wild red Dwarves in deep mines and caverns far beneath the forest floor: and then about summer when the woods were green and old Silenus on his fat donkey would come to visit them, and sometimes Bacchus himself, and then the streams would run with wine instead of water and the whole forest would give itself up to jollification for weeks on end.

So powerful is the Arcadian resonance in these books, that most readers—including the series' most famous illustrator, Pauline Baynes—persist in seeing Narnia as a landscape of rolling hills and meadows with the occasional picturesque stand of trees. Lewis, however, described it as largely forested. Its population consists of talking beasts, larger and visibly more intelligent than ordinary "dumb" beasts and treated by all good Narnians as free, sentient beings. Other Narnians include fauns, satyrs, dwarves (who come in "red" and "black" varieties), dryads and naiads (tree and water spirits), centaurs, and assorted mythical creatures, ranging from minotaurs to werewolves. The magical population concurs that while Narnia is "not men's country," it nevertheless ought to be ruled by a small elite of human beings in obedience to a decree made by Aslan at the dawn of the world (*The Magician's Nephew*, 1951).

Narnia is bordered on the west and north by rugged and sparsely inhabited mountains, and its marshy northern borders are occasionally harried by hostile, man-eating giants. To the south lies Archenland, a friendly nation populated by a feudal human society. A harsh desert separates Archenland from the vaguely Turkic empire of Calormen, whose dark-skinned and be-turbaned rulers frequently entertain imperial designs on the "Northern barbarians." The Calormenes own slaves, worship a frightening, multi-armed, and bird-headed god called Tash, and are described in *The Voyage of the Dawn Treader* as "a wise, wealthy, courteous, cruel, and ancient people." Some Lewis proponents have maintained that this depiction is not "racist" but merely a thoughtless borrowing of hoary Western literary devices concerning the East. Whether there's a substantive distinction between these two prejudices is debatable.

To the east of Narnia lies the Great Eastern Ocean, speckled with the allegorical islands visited in *The Voyage of the Dawn Treader*—the most medieval of the Chronicles and many readers' favorite. Because Narnia's world is flat, the furthest reaches of the Great Eastern Ocean abut on a wall of flowing water, beyond which is Aslan's country, home to the souls of the virtuous dead. Far beneath the surface of Narnia lies the land of Bism, whose gnome inhabitants live happily on the banks of a river of fire and pick diamonds like fruit to squeeze for their juice.

The marginal detail work on Narnia is pretty cursory; it's like an old-fashioned movie set, the facades just convincing enough to serve as a

setting for the narrative at hand. Even Narnia itself is scantily shaded-in. Narnia has no major cities—just two castles and a briefly mentioned market town, Chippingford. Despite the absence of any industry or agriculture to speak of, the inhabitants have somehow obtained such commodities as a sewing machine, orange marmalade, tea, and a seemingly endless supply of sausages and bacon.

Does this incongruity matter? Not to millions of young readers, that's for sure. Children, as a general rule, don't even detect the religious symbolism that many adults find so glaring in the Chronicles. We seldom notice the flaws in the object of our desire, and that is what Narnia is—a shimmering, delicious mirage, just out of reach. Within its elusive borders is collected every wonder that ever delighted Lewis in the thousands of books he read, every adventure he longed for, every brave prince and doughty badger, every enchanted pool and misted mountain, every mermaid and leafy-haired dryad, every spired castle and green hill. It would be a motley collection indeed if it were not unified by the intensity of his desire, which, because it is effectively a child's yearning, mysteriously preserved in the mind of a formidably well-read, middle-aged man, communicates most immediately to child readers.

That doesn't, however, make it merely childish. The desire to bring all of life's joys together in celebration is an impulse that even those who can't subscribe to Lewis's faith can nevertheless still understand and share. In the case of Narnia, it isn't the elaboration of the backdrop that casts the spell, that makes the place seem real in spite of its many absurdities, but the inexhaustible delight of the dancers who inhabit it, as well as the man who made it.

Opposite:
Pauline Baynes's map of Narnia, published in 1972 by Puffin Books.

ISAAC ASIMOV

I, ROBOT (1950)

As the science of robotics advances to an inevitable conclusion, the nine short stories of Asimov's I, Robot *chronicle a remarkably prescient future history from 1998 to 2052.*

First published by Gnome Press in 1950.

From robots being restricted to off-world use to becoming indistinguishable from humans, *I, Robot* anticipates the film *Blade Runner* by decades. Asimov's book is arguably as essential to that landmark film as Philip K. Dick's *Do Androids Dream of Electric Sheep?*, upon which *Blade Runner* is officially based.

The *Oxford English Dictionary* credits Asimov with the earliest usage of the words "robotics" and "positronic" (although the first use of the word "robot" belongs to Karel Čapek's 1920 play *Rossum's Universal Robots*).

Through nine stories originally published in the magazines *Astounding Science Fiction* and *Super Science Stories* between 1940 and 1950, the Russian-born American master of science fiction Isaac Asimov developed his vision of the future, our present, which now appears simultaneously naive and extraordinarily prescient. His foresight stems from an extraordinary imagination coupled to genuine facility for real science; he obtained a PhD in biochemistry in 1948 and joined the faculty of the Boston University School of Medicine.

The stories were published together in 1950 as *I, Robot* and together they present a future world of wonders, in which humanity is spread across the solar system: from flying cars, to mining operations on Mercury, to a network of interplanetary solar-power relay stations, and on to Hyper Base, where an experimental new warp drive will power a spaceship to the stars. The one unifying element to all these marvels is robots, specifically those designed by the monolithic corporation, U.S. Robots and Mechanical Men, Inc.

Lawrence Robertson founded U.S. Robots in 1982, the same year in which Dr. Susan Calvin, the scientist who eventually becomes the company's head robot psychologist, is born. Calvin does not appear in every story, but when Asimov "fixed up" his individual tales into a novel he devised a framing device in which the doctor, now seventy-five, is interviewed by a young journalist on the occasion of her retirement, offering the chance to reflect on her life and the intertwined history of robotics.

A handful of other characters recur through the stories—notably the troubleshooting robotics engineers Gregory Powell and Mike Donovan—but more consistent than any one character is the process of continual change realized by rapid technological progress. In the first story, set in 1998, Robbie is a humanoid metal machine who cannot speak, who serves as a companion to a little girl, Gloria. By "Runaround," set seventeen years later, talking robots are engaged in complex mining activities on Mercury.

It is with this story that Asimov made his most inspired and enduring contribution to popular culture, codifying the "Three Laws of Robotics" as an

A robot may not injure a human being or, through inaction, allow a human being to come to harm.

A robot must obey orders given it by human beings except where such orders would conflict with the First Law.

A robot must protect its own existence as long as such protection does not conflict with the First or Second Law.

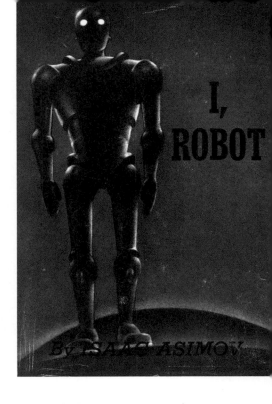

essential protocol to govern the increasingly sophisticated behavior of robots and with the aim of ensuring that human safety remained paramount. Rules in place, the stories unfold as logic puzzles, with either Powell, Donovan, or, later, Calvin, required to resolve a situation arising from a robot interpreting the Laws in an unanticipated way, often with dangerous consequences.

The cover for the first U.S. edition of *I, Robot* published in 1950 by Gnome Press. Opposite is shown the first UK edition (1952).

The robots have "positronic" brains. They are conscious, but there is a tension between cybernetic "free will" and programming. That Susan shares her name with the theologian John Calvin, who argued the individual's fate was predestined by God, does not seem coincidental. Indeed, the final story documents "The Inevitable Conflict."

Decades prior, in "Reason," QT1, nicknamed Cutie, rejects the human explanation for its existence and creates its own religion. The robot determines it was created by the power source of the space station it is on, which it calls Master: "There is no Master but Master, and QT1 is His prophet." By 2032, such are the advances in robotics that a political candidate is challenged to prove he is human. Finally, the machines become superior. Humanity barely notices.

Ultimately, for a work written through the years of World War II and the early Cold War, *I, Robot* offers a remarkably optimistic vision of a peaceful future, of a transition to a postcapitalist, post-statist global economy. Inevitably a product of its time, *I, Robot*'s future remains largely a man's world, with Calvin apparently the only successful woman, excepting a brief appearance by Madame Szegeczowska, co-coordinator of the European Region, and the fourth most powerful person in a society where all real power resides in the Machine.

RAY BRADBURY

FAHRENHEIT 451 (1953)

A masterwork of twentieth-century literature set in a bleak, dystopian future where literature is on the brink of extinction.

First published by Ballantine Books in 1953.

451°F is supposed to be the temperature at which book-paper will begin to burn.

In December 2015, a new Internet HTTP error code 451 was adopted to denote content that has been censored/blocked for legal reasons.

Ray Bradbury (1920–2012) wrote the first version of *Fahrenheit 451*, originally called "The Fireman," in 1949, in nine days, on a rented typewriter in the basement of the library on the University of California, Los Angeles (UCLA), campus. Surrounded by books as he wrote, grabbing them at random for inspiration, Bradbury liked to say that the library had written the story for him. The novel we know as *Fahrenheit 451* was published in 1953.

Although he loved movies, the new medium of television was, in Bradbury's view, a threat both to reading and to conversation, as people spent increasing amounts of time staring at a screen in their living rooms, rather than engaging with others or exploring ideas. He imagined the results after fifty years: giant "televisor" screens on multiple walls, social life replaced by soap opera families, tiny "Seashells" plugged into the ears providing a constant stream of music or chatter, and an increasing rejection of independent, critical thinking accompanying the fear of anyone being different.

Into this nightmare of bland conformity, Bradbury incorporated his personal dislikes: speed, team sports, and modern art. He never learned to drive, but the citizens of his dystopia are not allowed to travel at less than fifty miles per hour, often crash, and enjoy running down pedestrians. Sports have replaced books as the major part of school curricula, and are prescribed (along with easily available tranquilizers and stimulants) for anyone whose behavior is out of line. Only abstract paintings are on display.

In a powerful reversal of the norm, firemen start fires rather than putting them out. Their job is to seek out illegal caches of books and burn them. Since the Constitutional meanings of "happiness" and "a free and equal society" have been corrupted to mean that all must be *made* equal in order to be happy, firemen become the guardians of society.

Guy Montag is a fireman, delighting in his destructive power until he meets a neighbor, self-described "crazy" teenager Clarisse, who asks him "Are you happy?" He cannot answer and begins to question his life.

Montag's boss, Captain Beatty, explains that books are so dangerous to human happiness because not one of them agrees with another. Some are

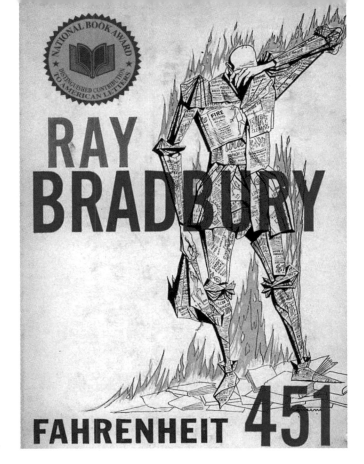

offensive to particular groups, some make you feel unpleasant emotions, some make you dissatisfied with your lot, others force you to ask questions—they are like loaded guns in the wrong hands.

When he sees a woman refuse to be parted from her books, choosing to burn with them, Montag believes they must be the thing that is lacking in his life. However, as another book lover, the philosopher Faber, tells him: "It's not books you need, it's some of the things that once were in books. The same things *could* be in the 'parlor families' today. The same infinite detail and awareness could be projected through the radio and televisors, but are not."

The city in *Fahrenheit 451* is unnamed, but is probably somewhere in California. The shadow of nuclear war hangs over all, yet the citizens are encouraged to believe that only "other people" die that way. But no matter how desperate things are, there is still a ray of hope. Outside the city, living simply in the countryside, former professors, librarians, and others have formed a resistance movement, not owning the banned books, but keeping them alive in their minds. They will pass the memorized texts on to their children by word of mouth, and they to their children, until the time is right for their return.

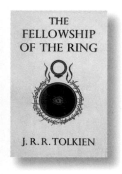

THE
FELLOWSHIP
OF THE RING

J. R. R. TOLKIEN

J. R. R. TOLKIEN

THE LORD OF THE RINGS
(1954–55)

*Classic and incredibly detailed fantasy world of Middle-earth;
created by a mild-mannered language professor as a hobby, it went
on to become the most influential imaginary world ever created.*

Initially published as three books by George Allen and Unwin: *The Fellowship of the Ring* (July 1954), *The Two Towers* (November 1954), and *The Return of the King* (October 1955).

The Lord of the Rings was preceded by *The Hobbit*, published as a children's book in 1937, and was intended as a sequel to it. When delivered seventeen years later, however, it was no longer a children's book and had become far longer and more ambitious. The background history to both works is contained in *The Silmarillion* (1977).

The Middle-earth of J. R. R. Tolkien's (1892–1973) *The Hobbit* and *The Lord of the Rings* is probably the best-known and most influential of all the many imaginary worlds of the twentieth century. The books have sold millions of copies in scores of languages, and yet the stories are remarkable for more than sheer numbers. Heroic fantasy existed before Tolkien, of course, but his success brought it into the mass-market. Very few later authors of fantasy have escaped his imprint—even those who have tried very hard to shed it—and many have testified that it was his work that made them writers.

Tolkien's commercial and popular success is ironic because he made almost no attempt to achieve it. No one could look less like a professional author. We know, now, that he started to write a version of his personal mythology as early as 1917, but although he rewrote it continually, he made little effort to have it published for twenty years, and then met with no success. *The Hobbit* (1937) might never have seen publication if a student of Tolkien's had not mentioned it to an employee of the publisher George Allen and Unwin. When *The Hobbit* became moderately successful, Stanley Unwin asked him for a sequel. Tolkien started work on it right away, at Christmas 1937, but it was years before the sequel began to be published, in three volumes 1954–55, and by then *The Lord of the Rings* had ceased to be for children. Unwin expected the work to make a loss, but was prepared to take a chance on it—because the other side of the author's apparent amateurishness is his originality.

The Lord of the Rings is not the story of a quest, but of an anti-quest. The hero, the hobbit Frodo Baggins, is not trying to recover some lost object of power, like the Holy Grail, but to destroy forever one that he already has—the One Ring, found accidentally in the course of *The Hobbit* by his older cousin Bilbo Baggins. If the Dark Lord, Sauron, regains it, his power will become irresistible; if it is destroyed he will crumble—but the only place where the Ring can be destroyed is where it was forged, in the Cracks of Doom in the heart of Sauron's own country of Mordor. Frodo, with his companion Sam, has to get there on his own. The wars and battles that occupy his

other companions, though much more dramatic than Frodo's stealthy journey, are secondary.

Tolkien's hobbits are a race or subspecies of small humans, rarely more than four feet tall, but in almost every other respect—including behavior and mindset—identical to the rustic English people of his own Victorian youth: cheerful, practical, unintellectual, and unadventurous. They live in the Shire, very like Tolkien's home county of Worcestershire, and take no interest in the wider world of Middle-earth. It is Gandalf the wizard who decides, in *The Hobbit*, to shake them up by recommending Bilbo as a professional burglar to a company of dwarves, setting off to recover their ancestral treasures from the dragon Smaug.

The Lord of the Rings opens up far wider perspectives of space and time than *The Hobbit*, beginning with Gandalf explaining to Frodo what the Ring really is and what must be done to ensure its destruction. But a third and critical invention was there in the earlier work as well—the concept of Middle-earth. It has been rightly said that the hero of *The Lord of the Rings*

Tolkien's sketch of Orthanc, the impenetrable tower of Isengard, in an early manuscript of *The Lord of the Rings*.

is not Frodo, nor Aragorn, nor even Sam Gamgee, but Middle-earth itself. It is Middle-earth with which so many millions of readers have fallen in love. An initial feature of this mystical land is the variety of physical environment that it encompasses: the Misty Mountains, the prairies of the Riddermark, the Great River of Anduin, the Dead Marshes, but most of all, the forests: Mirkwood, the Old Forest, Fangorn Forest, and Lothlórien, all different, all lovingly described.

Along with physical environments comes a variety of species. Tolkien would have been the first to acknowledge that his Middle-earth was not purely his own creation, but a re-creation, backed by his own unique professional knowledge of the lost world of early Northern fable and myth. From these tales Tolkien drew his cast of elves and dwarves, trolls and dragons, and even orcs and ents—both words that existed in Old English, and which moreover meant nothing (like hobbits) until Tolkien gave them life.

Tolkien was a Professor, first of English Language at the University of Leeds, then of Anglo-Saxon at Oxford, finally moving to the Merton Chair of English Language and Literature, also at Oxford. All his fiction is animated by his awareness of early Northern literatures—primarily, but not exclusively, Old Norse and Anglo-Saxon—and even more by his attempt to make sense of what they said, which is often said to be self-contradictory or inadequate. Tolkien never accepted this. He believed instead that old authors and old ideas had simply been misunderstood, badly copied, or gone missing, and if he had to write a story or a poem to explain a problem or fill a gap—as he did with *The Legend of Sigurd and Gudrún*, published in 2009 nearly eighty years after it was written—then so be it. It should certainly not be forgotten that, quite apart from his fiction, he was in some areas the most learned man in the world.

It is this knowledge that gives Middle-earth one more distinctive quality, and that is its sense of great age and complex history. Tolkien's work made it almost mandatory for fantasy authors after him to include maps of their imaginary worlds, but further to this, at the end of *The Lord of the Rings* he also gave a hundred pages of history, chronicle, and family tree, with carefully considered alphabets and language-commentaries to boot. No one has had the resources to imitate this. As well as his vast learning, Middle-earth was, in his own mind, at least twenty years old by the time he started writing the trilogy, with already developed Elvish languages, characters, and even poetic traditions—*The Lord of the Rings* is full of poems, in many modes, mostly now quite unfamiliar. But Frodo and Sam and the other hobbits, as soon as they leave the Shire, recreate the experience of modern readers as they find themselves plunged into a world with a deep sense of history, often of ancient grudge. Bilbo's dwarf-companions want revenge on Smaug the dragon, the Mines of Moria preserve the memory of the underground wars of orcs and dwarves, elves and dwarves also have old and recent enmities, the very landscape (like the English landscape) is covered with old barrows, ruined castles, memorials of forgotten people—all of them provoking a wish to know more, which is left unsatisfied. This thirst for a greater and deeper understanding of the roaming history that Tolkien created has been a major stimulus for later writers, poets, artists, and even composers.

One last feature deserves to be considered as an explanation for Tolkien's extraordinary success, and that is—rather surprisingly, in view of what has just been said—his contemporary relevance. Most of Tolkien's own life was uneventful. He held one academic post after another for forty years, married the sweetheart of his teenage years, raised four children, and enjoyed popular fame only in retirement. However, his early life was unremittingly sad. His father died when he was four, his mother when he was twelve. Family life was replaced for him by life at school, but many of his school friends were killed during World War I when Tolkien also saw active service at the Somme with the Lancashire Fusiliers, until he fell victim to "trench fever," a disease probably carried by lice. He rejected scornfully suggestions that the Ring was in some way an allegory of the A-bomb (his work was mostly complete before Hiroshima), but it resonates with the themes of power and dictatorship and the inevitable corruption of good intentions backed by power, which have been such a feature of twentieth-century life. Those who use the Ring become Ring-wraiths, eaten up by their cause and their obedience: a fantastic version of something all too familiar in reality.

Along with this political suggestion goes unusual emotional depth. *The Lord of the Rings* includes a victory, but does not end with it. Frodo cannot be cured in Middle-earth, and has to leave for the Undying Lands. Not everyone can follow him. The elves, potentially immortal though they are, will die or dwindle if they stay, and if they leave will lose forever Middle-earth and the trees they love. The tree-herding ents are also doomed to species-extinction. If the dwarves and hobbits survive, it will be marginally and invisibly. Tolkien does death scenes brilliantly, even in the children's book *The Hobbit*, but even stronger than his sense of death is his sense of loss, of which death is only a part. One can lose memories as well as people, and the loss even of Gollum is sad: He had a chance to save himself before he died, but failed to take it.

Yet the counterpart of loss is determination. Tolkien's work is studded with heroes of very different types: warriors and dragon-slayers like Aragorn and Bard the Bowman or Túrin in *The Silmarillion*; Beorn the were-bear in *The Hobbit*; Théoden King charging to death and glory in *Lord of the Rings*; and, throughout, the hobbits—not very aggressive but plugging gamely and cheerfully along like overburdened soldiers in the trenches. They are heroes, too, both hobbits and soldiers. In all Tolkien's work, archaic and modern concepts interpenetrate, showing continuity beneath change, something in which he firmly believed. He brought back a whole inheritance of myth and legend in his vast world, and made it work for the present day.

JUAN RULFO

PEDRO PÁRAMO (1955)

In this hugely influential novel, Juan Preciado sets out across Mexico to the spectral town of Comala, where dream and reality, past and present, and the realms of the living and dead, merge and overlap.

First published by Fondo de Cultura Económica in 1955.

Rulfo's full name was Juan Nepomuceno Carlos Pérez Rulfo Vizcaíno, and he was also a screenwriter and photographer.

He is best known for *Pedro Páramo* and a collection of short stories, *El Llano en llamas* (*The Plain in Flames*, 1953).

Although Juan Rulfo (1917-1986) authored little more than two slender volumes of fiction in his lifetime—a short novel and a collection of short stories—he remains a towering literary figure to contemporary Latin American and Mexican authors. Rulfo is largely unknown outside of Spanish-speaking countries, though authors such as Gabriel García Márquez and Jorge Luis Borges have credited him as being one of the world's greatest writers. The imaginary world Rulfo created in *Pedro Páramo* sent shock waves through the literary milieu and, although critics did not initially respond well to his work, Rulfo became a beacon to authors who were eager to engage in a type of writing that was unlike anything that came before.

Pedro Páramo uses the layering of many alternate and alternating narrative voices, flashbacks and flash-forwards, and jumps around in time. The point of view of the first-person narrator, Juan Preciado, begins us on our journey, which alternates from character to character without warning, moving between first- and third-person narration, and from the living to the dead. It leaves the reader in a permanently perplexed, dreamlike state. Rulfo's novel transports the reader to the imaginary and poignant wasteland of Comala—a journey that the reader may interpret as a descent into hell (the word itself means griddle, grill, or brazier)—as Juan attempts to carry out his mother's dying wish for him to find his father. *Pedro Páramo* (the name means wasteland or barren plain) forces the reader to distinguish between the original narrator's voice, the whispers of the dead in their crypts, Pedro Páramo's frequent flashbacks to his own childhood and his love for Susana San Juan, Susana's senseless musings in life and in death, the repeated phrases of Juan Preciado's dying mother—who lauds the lush beauty of her native city, Comala—and Juan's present, voiced perceptions of the city as a deserted and burned-out wasteland.

Described as one of the most haunting works in the Spanish language, Rulfo's use of time encapsulates a way of life that was and always will be recognizable as Mexican, with its unique cultural presentation of pre- and postrevolution life. The reader is continually involved in a process of

A scene from the film adaptation, loosely based on the novel and directed by Carlos Velo in 1967.

orientation and reorientation with regard to space and time, until a sense of disorientation becomes the standard mode through which Rulfo's narrative is framed. Rulfo uses the cacophony of narrative voices to portray the community of the crypt, where people are buried nearly on top of each other (especially if they are poor), and demonstrates that the dead seem to be more concerned with the cares of the living (or of the dead when they were living). They attempt to overhear Susana San Juan speaking aloud in the sleep of death in her crypt—as a person of means, she is farther away from the rest of the buried community so that the others have to strain to hear her.

Rulfo jerks the reader in and out of linear time as he leapfrogs from one narrator to another, from one time period to another (and sometimes within another time period, like Borges's box within a box within a box), to a flashback or even a flash-forward to the future from the perspective of the past, and always without the slightest notice. Rulfo knows that by keeping the reader disoriented in terms of causality we cannot grow comfortable with any sense of reliability in the novel. Yet the portrayal of many different narrative voices helps to create a simulacrum of the world and society. This simulacrum cannot be anything but a fantastic representation; however, the ghosts of Comala linger in our minds in the same way that a powerful event lingers in consciousness. No reader ever leaves Comala completely behind.

Sadly Rulfo is not well-known to a popular audience outside of Spanish-speaking countries, although authors such as Gabriel García Márquez and Jorge Luis Borges have credited him as one of the world's greatest writers, and the international literary intelligentsia, as Susan Sontag has pointed out, read and praised his work.

STANISŁAW LEM

SOLARIS (1961)

Lem's powerfully intelligent and influential science-fiction story asks the fundamental question of whether we can begin to understand the mysteries of the universe without first coming to understand ourselves.

First published by Wydawnictwo Ministerstwa Obrony Narodowej in 1961.

The word "solaris" is a Latin adjective meaning "sunny."

It used to be believed that consciousness would always require a "hard" or fixed system on which to run, like the pattern of neurons in the brain, or the circuits of computers. Some more recent thinkers like Stuart Hameroff have theorized something more like fluid- or quantum-based consciousness, much closer to the idea Lem advances in this novel.

Polish-born Lem (1921–2006) was an astonishingly prolific and varied writer, but there are good reasons why his novel *Solaris*, published in 1961, remains his best-known work. Always restlessly intelligent and inventive, as much a philosophical thinker as a writer of fiction, many of his stories are thought-provoking on an intellectual level. But this account of explorers from Earth attempting to make contact with the radically alien intelligence represented by the planet Solaris is more than just thought-provoking: it is poetic, moving, and liable to haunt your dreams.

In the novel, human space explorers have been studying the baffling world of Solaris for decades. The whole planet is covered in a globe-spanning ocean that itself seems to be conscious and intelligent, although all attempts to make contact have failed. Indeed, the ocean-world appears indifferent to humanity, and the observing scientists have been reduced to recording and cataloging the complex phenomena that appear on the planet's fluid surface. The mental health of the space station crew is suffering, and a psychologist named Kris Kelvin is dispatched from Earth. Kelvin's wife has recently committed suicide, and when he arrives on the Solaris-orbiting space station he sees her again. Several of the crew report similar apparitions—physical manifestations of people they have lost. It seems that bombarding the planet with x-rays has caused it to respond by creating these eidolons: artificial people, gifted with minds and emotions read telepathically from the memories of the humans.

Two well-regarded films have been made based on *Solaris*: the first by Russian director Andrei Tarkovsky in 1972, and the second by Steven Soderbergh in 2002. Both are haunting and beautiful works of visual art, but both focus much more on the relationships between the human characters than does the original novel. It's not that Lem neglects that aspect of his story, it is just that he is much more interested in the sublime mystery of the planet. As Lem said in interview, having seen the first movie adaptation: "But the book was entitled *Solaris* and not *Love in Outer Space*!" In other words, *Solaris* is centrally about an encounter with an almost overwhelming radical

A poster for Andrei Tarkovsky's 1972 film adaptation.

alienness and otherness. Most science-fiction aliens look rather like humans or, if they differ from us physically, we are nonetheless able to communicate and interact with them. Science fiction is full of stories of human–alien trade, or wars, or intermarriage. *Solaris* is nothing like this.

Early observers of Solaris assumed, the novel tells us, "that the thinking ocean of Solaris was a gigantic brain, prodigiously well-developed and several million years in advance of our own civilization," which had "long ago understood the vanity of all action and for this reason had retreated into an unbreakable silence." But as the novel goes on, we realize that "the living ocean [is] active."

Not active according to human ideas, however—it did not build cities or bridges, nor did it manufacture flying machines. Nor was it concerned with the conquest of space. It was engaged in a never-ending process of transformation, an ontological auto-metamorphosis.

That last word is key to the novel's success as a work of fiction: Solaris as imagined keeps changing, redefining itself, and, therefore, redefining its human observers. This is why Lem imagines it in terms of an ocean: its consciousness is not fixed and benchmarked by static points of science, convention, or ideology, the way human minds are. It is in a process of continual flux. There is no world in the whole of science fiction like it.

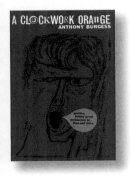

ANTHONY BURGESS

A CLOCKWORK ORANGE (1962)

A study of youth, violence, and free will, A Clockwork Orange *creates a new language in order to build a world where children and adults are incomprehensible to each other.*

First published by Heinemann in 1962.

For many years, the UK and U.S. editions of *A Clockwork Orange* had different endings, with the UK edition printing an extra chapter of epilogue, in which Alex matures and chooses to change his ways.

The word "nadsat," for the youth language of the book, derives from the ending of the numerals eleven through nineteen in Russian.

A Clockwork Orange begins with a question ("What's it going to be then, eh?"), which will be repeated throughout the novel, and which will resonate differently each time it appears. It's the next sentence, though, that plunges the reader into the book's world: "There was me, that is Alex, and my three droogs and we sat in the Korova Milkbar making up our rassoodocks what to do with the evening. . . ." More unfamiliar words are used: *mesto, skorry, veshches, moloko, peet*. In addition, the diction is also unusual: "the evening, a flip dark chill winter bastard though dry," "and you may, O my brothers, have forgotten," "admiring Bog And All His Holy Angels And Saints."

This is "nadsat," an argot Anthony Burgess (1917–93) invented, mostly from anglicized Russian root words. The words create not only the voice of a person, they also evoke an entire world. It becomes clear that nadsat is a language used only by certain young people. Children who speak in nadsat make themselves all but incomprehensible to adults, who speak a standard version of English. With nadsat, Burgess makes the generation gap literal.

In 1962, Anthony Burgess was already an established novelist, but *A Clockwork Orange* shot him to international fame, and particularly so after Stanley Kubrick's film adaptation was released in 1971. A prolific, polymathic writer, Burgess would go on to write a total of thirty-three novels, dozens of nonfiction books, plays, screenplays, autobiographies, translations, and musical compositions, making him one of the most prominent, celebrated, and controversial British writers of the later twentieth century.

A Clockwork Orange is set in what was, when the book was published in 1962, the future, but the exact date isn't clear, and the world is not significantly different from England in the 1960s. There are "worldcast" TV shows and other items that were more speculation than reality when the book was written, but the feeling of science fiction is mostly derived from the nadsat terms, which create an alienating effect easily as strong as warp drives and ray guns in conventional science fiction.

There is also the ultraviolence. The word is Alex's own for what he and his droogs get up to. They vandalize, they assault, they rape. In Kubrick's

film, the shock comes from just how much joy their sadism brings them, but in the novel the effect is somewhat different, and suggests much about this world. Alex brings girls home, plays Beethoven's *Ninth Symphony* for them, gives them drugs, and rapes them. There is a similar scene in the film, but in the book a key point is different: the girls "couldn't have been more than ten [years old]." After the murder that will land him in jail, Alex reveals information previously unknown: he is only fifteen years old.

The youth violence that the politicians and scientists try to solve (which renders Alex into the titular "clockwork orange," incapable of committing any sort of aggression without being crippled by pain and nausea) is not small stuff. Alex is a monster, living a monstrous life, and such a life does not seem uncommon in this world. Whether Alex ought to be programmed against violence or left to his own free will is one of the questions the novel raises.

Alex becomes a political symbol for a group opposed to the government's plans for controlling violence. The government, too, wants to use him. Neither side consider him as a person, he is merely a symbol to be broadcast for political gain: a clockwork orange of another sort.

A Clockwork Orange is often described as depicting a dystopia, but that's not quite right. In its characters' eyes, it is a world heading that way. To the government and many citizens, the out-of-control children are leading the country toward chaos; to radicals, the government is trying to destroy free will and individuality. All we can know is that the world becomes a different one after the events of the story; in one of the first sentences of the book, Alex complains about "things changing so skorry these days and everybody very quick to forget." He has not forgotten, nor could he, and so he helps us remember a world we never experienced.

"The Korova Milkbar sold milk-plus, milk plus vellocet or synthemesc or drencrom, which is what we were drinking. This would sharpen you up and make you ready for a bit of the old ultra-violence." Alex (played by Malcolm McDowell in Stanley Kubrick's 1971 film) makes his plans for the evening ahead.

VLADIMIR NABOKOV

PALE FIRE (1962)

"Nabokov's most perfect novel" and a postmodern masterpiece, Pale Fire *presents a wildly original narrative structure in the form of a 999-line poem, with an extensive, and very subjective, commentary that reveals the politics and petty jealousies of academia.*

First published by G. P. Putnam's Sons in 1962.

Frequently appearing on lists of the best novels of the twentieth century, *Pale Fire* received a mixed reception, with one critic labeling it "unreadable."

Multifaceted and heavy with allusion to other works, *Pale Fire* also incorporates references to Nabokov's previous novels, such as *Lolita* and the eponymous hero of *Pnin*, who appears here as a minor character.

The title of John Shade's poem is taken from Shakespeare's *Timon of Athens*: "The moon's an arrant thief,/And her pale fire she snatches from the sun."

What can be said about *Pale Fire* to someone coming to it for the first time—someone who doesn't have all day, much less the lifetimes needed to dig down to all its different levels? To start with, it's a very fancy and very funny fairy tale, told partly by an imaginary poet and partly by an imaginary critic, who is supposedly explaining the imaginary poet's poem, but is mostly trying to shape the poem, which is a combination of fantasy and autobiography, into a reflection of his own imagination.

Pale Fire is full of tricks and mirrors and false bottoms, and also people you'd never find in your usual wonderland. Look! There's Dr. Samuel Johnson! He's dressed as a suburban English professor, and pontificates in an upstate college town instead of eighteenth-century London. And then there's a trained assassin, sent from pre-Soviet Russia to kill an exiled king. When they're not turning on one another, people are turning into one another by the strange lights of *Pale Fire*—reformed and transformed, but never so you don't recognize them. There's a home-run hitter named Chapman (in reference to the Chapman of Keats's poem, "On First Looking into Chapman's Homer," an old-time, big-league translator of Homer) who becomes a character in the poem, where his achievements are published in a newspaper and nailed to a door:

> . . . from the local *Star*
> A curio: Red Sox Beat Yanks 5-4
> On Chapman's Homer . . .

Look again at that king killer come from far away; he's reborn as a garden-variety lunatic, just escaped from the local asylum. And a closer look at that exiled monarch from a kingdom called Zembla (somewhere between Iceland and the Garden of Eden) shows a pedantic, semi-certifiably psychotic, perennially "visiting" professor, a bizarrely and bravely unapologetic vegetarian, homosexual émigré, living in the middle of the last century, before those things were accepted.

By all accounts, the world of *Pale Fire* is hilarious. The poem "Pale Fire," written by the imaginary poet, is a pretty good poem, although the imaginary poet (his name is Shade) would be the first to tell you it's not what a lot of people would call great the way *Paradise Lost* is great: "Pale Fire" (and *Pale Fire*, for that matter) won't explain the mysteries of the deep to you. It won't serve up Eternity, much less promise eternal life. (That's partly why the critic—his name is Kinbote—tries to make the poem into something it isn't: an epic of his sorely missed, wholly imaginary Zembla, stocked with winter palaces and seaside dachas, 24/7 pomp and circumstance, and teams of costumed young athletes. This is Kinbote's own, his native land, all the more beloved for living only in his mind.)

About as far from Zembla or any "kingdom by the sea" as anything could be, the poem itself makes no promise of happiness. "Pale Fire" makes no promise to enlighten or assure, or put an end to all that ails. The poet is very imaginative—he can turn a phrase so that the most ordinary sight or sound is magically transformed into a thing of beauty and a joy, albeit not forever. This lack of "forever" is the problem in a nutshell: it's the pain that no amount of pretending can keep out of any wonderland:

> And suddenly a festive blaze was flung
> Across five cedars, snowpatches showed,
> And a patrol car on our bumpy road
> Came to a crunching stop . . .

That festive blaze—police lights—is a cool transformation, but no amount of poetic dancing can keep that patrol car from its appointed round: It's come to tell the poet and his wife that their daughter has taken her own life. The pain at the heart of *Pale Fire*—the loss of the will to live, the loss of that which you love—never goes away. And the greatness of Nabokov's greatest pretending is to never pretend that it can.

This cryptic detail of messages and paperwork from a 1943 painting by Meredith Frampton was used to great effect on the cover of a recent Penguin edition of Nabokov's classic.

PIERRE BOULLE

PLANET OF THE APES (1963)

At once a biting satire and unsettling critique of modern civilization and arrogance, the story of a planet ruled by primates has become one of the most well-known tales of the twentieth century.

First published by René Julliard in 1963 in French, the first English edition was translated by Xan Fielding in 1963 in the U.S. by Vanguard Press. In the UK, the book was published as *Monkey Planet* but returned to the original title to tie in with the film franchise.

Boulle is also known for his novel, *The Bridge over the River Kwai* (1952), which was adapted into an award-winning film, garnering seven Oscars.

Opposite: Charlton Heston in the legendary film adaptation from 1968, directed by Franklin J. Schaffner and produced by Arthur P. Jacobs.

Ulysse Mérou, the central character in Pierre Boulle's 1963 satirical novel, *La Planète des Singes*, is a journalist who shares his name with the hero of Homer's *Odyssey* (c.725–675 BCE, page 18) Like his Greek namesake, he is a traveler—in his case journeying through deep space in the year 2500 to a planet orbiting the star Betelgeuse—and, like him, he is unexpectedly taken prisoner by strange creatures. He shows a similar degree of cunning in first winning the trust of his captors and then contriving his escape. But there the similarity with the *Odyssey* ends. While Homer concentrates on the journey that finally takes his hero home, Boulle's focus is on the world in which Ulysse and his companions find themselves.

Although Boulle puts the distance they travel at three hundred light years—less than half the actual distance to Betelgeuse—the fact that their spaceship almost reaches the speed of light means that, because of the effects of relativity, the journey takes them only two years. They land on a planet that is markedly like the one they left behind, and are so struck by the immediate similarities that they call it Soror, the Latin word for sister. However, they discover that humans in this new world have degenerated into the condition of wild animals, and apes have taken their place as the dominant species.

Even before they land, the explorers' instruments tell them that the atmosphere, like that of Earth, contains oxygen and nitrogen; although Boulle's Betelgeuse is three or four hundred times as big as the sun, the distance of the planet's orbit means that levels of radiation are also comparable. The countryside spread out below as their spaceship approaches confirms these early impressions. First, they see continents surrounded by a blue ocean. As they get nearer, there are towns with houses and tree-lined streets with cars, and a thick russet-colored forest reminiscent of Earth's equatorial jungles:

There was no doubt that we were on a twin-planet of our Earth. Life existed. The vegetable realm was in fact particularly vigorous. Some of these trees must have been over a hundred and fifty feet tall. The animal kingdom was not slow to manifest itself to us in the form of some big black birds, hovering

in the sky like vultures, and other smaller ones, rather like parakeets, that chased one another chirping shrilly.

However, it gradually becomes clear that the men and women who emerge, naked, from the jungle and finally take them prisoner have neither speech nor civilization. When Ulysse and his companions, along with their captors, are chased through the jungle in a terrifying hunt in which many of the humans are killed, he realizes to his horror that humans and apes have changed places.

Even in the towns to which he is eventually taken by his ape captors—initially led on a chain like a pet—occasional differences from life on Earth (such as the aerial crossing places in the streets where pedestrians simply swing above the traffic) serve only to highlight the overall similarity between Soror and his home.

The gorillas, orangutans, and chimpanzees who hold Ulysse captive believe that man has never evolved beyond his savage condition, because of the physical disadvantage of having only two hands, rather than the four an ape possesses. It is only later that highly controversial research comes to light, revealing that the apes actually achieved dominance by copying the achievements of a scientifically advanced but idle and feckless race of men.

There are no wars, no armies, and no nations on Soror, which is ruled by a council of ministers under the leadership of a triumvirate consisting of one gorilla, one orangutan, and one chimpanzee. There is also a tri-cameral parliament representing the three different species.

Long ago, the gorillas used to reign by sheer physical force, but now, at least in theory, all the different species have equal rights. In practice, despite the general ignorance of the gorillas, they remain the most powerful class, because of the cunning ways in which they manipulate the others. They also work as guards or law-enforcement, and in other roles that require physical strength, and retain a passion for hunts like the one in which Ulysse is captured and scores of other humans are killed, including one of his companions.

The orangutans—less numerous than either gorillas or chimpanzees—form a class of scientists and scholars, although Ulysse dismisses them as "official science," unoriginal, opposed to any innovation, and content to use their highly retentive memories to learn vast amounts of information from books.

The true intellectuals are the chimpanzees, who are imbued with a powerful spirit of research, and who have been responsible for most of Soror's great discoveries. The apes have electricity, industries, motorcars, and airplanes, but Ulysse notes that, technologically, they still lag behind the civilization he left behind.

However, they have classical, impressionist, and abstract artists, sports such as soccer and boxing, and zoos filled with various species of animals, including men, in cages. Apart from hunting, killing, and imprisoning men, the apes use them for gruesome medical experiments and generally treat them with cruelty and contempt. Explaining his origins to a scientific congress on Soror, Ulysse declares:

> I come from a distant planet, from Earth, that Earth on which, by a whim of nature that has still to be explained, it is men who are the repositories of wisdom and reason. . . . It is man who settled my planet and changed its face, man in fact who established a civilization so refined that in many respects, O Monkeys, it resembles your own.

By this time, the novel has demonstrated that words such as "wisdom," "reason," and "refined" are deeply ironic. The apparent similarity of the environment is a constant implied reproach as Boulle highlights the barbarity with which animals are treated both on Soror and on Earth.

When Boulle wrote *La Planète des Singes* in 1963, he had already achieved worldwide success with his other best-seller, *The Bridge over the River Kwai* (1952). Both books became successful films. *The Bridge over the River Kwai* drew directly on his time in a Japanese prisoner-of-war camp, and critics also see echoes of these experiences in the cruel domination of humans by the ruling apes on Soror.

The original 1968 film of *The Planet of the Apes*, loosely based on the novel, was directed by Franklin J. Schaffner, and has been followed by several sequels, a television series, comic books, and various profitable merchandising deals. A remake in 2001 was also successful, and since then there have been *Rise of the Planet of the Apes* (2011) and *Dawn of the Planet of the Apes* (2014). *War of the Planet of the Apes* is due for release in 2017.

Boulle, who died in 1994, criticized the original film. It lacked the subtlety and ironic bite of the novel, which ends with a surprise twist making clear that the similarities between Earth and Soror might prove to be even closer than the story has suggested. Where Franklin J. Schaffner was directing an action movie, Boulle had written a finely judged satire that deserves to be judged in the tradition of Voltaire.

GABRIEL GARCÍA MÁRQUEZ

ONE HUNDRED YEARS OF SOLITUDE (1967)

Seven generations of the Buendía family are traced in the magical and surreal location of Macondo known as "the city of mirrors," in the South American countryside.

First published by Editorial Sudamericana in 1967.

"Gabriel García Márquez" appears as a minor character in the novel. Unlike the author, this Márquez emigrates to Paris, where he makes a living "selling old newspapers and empty bottles."

Márquez was awarded the Nobel Prize for Literature in 1982.

Gabriel García Márquez (1927–2014) grew up in rural Colombia and, whenever critics suggested he had imagined the fantastical and implausible elements in his writing, he always insisted "there's not a single line in all my work that does not have a basis in reality." He began work as a journalist, moving onto writing novels when the newspaper he worked on was shut down by the Colombian authorities, but it was *One Hundred Years of Solitude* that established him as one of the most important writers in the world.

In one sense Márquez's immensely subtle and complex novel is quite straightforward: the "patriarch" José Arcadio Buendía, leaves Riohacha, Colombia, with his wife in search of a better life. One night, camping beside a river, he has a prophetic dream about a city made of mirrors. He decides to found this city and to call it Macondo. The novel then tells the stories of Buendía's many descendants.

There is little, however, by way of conventional narrative, beyond a list of the strange things that happen in the town, and the rise and fall of the doomed Buendía clan. Seven generations, each of which contains many individuals, makes for a crowded *dramatis personae*, but although it is possible to trace the family tree underpinning the story's many episodes, this may not be the best way of reading the text. Márquez's achievement lies in the atmosphere he creates, and the many evocative, even poetic moments of narrative intensity. Part of that atmosphere has to do with a certain intricacy, of busyness, of texture, which in turn speaks to a vision of life as rich, and complex, and involved, and endlessly surprising.

An example is the character of Colonel Aureliano Buendía, the founder's second son. The novel's famous opening sentence introduces him: "Many years later, as he faced the firing squad, Colonel Aureliano Buendía was to remember that distant afternoon when his father took him to discover ice." In addition to being a soldier, Aureliano is a poet, and the maker of beautifully crafted golden fish. He has fathered seventeen illegitimate sons, all named Aureliano, by seventeen different women. All seventeen come to his house on the same day. Four of them decide to settle in the town, but all of them,

"Houses in Aracataca (Macondo), Colombia," c.1950. Photograph by Leo Matiz. The town in the novel, Macondo, is closely based on Márquez's childhood hometown of Aracataca, which is located near the northern Caribbean coast of Colombia. In June 2006, the town proposed a referendum to change its name to Macondo.

whether they stay or go, are murdered by mysterious assassins before they reach the age of thirty-five.

Such things are unlikely, but possible. Other aspects of the novel partake of a dream logic. Remedios the Beauty is a girl so beautiful that men break down and die at the sight of her. Apparently mentally vacant, she eventually floats off into the sky. A character called Melquíades travels to Singapore and dies, although he later returns to Macondo, declaring that he "could not endure the solitude of death." He then dies a second time, and is buried. All these things are treated by Márquez as if they were perfectly normal.

This last point is important, because the experience of reading the novel is not in the least whimsical, random, or bizarre. On the contrary, the world Márquez creates feels exceptionally grounded and real. The textures of every-day life are precisely evoked: the weather and the landscape, infestations of red ants in the houses, the physical intensity of sexual desire. The surreal elements of the story do not contradict the realist elements; the two complement one another, just as the town contains both a character who is an aviator, and who plans to establish an airmail service, and a functioning alchemical labor-atory in the main Buendía house.

In the end, a hurricane destroys Macondo, a fitting end for this place of South American heat and intensity, prone to floods and tempests. Márquez re-imagines his homeland as a place worked into strange shapes by the forces of individual desire and despair, by love and lust, by pride and willpower and family ties. Because those forces are so central to human life, we instinctively understand the magical logic of his City of Mirrors. *One Hundred Years of Solitude* is a foundational novel in the literary tradition known as "magical realism" and remains to this day one of the most influen-tial examples of this mode.

URSULA K. LE GUIN

A WIZARD OF EARTHSEA (1968)

This classic heroic journey features a young man who has to confront a frightening shadow he has released into the world in order to accept that this darkness is a part of him and to grow into his power.

A Wizard of Earthsea is the first novel in a six-part epic fantasy series.

Le Guin based this novel, first published by Parnassus Press in 1968, on two short stories she had written earlier: "The Rule of Names" (1964) and "The Word of Unbinding" (1964).

A Wizard of Earthsea introduces the idea of a school for wizards, inspiring writers like Diana Wynne Jones and J. K. Rowling.

A Wizard of Earthsea has all the vital aspects of a heroic journey, and the world in which it is set has magic as a part of daily life—it is "a land where sorcerers come thick." Magic is respected, its users trained to be a vital part of society, be it as healers of the sick or engineers of safe boats and ships. Earthsea has its own creation myth; it has a political system; there is an economy; a social hierarchy even where the "wizard born" consider themselves superior; there is disease, piracy, and war-mongering that endangers lives; a shipping trade; smiths who work in bronze and iron; livestock and farming. There are also dragons to fear, huge ancient magical beasts that sound like an avalanche when they speak and "have their own wisdom [and] they are an older race than man." Earthsea is a classic example of Le Guin's (b.1929) strong world building, which is rock-solid yet never heavy-handed.

The journey of central character Ged begins in a way that is now standard for a hero's epic fantasy journey. He is a lonely young goatherd who doesn't have much, lives in a poor village, is motherless but has magical abilities greater than he can perceive. He is partly trained by his aunt who is a witch, but her skills are far less than his, and she has only a superficial understanding of the craft. Ged eventually reaches a school for wizards, where he finds himself among other young men with similar abilities. In attempting to impress them with his power, he sets free an evil that nearly kills him, one that he then has to struggle to find and face among the islands of Earthsea.

Earthsea is a large archipelago; three of the islands are named for Le Guin's children's pets, the others named in ways that sounded "right" to her. Earthsea's civilization is pre-industrial but literate, with an inbuilt, accepted system of magic as part of its history and culture. The magic system is such that knowing the true name of something or someone in "Old Speech" gives you power over it or them. It is not possible to lie in true speech, so to speak a truth is to make it happen, though of course only those with powerful abilities can force such transformations, and each have repercussions. Earthsea's magic isn't without its checks and balances.

A map of Earthsea drawn by and used with permission of author Ursula K. Le Guin.

Language is important in Earthsea, and the idea of words as power and that of true names can be traced back to many real-world tribal societies and to Le Guin's interest in anthropology. The people of Earthsea are genuinely multiracial and multicultural, without any implication that the few who are of lighter skin are superior in any way. Le Guin has openly criticized the common assumption that sets much Western fantasy in a Eurocentric version of the Middle Ages. Earthsea is, in a way, the anti-Middle-earth. It's an archipelago, it is home to many people of color, and, in it, Le Guin is more focused on the personal development of its individual residents than large-scale wars. Ged isn't in a constant battle with a large army—his battle is with his shadow self and, along the way, he must complete tasks that fade in comparison to his ultimate quest.

Magic may be a part of Earthsea's culture, but so is spirituality. Le Guin has based the spiritual systems of her world more on psychology and anthropology than on a monotheistic religious model. Through in the entire series, there is a very strong element of Taoism, especially in regard to the magical balances required. In *Wizard of Earthsea*, Ged's battle with his shadow self is clearly Jungian, though he, too, believes in the Taoist idea of Dynamic Balance. As he is taught, to light a candle is to throw a shadow.

PHILIP K. DICK

DO ANDROIDS DREAM
OF ELECTRIC SHEEP? (1968)

*On a post-apocalyptic Earth, a bounty hunter questions his own
humanity as he attempts to "retire" a group of renegade androids
masquerading as human.*

First published by
Doubleday and Company,
Inc., in 1968.

According to Dick, his
androids were inspired by
the journals of Gestapo
officers he researched for his
novel *The Man in the High
Castle* (1960).

In an earlier, then
unpublished novel, *We
Can Build You* (1972), Dick
wrote about the invention of
androids by the Rosens, who
created the first humanoid
robots as replicas of
important historical figures.

Dick's book was the basis for
Ridley Scott's film *Blade
Runner* (1982). However,
many elements of the book
were left out of the film.

A destroyed earth, ruined by a war for which no one can remember the reason; a planet irradiated and only just habitable; a population that has mostly migrated to off-world colonies in order to protect the genetic integrity of humanity, incentivized by the offer of an android servant, leaving a small remaining population of people on Earth to survive in the radioactive dust, living with corrupted genes and decreased intelligence; a broken, sad city filled with vacant apartment blocks—this is the anxious, depleted world of *Do Androids Dream of Electric Sheep?*

Richard Deckard is a bounty hunter who must track down and "retire" six Nexus-6 androids, a model that has come close to passing as entirely human. These particular androids violently escaped from Mars and are attempting to hide out on Earth, settling in amid the remaining human population, who are doomed to eke out a life in clustered settlements in what were previously bustling cities. Deckard must ensure the humanoid body he kills is an android before he retires it. The only way to differentiate androids from humans is by the "Voight-Kampff" test, which gauges the instinctual, empathic response to questions asked primarily about animals. The test isn't entirely accurate—schizophrenic humans may well fail it, too. But in a world where the care for now-endangered creatures is sacrosanct, a lack of empathy toward animals is enough to separate humans from other biological organisms created by them, no matter how lifelike they may be, or the range of emotions they display.

Do Androids Dream of Electric Sheep? is about what it means to be human, which is even more important in a post-apocalyptic world with a bleak future. The androids Deckard hunts want more than they have been allowed, and have chosen some form of independence on a ravaged planet over subservience to humans elsewhere. The humans left on Earth, on the other hand, are losing sense of their emotions, often depending on artificial mood enhancers to guide their daily behavior. Dick's love for absurdity has to be appreciated, even in the broad, effective strokes with which he creates the world of this book—he's never without humor, even when he's writing about the steady disintegration of society and individuality.

Harrison Ford plays Richard Deckard in a scene from the Warner Bros. movie *Blade Runner* (1982), directed by Ridley Scott.

The world of *Do Androids Dream of Electric Sheep?* is a believable, not too far away future, albeit one with hovercrafts and the colonization of other planets. But this vision doesn't feel dated. Dick's future of vidphones and mood controllers is, in many ways, very much our present too. His San Francisco is a strange but believable construct—a city shrouded in dust that is slowly killing its inhabitants, residents who will do anything to own and care for live animals, almost all of which are endangered after the plagues following World War Terminus. The city is half-empty and full of vacant apartments where sinister junk known as "kipple" collects and seems to breed overnight.

And yet the show goes on—Deckard finds one of the androids performing as an opera singer in *The Magic Flute* and museums still exist. So Dick's world-building often feels a little incongruous, but it always works, not just because his characters carry the narrative, but because this is what humanity is: inconsistent, resilient, and always creating something more.

In his 1978 essay *How to Build a Universe That Doesn't Fall Apart Two Days Later*, Dick wrote of how he enjoyed creating universes that fell apart, become unhinged, unglued and how he had a secret love of chaos. "Do not assume that order and stability are always good, in a society or in a universe," he wrote, insisting "objects, customs, habits, and ways of life must perish so that the authentic human being can live."

During his search, Deckard finds himself face to face with Munch's *The Scream*, and Dick's description of the painting is one that perfectly describes not just the world as his reader may know it, but the taut, grim one he has created too: "The painting showed a hairless, oppressed creature with a head like an inverted pear, its hands clapped in horror to its ears, its mouth open in a vast, soundness scream. Twisted ripples of the creature's torment, echoes of its cry, flooded out into the air surrounding it; the man or woman, whichever it was, had become contained by its own howl. It had covered its ears against its own sound. . . . The creature was in isolation. Cut off by—or despite—its outcry."

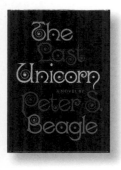

PETER S. BEAGLE

THE LAST UNICORN (1968)

Voted one of the "All-Time Best Fantasy Novels," Beagle's novel describes a series of fairy tales through which the last unicorn must pass in search of others of her kind.

First published by The Viking Press (U.S.) and The Bodley Head (UK) in 1968, Beagle's novel has sold more than six million copies, and has been translated into more than twenty-five languages.

The Last Unicorn became an animated movie in 1982, featuring the voices of Mia Farrow, Christopher Lee, Angela Lansbury, Jeff Bridges, and Alan Arkin, and an original score by American singer-songwriter Jimmy Webb.

Beagle wrote a sequel to *The Last Unicorn* entitled "Two Hearts," which was published in *Fantasy and Science Fiction* magazine in 2005. It won both the Hugo and the Nebula award.

Peter S. Beagle's (b.1939) *The Last Unicorn* follows the titular character as she embarks on a series of episodic adventures. The unicorn's wanderings take her through a deliberately generic, if forlorn, fairyland, with indications and slight hints that it is—or is steadily becoming—the "real" world. Although her encounters have a distinctly medieval flavor, fragments of other times and places bleed through: a glimpse of the Midgard Serpent, a passing reference to "Anglo-Saxon folklore," and a chattering butterfly that references song lyrics and the "A Train."

The unicorn begins her journey in a "lilac wood," a beautiful and secluded forest that flourishes in part due to her magical presence. Yet, remote as it is, a pair of hunters visits the wood one day. Over the course of their conversation, they reveal their belief that there's—at most—a single unicorn left in the world. In one of the book's recurring themes, they compare previous generations to their own, describing the gradual loss of magic. The unicorn overhears them and decides to leave her home in search of her kin.

The unicorn discovers a world where the existence of magic, including unicorns, is no longer taken for granted. Her wandering—along a long road that "hurried to nowhere and no end"—takes her over vast distances, through lands that are either unknowable or unrecognizable in the unicorn's eyes. The feeling is mutual: As the unicorn passes through towns and villages, the residents merely see her as a white mare, if at all.

Her journey is interrupted when she is captured by Mommy Fortuna's Midnight Carnival, a bedraggled traveling show that promises "Creatures of night, brought to light." The show is largely illusion, with two notable exceptions: the unicorn and a harpy. The world's tentative relationship with the supernatural is on full display with the carnival. The thrill-seeking attendees simultaneously wish to glimpse "magic," but are also reassured by the knowledge that the show is a fake. In parallel, Mommy Fortuna wrestles daily with the repercussions of having captured the uncapturable—she knows the harpy is bound to escape and that, with its departure, she will be destroyed.

You're in the story with the rest of us now, and you must go with it, whether you will or no. If you want to find your people, if you want to become a unicorn again, then you must follow the fairy tale to King Haggard's castle, and wherever else it chooses to take you.

The carnival is the first in a series of archetypal folkloric settings visited by the unicorn. In an outlaw-infested forest, she encounters a band of "Merry Men" so desperate for notoriety that they've begun composing their own ballads. In a cursed village, she finds a group of wealthy burghers who—like the inhabitants of Hamelin—have traded their children for a life of comfort. In all scenarios, the unicorn finds people trying to manipulate the world by interfering with the power of stories. Mommy Fortuna imprisons "legends" in her search for power. Captain Cully, leader of the outlaws, seeks immortality by creating his own myths. The burghers strive to prevent the resolution of a curse, knowing that having it lifted will impoverish them.

It is at the crumbling castle of King Haggard, however, that the unicorn finds the truest intersection of the land's geography and her own story. Haggard and his Red Bull are behind the disappearance of the unicorns, and the unicorn's journey to find them takes her to the very heart of his dismal kingdom. Haggard's castle is a bleak location, teetering on the edge of the sea, abandoned by servants and courtiers alike.

At this point, the unicorn is transformed into a human girl. Yet, even in mortal form, she still inspires change in her surroundings. The grim atmosphere of the castle is not enough to stifle the love of the King's son for the mysterious newcomer and, despite their ominous surroundings, the remaining guardsmen and the unicorn's friends make the castle into a cozy home. Everywhere she goes, the unicorn acts as an agent of change and, despite King Haggard's best efforts, his keep is no exception.

The Last Unicorn by Rebekah Naomi Cox, 2005. Beagle has commented of Cox's work: "... unicorns look nothing at all like horned horses, and, while magically beautiful, they are also, from certain angles and under certain circumstances, just a little funny-looking. Rebekah is the only artist who has ever captured this."

KURT VONNEGUT

SLAUGHTERHOUSE-FIVE (1969)

Considered Vonnegut's most popular work, and inspired by his own experience of the Dresden firebombings, the story follows the time-traveling adventures of Billy Pilgrim, a soldier who becomes "unstuck in time."

First published by Delacorte in 1969.

The book has often come under censorship in the U.S. because of its perceived vulgarity and obscene content. A film adaptation was released in 1972.

Vonnegut's other notable works include *Cat's Cradle* (1963) and *Breakfast of Champions* (1973).

On the night of February 13, 1945, three months before the end of World War II, Kurt Vonnegut (1922–2007) was a prisoner of war, sheltering in an underground abattoir during the devastating firebombing of Dresden. "Slaughterhouse-Five" (*Schlachthof-fünf*) was, ironically, shelter from the slaughter. The next morning, Vonnegut and his fellow prisoners of war were set to work excavating blackened bodies for cremation on open piles.

In the novel, Billy Pilgrim, the unheroic hero, is a POW in the same shelter as Vonnegut during the devastating firebombing. He, too, survives, but he goes crazy: he cannot make sense of the event.

Fiction, like history, has been generally silent about Dresden. As Hitler said, "The victor will never be asked if he told the truth." Vonnegut himself had almost insuperable difficulty writing his "Dresden novel." He had to forge an entirely new "schizophrenic" technique, weaving realism, sci-fi schlock (little one-eyed green men from Tralfamadore, resembling toilet plungers), and slapstick social comedy into a startlingly innovative pattern.

The novel's composition accompanied a catastrophic crisis in the author's family life. His marriage broke up, his son developed schizophrenia, and Vonnegut himself was afflicted with depression. *Slaughterhouse-Five* was finally published, out of this crisis, to huge acclaim in 1969. It shot to the top of the *New York Times* best-seller list, and has since been awarded a place in the canon of American classic fiction.

The thesis of *Slaughterhouse-Five* is essentially that humankind cannot bear too much reality. Life is so horrible that only fiction can deal with it, and, crucially, the more horrible the life experience, the more fantastic the fiction. After Auschwitz, Theodore Adorno famously declared, poetry was impossible. One of the underlying contentions of *Slaughterhouse-Five* is that after Dresden, fiction, or at least realist fiction, is impossible.

A way out of this impasse was science fiction. Billy Pilgrim, a time and intergalactic traveler (or, more likely, merely nuts) ends his post-Dresden pilgrimage incarcerated no longer by Nazi Germany, but by aliens from the planet Tralfamadore.

Billy's prison is a geodesic dome (a style favored by hippy communes in the 1960s); it is made tolerable by furniture from Sears, Roebuck (less favored by hippies), and the presence of starlet Montana Wildhack, who is similarly transported across space to be Billy's "mate." They will be earthling specimens in the Tralfamadorian national zoo.

The city of Dresden after the bombing. Churchill had decreed that Dresden was a strategic target. It wasn't, but was razed just the same.

The Tralfamadorians, like the RAF, are dangerous bombers. Billy asks his little green mentor whether earthlings will go on to destroy the universe, since they are so good at destroying their own planet? Their philosophy in the face of this inevitable doom? "We spend eternity looking at pleasant moments—like today at the zoo." Earthlings should learn to do the same. Forget Dresden. Enjoy Disneyland.

When Vonnegut was asked about his decision to process the horror of historical events through slapstick, black comedy, and science fiction, he noted these tropes were just like the clowns in a Shakespearean tragedy: "Trips to other planets, science fiction of an obviously kidding sort, is equivalent to bringing on the clowns every so often to lighten things up." Yet, the novel clearly has more serious intentions. Vonnegut, in writing *Slaughterhouse-Five*, was influenced, the author acknowledged, by Joseph Heller's *Catch-22* (1961). War in *Catch-22* is conceived as a madhouse. The hero, Yossarian, can only escape the madness by being diagnosed mad himself. But to report his madness to the medical services would be to prove himself sane. This double bind is the *Catch-22* by which the military machine works. It is absurdity institutionalized, and only comedy can effectively handle it.

The other likely, but unacknowledged influence on *Slaughterhouse-Five* was Stanley Kubrick's comedy film about nuclear annihilation, *Dr. Strangelove* (1963). It's so deadly serious, you have to laugh.

LARRY NIVEN

RINGWORLD (1970)

Members of three galactic species explore an ancient artificial "world,"
a vast flattened ring encircling its sun, to see if it is a threat or an
opportunity, or both.

Ringworld, first published
by Ballantine Books in 1970,
won the Nebula Award
that year, and, in 1971, both
the Hugo and Locus Award.

Four sequels and four
prequels extend the
Ringworld narrative, and
form part of Niven's wider
Known Space universe,
detailed across various
novels and short stories.

Niven's iconic world has
influenced authors
including Iain M. Banks,
and its engineering and
physical properties have
been the subject of heated
debate among expert fans.

Ringworld stands as the climax to the first volumes of Larry Niven's
"Tales of Known Space" sequence. The narrative unfolds on two inter-
acting levels. Before arriving at the Ringworld itself, readers are
given back-story from earlier tales to make the complicated relationships among its cast understandable. This cast comprises two humans,
the restless 200-year-old Louis Wu and the twenty-year-old Teela
Brown, who has been genetically engineered to impose her good luck
on events; a warrior Kzin who is deemed a coward by his civilization
for consorting with other races peaceably; and a Pearson's puppeteer,
a two-headed tripodal figure described as insanely brave because of his
ability to consort with dangerous alien species without fleeing from such
contact. If these characterizations seem mechanical, that is, in a sense,
Niven's intention. Through his long career, he has created many species
defined in terms of their high level of adaptability to niche habitats, which
renders them highly potent when they are in their comfort zones, but vul-
nerable when threatened with change. Humans—less martially formidable
than Kzins and stupider than puppeteers—are relatively free of niche constraints; indeed, Teela adapts both the voyage and the Ringworld itself
to her needs.

The Ringworld itself is explored through sequences heightened by, and
comprehended through, interactions among the three species, each event
moving the story forward while simultaneously broadening the reader's
vision of the great ring, 600 million miles around and one million miles
wide, with a habitable inner surface. The lifeless outer surface is a virtually
impermeable material, designed to hold the structure together, and to defend
against collisions with asteroids or even planetary bodies; from beyond the
ring, observers can detect in reverse the contours of the inner land: oceans
cause bulges, while mountains create vast dimples gazing into the void.
To contain atmosphere, the walls of the rim are one thousand miles high, and
contoured in the form of mountains and ridges. Great opaque rectangular
sheets between the Ringworld and its small sun slide longitudinally over the

surface, which they darken into night. The habitable surface of the Ringworld is the equivalent of three million Earths.

It would have been impossible for one novel to provide a close-up conspectus of a landscape too large to comprehend, and Niven does not risk attempting to do so. The puppeteer starship the crew has traveled in is soon, therefore, incapacitated and crashes to the surface, leaving the four to navigate in one-person, extra-vehicular scouts. All but Teela are immediately overwhelmed, and threatened, by the sheer scale of what they are, even disabled, capable of perceiving. There is no visible curvature, no horizon: all perspectives end, dizzyingly, in vanishing points. The arch of the ring is visible in the sky: if you had a million years you could walk there. Fauna is initially absent from view; nearby flora is subtly unlike Earth's, but similar enough to understand.

When the crew discover humanoid beings, they find them to have suffered a catastrophic loss of civilization, almost certainly due to a failure in the overall power system. (There are no natural resources except for rimrock; the inhabitants of the Ringworld face the same lack of resources that would make recovery so difficult were civilization to fall on Earth.) The novel ends in the discovery of an archaic tyranny or two. The original Ringworld engineers are nowhere to be seen, and their creation is seemingly on its last legs. The reasons for Ringworld's creation are supposititious. All we know is that a playground for trillions of people should last forever.

Engineers Chmeee and Louis investigate the enormous spacecraft parked at the spaceport on the ring walls. Illustration by Paul Marquis.

ITALO CALVINO

INVISIBLE CITIES (1972)

The merchant Marco Polo recounts impressions of fifty-five fabulous cities he has visited, or claimed to have visited, to the emperor of the Tartars, Kublai Khan.

First published by Einaudi in 1972.

The city of Leonia refashions itself every night so that its inhabitants wake to a reconfigured world. This would seem a clear inspiration for the science-fiction film *Dark City* (1998).

At one juncture, Kublai Khan himself imagines a "city of stairs," anticipating the titular city of the first volume of Robert Jackson Bennett's *The Divine Cities* series of urban fantasy novels (2014).

If the protagonist of *Le città invisibili* (published in 1972; translated into English in 1974 and entitled *Invisible Cities*) is Italo Calvino's (1923–85) post-modern version of the real historical traveler Marco Polo, it is, as the title suggests, the places the Venetian merchant visits that are key. Calvino, a veteran of the Italian Resistance in World War II, rejected his family's Catholicism, becoming a member of the Italian Communist Party, later withdrawing from active political engagement. By nature a city dweller, he lived in Turin, Florence, Milan, Paris, Rome, and once wrote, "I always felt a New Yorker. My city is New York."

Though the book has its roots in *The Travels of Marco Polo* (1300, the merchant's adventures as told to Rustichello da Pisa while both men were imprisoned in Genoa), Calvino's work is neither travelogue nor biography. Rather, it is a fabulous directory, preserving for posterity this fictional Marco Polo's highly unreliable accounts of distant cities as told to Kublai Khan during his sojourns in the imperial palace.

Marco's accounts are divided into nine chapters, while the metropolises themselves are, ambiguously or ironically, sorted by eleven criteria: Thin, Hidden, Continuous, and Trading Cities, and Cities devoted to the Sky, Memory, Eyes, Signs, Desire, and the Dead.

While the chapters themselves are presented as straightforward, beautifully written accounts, it soon becomes clear that, in our world at least, these places do not, often could not, exist. Either the world of the novel is not our world, but a world of fantasy, or Calvino's Polo is a vastly accomplished fabulist, conjuring illusions to beguile, entertain, amuse, or otherwise deceive the emperor for his own purposes. Indeed, the first words of the novel are:

> Kublai Khan does not necessarily believe everything Marco Polo says when he describes the cities visited on his expeditions . . .

An additional dimension of complexity is lent to the novel by the passages inserted between chapters, which recount the meetings between Polo and

Kublai Khan. These sections are composed in a different voice, which appears to belong to a later emperor, one who understands the "sense of emptiness which comes over us at evening," reflecting on Khan's realization of "the desperate moment when we discover that this empire, which had seemed to us the sum of all wonders, is an endless, formal ruin." Or the author could, perhaps, be Khan himself, observing in the third person, seeking detachment, recording his memories of the elusive, elliptical dispatches of Marco Polo with as much objectivity as he can muster.

On one level *Invisible Cities* can be taken as a sly critique of the inherent untrustworthiness of travel writing, and by extension, all texts; at the literal center point of the book Khan himself makes a rare visit, traveling to Kin-sai, a city of canals very much like Venice. Polo says, "I should never have imagined a city like this could exist." A little later, "Every time I describe a city I am saying something about Venice."

This is the heart of *Invisible Cities*, that imaginative visions can offer deeper truths than unvarnished facts. Calvino's cities are akin to Jorge Luis Borges's labyrinths and libraries. The thirteenth-century merchant reports of motorcycles, skyscrapers, and radar. Marco lands in the city of Trude by plane. The city covers the world. Only the name of the airport changes.

Invisible Cities is a book with a strong heteronormative, male perspective. Women appear almost entirely as beautiful, usually unobtainable, objects of desire. Glimpsed fleetingly, they haunt the traveler's imagination, inspire him, but ultimately evade or disappoint. The cities themselves are often graced with feminine names, being called variously Cecelia, Clarice, Esmeralda, or Phyllis, and seem to embody the impossibility of fully knowing and possessing. Polo is always in pursuit, arriving only to leave, to travel ever onward to the next invisible city.

Isaura, the city of the thousand wells, sits over a deep, subterranean lake. Illustration by Colleen Corradi Brannigan.

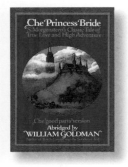

WILLIAM GOLDMAN

THE PRINCESS BRIDE (1973)

Goldman's metatextual comedy envisions a world within a world, filled with swordplay, Rodents of Unusual Size and, most of all, romance.

First published by Harcourt Brace Jovanovich in 1973.

Goldman returned to the S. Morgenstern pen name in 1983 with *The Silent Gondoliers*.

Goldman's family—his wife "Helen" and son "Jason"—although key figures in the introduction, are fictional. He also revisits them in the twenty-fifth anniversary edition.

The adventure of *The Princess Bride* is set primarily within the fictional European nations of Florin and Guilder, located between "where Sweden and Germany would eventually settle." In a tale later made popular by the classic film, the titular princess, Buttercup, is betrothed to the land's conniving prince, Humperdinck. Her childhood lover, Westley, aided by a band of talented rogues, returns from overseas in an attempt to save her from Humperdinck's clutches. Hijinks ensue.

The Princess Bride's events take place at time in history that not only doesn't exist, but is deliberately and provocatively impossible. "A time before Europe but after Paris" is only one of the many self-contradictory explanations provided by William Goldman (b.1931). The book freely references locations such as Spain, Turkey, and Scotland, but invariably and meticulously mentions that these places, and the activities therein, may or may not have existed, thus creating a sense of historicity that is, at best, utterly chaotic.

The world within the book is deliberately maddening, rife with anachronism and self-contradiction. In one breath, Goldman will note that everything in it is historically accurate, and challenge the reader to check the source against any Florinese history. Yet, at the same time, *The Princess Bride* gleefully references fire swamps, miracle men, King Bats, Blood Eagles, Sucking Squid, and the immortal Rodents of Unusual Size. Florin, with its castles, forests, fleets, and European neighbors is a prototypically generic Western fantasyland, littered with impossibilities.

Adding to the chaos of *The Princess Bride*, the book itself is a fictional construction. The central text comes complete with a lengthy introduction—and many interruptions—by Goldman, who sets up his version of *The Princess Bride* as an abridgment of the original by "S. Morgenstern." This metatextual wrapping comes complete with a fictionalized version of Goldman's own family and re-imagination of his childhood. This allows Goldman to comment on the book's themes even as he presents them, including frequent and pithy interjections from his youthful and adult selves.

Goldman states in one open aside that "life isn't fair," and this theme is reflected through the people and the locations described in the book. Buttercup is *objectively* the most beautiful; the mighty Fezzik the strongest. Terrible things happen to deserving people, most prominently in the case of Westley's mid-book demise. Westley is faced with one unequal challenge after another: he is forced to out-brawl a giant, out-fight a "Wizard" swordsman, out-think a genius, hide from a master huntsman, and keep secrets from an uncanny interrogator. Even the geography of Florin and Guilder conspires against our heroes, ordeals range from trudging through fire swamps to falling down snow sand, to climbing the Cliffs of Insanity.

When the heroes aren't menaced by some sort of external force (from King Bats to Humperdinck), they go out of their way to create their own problems. The evening that Buttercup and Westley declare their love for one another is immediately followed by Westley's decision to depart and seek his fortune: A choice they both agree is unquestionably right. This moment is bookended by the story's conclusion, when the traditional statement of "and they lived happily after ever" is immediately decried by Goldman's childhood self as inherently dissatisfying.

While the land in *The Princess Bride* isn't real, Goldman's conceit is that it *should* be. This is why he created a fictional and very dull history: so he could abridge it into an inspiring adventure. Similarly, the land of *The Princess Bride* is intentionally unfair—it is the triumph over the impossible that creates the romance and adventure that we require. The setting is an elaborate, improbable mechanism that exists to produce thrilling stories.

Wallace Shawn and Robin Wright Penn are forever remembered as Vizzini and Princess Buttercup in the film adaptation of *The Princess Bride* (1987).

SAMUEL R. DELANY

DHALGREN (1975)

A surprise best seller, Dhalgren *presents an apocalyptic city outside of time,*
Bellona. What is Bellona? Each reader must decide.

First published by Bantam
Books in 1975.

In its first year of publication,
Dhalgren went through
seven printings and sold
in the vicinity of half a
million copies.

When editor Frederik Pohl
was asked why he published
Dhalgren, he would say,
"Because it's the first book
that told me anything I
didn't know about sex since
Story of O."

Bellona was the name of a
Roman goddess of war,
sometimes described as the
sister or wife of Mars.

Samuel R. Delany's (b.1942) *Dhalgren* begins with the end of a sentence:
"to wound the autumnal city." The phrase repeats throughout as a line in
a mysterious notebook, puzzled over and relished. The beginning of the
sentence is the final sentence of the book: "Waiting here, away from the terrifying weaponry, out of the halls of vapor and light, beyond holland and into
the hills, I have come to." We encounter a variation on the complete sentence
earlier in the book's long last section: "I have come to wound the autumnal
city: the other side of the question is a mixed metaphor if I ever heard one."
The repeated, stuttered *to* is a latch or a skip or a jump. Is the *to* of "to wound
the autumnal city" the same as the one in "I have come to"? Should we link
them, should we not? Choose your own adventure.

Delany wrote *Dhalgren* from January 1969 to September 1973 between
various cities. He was already an award-winning science-fiction writer by this
time, having published his first work of fiction aged just twenty, and titles
such as *Babel-17*, *The Einstein Intersection*, and *Nova* would be among the
most celebrated works of science fiction of the 1960s. After *Nova* was published to much acclaim in 1968, the world waited with great anticipation
for Delany's next novel, which would not be published until almost seven
years later, and would be unlike anything anyone expected. *Dhalgren* was
huge, strange, and sexually explicit. On its publication in 1975, the *Los Angeles
Times* critic Harlan Ellison denounced it as "sorry compendium of pointless ramblings," while in *Galaxy* magazine, Theodore Sturgeon declared
it "the very best to come out of the science-fiction field" and compared
Delany to Homer, Shakespeare, and Nabokov. It became Delany's best-
selling work, embraced by adventurous readers who were entranced by the
city of Bellona.

Bellona is a city created by words, but not necessarily words with refer-
ents. Bellona is an idea as much as a place. When asked his purpose, the Kid,
our protagonist (whose name is also not the Kid), replies, "I want to get to
Bellona and—" His sentence doesn't finish; like so much in the book, like so
much in Bellona, it is a fragment. He then restarts explaining his purpose:

"Mine's the same as everybody else's; in real life, anyway: to get through the next second, consciousness intact."

Can anyone get through Bellona with consciousness intact? There's little evidence for it. Bellona is a place of shattered pavement, ruined buildings, ash. Its people are as wounded and mercurial as the city itself. It is a place with no time in any historical sense, a place that does not make the news: "Very few suspect the existence of this city. It is as if not only the media but the laws of perspective themselves have redesigned knowledge and perception to pass it by." Throughout are references to prisms, mirrors, and lenses. Bellona is all of these at one point or another.

The ashes in Bellona are not only those of buildings, but of texts. *Dhalgren* is a novel endlessly interested in writing and what has been written, in the trace that fiery writing leaves behind. Its words are other words. Fragments of countless stories, poems, and books make their way through its pages, some as transients or tourists, some as lifelong citizens.

Many things happen in the novel, but there is no plot in the traditional sense, no rising and falling action, no denouement. It often seems that life in Bellona is just one thing after another, with people wandering around, having conversations, having parties, having sex, having fights. (Maybe having hallucinations, dreams, nightmares—but when reality isn't tightly fixed, how do you know you're out of your mind?) The prose and the people meander.

Why is Bellona the way it is? If this were a traditional novel we would know: there would be a neutron bomb or an invasion from space. But this is not a traditional novel. Bellona is a science-fictional effect without a science-fictional cause. If there is a cause of Bellona, or at least of Bellona's apocalypse (its time out of joint, its existence apparent only to its residents, its landscape of fires and ash), the cause is that it is a city in a novel marketed as science fiction. Bellona is an experience more than it is a place: an experience of the characters and an experience of the readers. What Bellona gives us depends on what we bring to it.

Bellona is, more than anything, a city in a novel, which is to say it is a city in the mind of whoever finds its words.

A letter from Delany to Kirkpatrick Sale, thanking him and Thomas Pynchon for their "enthusiasm." He then asks Sale to "take a look at the novel I am working on," and his brief description must allude to *Dhalgren*: "In a burning city, all but evacuated, a young man is introduced to a variety of sexual / mythical / mystical experiences."

GEORGES PEREC

W OR THE MEMORY OF CHILDHOOD (1975)

Perec's semi-autobiographical novel intertwines uncertain personal memories with the story of W, a fantastic, seemingly utopian island state governed through sporting competition.

First published by Editions Denoël in 1975.

Perec was a member of OuLiPo, a group that sought to impose constraints on their work to generate inspiration. Other notable members included Raymond Queneau, Harry Matthews, and Italo Calvino.

Perec once wrote an entire book, *La Disparation* (1969), without using the letter "e." It was, remarkably, translated into English by Gilbert Adair as *A Void*.

Perec loved puzzles of every kind, and devised many crosswords. His most well-known book, *Life: A Users Manual* (1978) features a vindictive jigsaw maker, and is full of hidden games for the reader.

Georges Perec (1936–82) is celebrated as one of the finest authors of his generation, and was one of the most innovative writers of the twentieth century. In Perec's work the form of the story closely reflects its themes. In *W* he intertwined autobiographical chapters about his childhood with chapters about "W," an imaginary fascist society devoted to sports, and slowly draws the two stories together.

The autobiographical strand focuses on the author's childhood in France during World War II. Both Perec's parents died during the war; his mother was sent to Auschwitz. However, it is only in the parallel strand about the imaginary land of W that Perec is able to approach these subjects, and even here he keeps his distance from it by having this part of the book told by Gaspard Winckler. Winckler, like Perec, is an orphan, and this is one of many correspondences between the two narratives, which frequently share words, names, and phrases. For Perec, it is this very overlapping that matters most, a point made by the novel's title, which in French is "double-vé," describing the overlapping Vs that create a W. By overlapping fiction and truth, Perec intentionally generates an uncertainty about both narratives, one that paradoxically made it easier for him to face his experiences of the Holocaust.

W is located near Tierra del Fuego at the southernmost tip of South America, on a tiny island shaped "like a sheep's head with its lower jaw distinctly out of joint." The society of W is organized around a series of regular sporting events modeled on the Olympics. The male athletes live in villages that compete with each other, while those associated with the contests live either in giant stadiums or in the "Fortress," which is also the seat of W's government.

In W there is no division between sports and life—its whole society claims to celebrate "the greater glory of the Body." But it soon becomes clear to the reader that these lofty ideals are a thin justification for a system of institutionalized cruelty. All W's athletes are permanently malnourished—only the victors are fed properly. Losers are stripped naked and attacked with sticks and riding crops, and can be condemned to death by the downturned

> I have no childhood memories. . . .
> A different history, History with a capital H, had answered the questions in my stead: the war, the camps.

Werner Bischof, *Children's drawing representing Adolf Hitler and a swastika, Rhone-Alpes region, Vercors, 1945.* The area was well known for its Resistance to the Nazis. This image was used to illustrate the cover of a 2013 Swedish translation, *W eller minnet av barndomen*, published by Modernista.

thumb of a single spectator. There are even sporting contests whose only purpose is to mock the injured or handicapped. Though there are women on W, their numbers are strictly limited—eighty percent are killed at birth. The rest are locked up, except when they are deemed to be fertile, and then the best athletes violently compete for the chance to rape them.

In addition to the structured humiliation and cruelty, the land of W also contains many specific parallels with the Nazi concentration camps. In W, athletes are selected for contests, just as prisoners were selected for work or extermination; novices in W have to wear a triangle on their jackets, just as Jews were forced to wear a yellow star. At the end of the book, the Fortress is revealed to contain "piles of gold teeth, rings, and spectacles" and "stocks of poor quality soap."

Yet for all the nightmarish excesses of Perec's imaginary land, the novel's most powerful act of imagination takes place within the autobiographical narrative. While W is clearly an imaginary land, so in many ways is Perec's memory of his childhood. He is candid about his inability to remember many aspects of it accurately, and freely admits that many of the memories he offers are implausible and distorted. These admissions and omissions, along with many intentional factual errors, obliquely highlight the novel's theme of saying something by not saying it directly—such as when Perec gives May 1945 as the date of the Japanese surrender, when it was the date of the fall of Berlin.

In *W*, Perec's greatest fantasy is not the imaginary island, but something far more ordinary. He wanted to be able to clear the dinner from the table with his mother, then to fetch his satchel and do his homework. He wanted this to be a memory.

GERD MJØEN BRANTENBERG

EGALIA'S DAUGHTERS: A SATIRE OF THE SEXES (1977)

A classic text of modern feminist satire depicting a fantasy matriachry in which wim hold the power, and the menwim are the oppressed.

Egalia's Daughters was first published by Norwegian publishers Pax in 1977.

Director of the Norwegian Author's Union from 1981 to 1983, Brantenberg was also co-organizer of four International Feminist Book Fairs between 1984 and 1992.

Brantenberg is active in the gay rights movement and was a board member of Norway's National Association for Lesbian, Gay, Bisexual, and Transgender People in its early form, as the Forbundet av 1948.

Since the rise of first-wave feminism in the late nineteenth century, numerous writers have imagined worlds where women hold sway. Many, from Charlotte Perkins Gilman's *Herland* (1915, page 134), to Doris Lessing's troubling vision of an early society rent by the birth of the first male in *The Cleft* (2007), are women-only communities where life proceeds without the violence and oppression traditionally attached to patriarchal structures.

Norwegian author Gerd Mjøen Brantenberg's (b.1941) Egalia is rather different. The society depicted in *Egalia's Daughters: A Satire of the Sexes* (first published in Bokmål as *Egalias døtre* in 1977 and translated into English in 1985) is a matriarchy where gender bias is seeded into everything, right down to the words people use to describe themselves. This is a skewed mirror world of wim and menwim, sheroes and maidmen, menwim's coffee mornings and gentlewim's clubs where the powerful gather to debate the issues of the day without their housebounds worrying their pretty little heads and getting their beard bows in a twist.

Brantenberg's subversion of traditional gender inequality is ingenious and often very funny. Descriptions of the music of Womfred Womm playing in a gay club, for example, or references to the writings of eminent psychologist Sigma Floyd are guaranteed to raise a smile, as are exclamations such as "Well I'll be a daughter of a dog!" The portrayal of the fraught process of buying a first peho—the cupping device required to hold male genitalia in place for decency's sake—is also amusing with its involved discussion of the importance of balancing tube size against strap measurements.

For all the laughs, though, readers are left in no doubt as to the seriousness of Brantenberg's intentions. Through her inverted world, she holds received wisdom up to a new, searching light and repeatedly finds it wanting. We see, for example, the holes in the arguments of those who try to use nature as a justification for the power imbalance between the sexes: in Egalia, wim use the natural order to argue it is menwim's duty to take sole responsibility for contraception, childcare, and homemaking because "menwim engender children" and are thus "eternally imprisoned within their own biology,"

The boys said it was awkward and uncomfortable .... And it was so impractical when you had to pee. First you had to loosen the waistband which held the peho in place. The waistband was fastened under the skirt, so you stood fumbling for a long time ... Moreover, you had to sew a slit into each of your skirts so the peho might hang freely outside.

Gerd Brantenberg

EGALIAS DØTRE

Den utrolig morsomme satiren om landet Egalia, der kvinnene hersker og mennene undertrykkes, har lavt-lønnsjobbene, går med PH (penisholder) og legger skjegget for å behage kvinnene.

and because they are physically stronger are better suited to the demands of housework. In addition, the cruel preoccupations about body image that have boys obsessing over their figures and looks, and the abuse the young hero, Petronius, realizes he has been taught to regard as normal, reveal how we internalize fear and vulnerability. Cumulatively, the novel demonstrates how apparently innocuous habits—and even the words we use—can keep human (or "huwom") beings trapped behind the barriers to free thinking.

Alongside her robust criticism of patriarchy, however, Brantenberg works hard to avoid her book becoming an attack on the male sex. As Petronius and his "masculinist" allies realize when they try to organize themselves to protest against Egalia's inequality, such generalizations are meaningless because "as long as they lived in a society that was ruled and dominated by one sex, it was absurd to make use of such concepts as 'menwim's nature' or 'wim's nature.' As long as one sex held power over the other, they would never be able to find out what differences there really were between the sexes—psychically—if there were any at all."

The real evil in Egalia is not the notion of women having power over men (or vice versa). Instead, it is power itself.

A Norwegian paperback edition from the 1970s, featuring a crocheted "peho," the tagline reads "A hilarious satire about the country of Egalia, where women rule and men are suppressed, work menial jobs, wear a PH (Penis Holder) and grow their beards to please women."

ANGELA CARTER

THE BLOODY CHAMBER AND OTHER STORIES (1979)

A groundbreaking collection of stories about power, agency, desires, and inner demons, presented as a subversive reformulation of classic fairy tales.

First published by Gollancz in 1979.

Carter sometimes called these stories "reformulations" of fairy tales and explained that they were not "retellings" but rather her attempt to draw out the existing latent qualities in the tales.

The 1984 film *The Company of Wolves*, directed by Neil Jordan, was based on the werewolf stories included in *The Bloody Chamber*. Carter herself was involved in writing the script.

Opposite: From "The Tiger's Bride," in which a young woman is forced to live with a mysterious, masked man who is revealed to be a tiger. Illustration by Igor Karash.

Angela Carter (1940–92) was born as Angela Olive Stalker in the British seaside town of Eastbourne. After studying at the University of Bristol and working as a journalist, Carter began writing fiction in the 1960s. In 1969 she was won the Somerset Maugham Award for her novel *Several Perceptions* (which, along with *Shadow Dance*, 1966, and *Love*, 1971, comprises her "Bristol Trilogy"), and she later claimed that the prize money allowed her to divorce her husband, travel to Japan and become radicalized as a feminist.

Like that of Gabriel García Márquez, Jorge Luis Borges, and Salman Rushdie, Carter's writing is often described as a "magical realism;" a postmodern school of literature in which highly realistic and detailed settings are combined with fabulous or fantastic events.

The baroque, gothic world of *The Bloody Chamber and Other Stories* is held together almost entirely by the desires and the power of Carter's female characters. Even though they are often nameless archetypes, each are well realized in their motives and drive. Their transformative powers are what further develop the atmosphere Carter so deftly creates, with personal demons just lurking at the periphery. The idea of the beast within, a beast who will emerge whether silently or with a huge roar, but always, always just about to make its presence felt, is a powerful one—the mood of these stories is always one of something terrible, something incredible about to happen, the waiting, the knowing being very much part of the fearful excitement. The women who start off as sexual objects usually morph into something greater, taking back their agency, their power, and owning their desire.

Carter's settings for her stories may vary—from small apartments in Paris to grand castles on grim, sharp cliffs to desolate country houses to the archetypal cottage in the woods, but her worlds are all based in reality in the way any fairy tale's can be. Everything is just a little deeper, darker, more sexual—every room is a dark, lush, ornate space with secrets tucked away, while outdoors, every element of nature is pushed to its extreme. Her mise-en-scène for every story is always extravagantly theatrical and dramatic though never heavy handed and often tender and loving camp.

But it is Carter's fabulous, rich language that is what really details the world of her stories. Her voice is bold, fearless, unabashedly lush, and voluptuous. Each page rises with an orchestra of sensual colors, snarling sounds, tongues, tails, teeth, and skin. Every sensation is magnified until it is almost hallucinatory but beautiful, always beautiful, like a nightmare you don't want to wake up from. The ambience of each story itself is thick with wonder and heavy with mood, so bold, so daring, so relentlessly fearless.

Carter wrote about the importance of female heterosexuality and women taking control of their sexuality before anyone else did—these stories are erotic, but they aren't erotica—it isn't their primary purpose to titillate. Their primary purpose is to question our desires and how they define us. In understanding what she desires, Carter suggests, a woman will be able to understand who she is. Understanding and accepting desires, acknowledging them no matter how dark or strange they may be, will help women in knowing who they are. And desire, of course, isn't just about sex.

Of course, sex, with its undertones of violence and control, is always present in the world of *The Bloody Chamber*. There is a constant sense of mysterious impending doom caused by dangerous desires. But female sexuality is triumphant when Carter's heroines, with their wild hearts and sharp minds accept the beast within, the wolf or tiger or lion that desire makes of them. We see them navigate marriages as wives and daughters, we see their relationships with their mothers, we watch them take power from their sexual awakenings, transform into greater beings, survive strange transmutations, live among rot and decay, struggle with gender power dynamics, and manage the cruelty of their male lovers and oppressors.

These are girls and women who reclaim the night, who embrace the darkness and let it in so they can rise above it and claim the world as theirs.

Opposite: "Bluebeard and his wife" by Gustave Dore, 1862, illustrated to accompany Charles Perrault's tale *La Barbe Bleue* (1697), the inspiration behind Carter's *The Bloody Chamber.*

OCTAVIA E. BUTLER

KINDRED (1979)

A young, black woman writer is abruptly transported from twentieth-century Los Angeles to nineteenth-century Maryland where she learns hard truths about slavery and her own family.

First published by Doubleday in 1979.

Butler received a MacArthur Fellowship, popularly known as the "genius grant," in 1995, the first science-fiction writer to be so honored. Her other awards included a Lifetime Achievement Award from PEN Center West, the Langston Hughes Medal from City College of New York, two Hugos, and two Nebula Awards.

Although Dana is caught when she attempts to run away, some real-life slaves had better luck. Harriet Tubman (born about 1820) escaped to Philadelphia in 1849, returned to rescue family members, and helped almost 300 slaves take the "underground railroad" north to freedom.

Octavia E. Butler (1947–2006) began her career as a science-fiction writer in the 1970s, the only black American woman working in a genre then widely perceived to be the purview of white males. Her first three books were part of the "Patternist" series, featuring telepathic mind control, aliens, and power struggles between groups and individuals. *Kindred* was Butler's breakthrough novel and remains her best-known work: a powerful tale about race relations, which combines aspects of science fiction with the historic slave narrative.

Although it shares many common themes with her other novels, there are no psychic powers or aliens in *Kindred,* only humans shaped by social, historic, and emotional forces. Its time-travel element has led to it being classified as science fiction, but because she made no attempt to provide even a pseudo-scientific justification for the time travel, Butler disagreed, calling it instead "grim fantasy."

Dana, the main character and narrator, has her first experience of involuntary time travel on her twenty-sixth birthday, the day she and her husband move into their first house together. One moment it is the summer of 1976, and she is in Altadena, California, unpacking books; the next, she finds herself in a green wood on the shore of a river in which a child is drowning. She plunges in and saves him, and, after a short period of confusion and danger, returns home.

Later that evening it happens again, only this time she finds herself inside a house where the same child, now about four years older, has set fire to the curtains. Once again, she saves his life. Dana learns from the boy that they are in Maryland and the year is 1815. He is Rufus Weylin—a name she knows from the family Bible. He was the father of her great-great-grandmother, Hagar. Why did no one ever mention he was white? Probably because that knowledge died with Hagar in 1880, she thinks, for she cannot deny the strange connection between them. Rufus has the power to summon her whenever his life is in danger and, for the sake of her own existence, Dana knows she must do whatever she can to keep him alive, at least until Hagar is born. But her life and liberty, as a black woman in a slave state, are constantly under threat, and

even when she manages to return to her own time, she never knows when she will be pulled back to the past by her violent, unpredictable ancestor.

Slave quarters at l'Hermitage Plantation, Frederick County, Maryland.

The world in which Dana's adventures are set is not an imaginary land, but a well-researched, realistic reconstruction of an actual place and time. The historic sections of *Kindred* take place in Talbot County, on the Eastern Shore of Maryland, between 1811 and 1832. Butler chose Maryland rather than the Deep South because it was the only state from which a slave had any realistic chance of escape, with freedom possible across the border in Pennsylvania. A native Californian like her character, Butler journeyed to Maryland to do research, to get a feeling for the physical place, in addition to reading the writings of former slaves, and many books about the history of slavery.

Butler's aim was to make readers *feel* the reality of slavery, not as mere observers of a long-ago past, but more personally, through identification with a modern character forced to live in a world as alien to her as to them— a world that, although strange to us, was at once undeniably, physically real and inescapable.

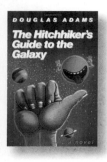

DOUGLAS ADAMS

THE HITCHHIKER'S GUIDE TO THE GALAXY (1979)

Adams's classic series begins with the demolition of Earth to make way for a galactic freeway. Everyman Arthur Dent is saved by the freewheeling alien Ford Prefect, and so begins a hilarious and wild ride through time and space.

First published by Pan Books in 1979.

Adams was a script editor on the BBC's *Doctor Who* when he wrote the original *Hitchhiker's Guide* scripts.

The joke around the name "Ford Prefect" is now somewhat obscure. The name refers to a make of car, manufactured from the 1940s to the 1960s, once very common on British roads, now very rare. Ford chose the name hoping to blend in, presumably because he assumed the sheer number of cars meant that they are the dominant form of life on Earth.

As a student at Cambridge University, Douglas Adams (1952–2001) became involved in the university's famous Footlights comedy club; and straight after university he wrote for the British TV shows *Monty Python's Flying Circus* and *Doctor Who*. It was while hitchhiking around Europe on a low-budget vacation in the 1970s that he got the idea of combining the surreal comedy of the Pythons with the science fiction of *Dr. Who*.

The result was the deeply funny space-opera fantasia *The Hitchhiker's Guide to the Galaxy*, which appeared in many different forms. Indeed, it might be easier to list the formats in which it *didn't* appear: it was first heard as a radio drama on BBC Radio 4 in 1978—six half-hour episodes, broadcast late at night. Despite this low-key launch the show quickly acquired a cult following. A second six-part radio series followed in 1980, and Adams wrote two novelizations, *The Hitchhiker's Guide to the Galaxy* and *The Restaurant at the End of the Universe* (1980). A television adaptation followed in 1981, and a video-game version in 1984. There was a movie (2005), three further radio series, more novelizations, a stage adaptation, comic books, and a general dissemination into fan culture. Even the title keeps changing, with *The Hitch-Hiker's Guide to the Galaxy*, *The Hitch Hiker's Guide to the Galaxy,* and *The Hitchhiker's Guide to the Galaxy* all used by different forms. Whatever else all this tells us, it shows how popular Adams's world was, and how adaptable.

That adaptability was key not only to its success but also to its own logic. As the *Hitchhiker's Guide* grew, its storyline proliferated in ingenious, absurd, and hilarious directions, but at its heart remains a simple fish-out-of-water story of an ordinary human being named Arthur Dent. Earth is scheduled to be demolished by an unpleasant alien species called the Vogons in order to make way for a galactic hyperspace bypass. Dent—still wearing his pajamas and dressing gown—is the only human to survive this catastrophe, having been rescued by his best friend Ford Prefect. Dent had assumed that Ford was from the English town of Guildford; in fact he was from the star Betelgeuse and had been living on Earth to research an entry on the planet for the titular encyclopedia-style guidebook.

From this bravura opening—it really does require chutzpah to *begin* a story with the end of the world—Dent and Ford embark on a peripatetic series of interstellar adventures, meeting the splendidly egotistical two-headed Zaphod Beeblebrox, onetime president of the Galaxy and now outlaw and barfly; Marvin, a hugely intelligent but chronically depressed robot ("Marvin the Paranoid Android"); Trillian, a human woman who happened to flee Earth a few years before its end; and various others. Their adventures take them back and forth through space and time, with increasingly complicated ramifications. They visit planets teeming with life and planets abandoned to spooky ruins; they visit the headquarters of the Guide's publishers only for the entire building to be ripped from the ground and flown through space by kidnapping robots; they travel forward to the end of time itself and backward to the epoch of cavemen. At all points they actualize a very English type of inventively deadpan humor: premises are logically extrapolated into absurdity, the arbitrary cruelty of the cosmos is illustrated from the largest scale—such as the abrupt destruction of the whole of Earth and all its people—down to the smallest (Dent finds it frustratingly hard to find that beverage most essential to the English, a nice cup of tea), but disaster is always treated in a drily comic manner. There is little slapstick, no vulgarity or obscenity, and often the jokes entail quite profound metaphysical consequences. This perhaps makes Adams sound like a forbiddingly intellectual humorist, which he wasn't at all. The funniest moments in *Hitchhiker's* depend upon character and situation, and the philosophy never treads upon the jokes.

As Dent and Ford's adventures continue, they discover that Earth was not actually a regular planet, but rather a gigantic computer that had been running a program for millions of years designed to solve one of the great cosmic

The original radio cast (from left to right, David Tate, Alan Ford, Geoffrey McGivern, [Douglas Adams, behind], Mark Wing-Davey and Simon Jones).

mysteries. This mystery is not the meaning of life, which had long ago been determined—it is "42"—but instead the meaning of the meaning of life. It is designed to determine, in other words, what the ultimate question could be that might lead to the ultimate answer "42." And by the end of the second series of the radio show, we discover what the ultimate question is; but without wishing to spoil that reveal, we can say that Adams's "42" works both as a neatly absurdist gag, and as a profound intervention into the metaphysics of meaning. What *can* the universe "mean," if its meaning could be summed up as a two-digit number?

The appeal of *Hitchhiker's* depends upon more than its comedy, endearing though that is. The imagined world Adams creates is fascinating, varied, and, above all, hospitable where fan engagement is concerned. The universe is full of the bumbling and the wisecracking but rarely with pure evil or cruelty: even the horrid Vogons compose poetry (although it is poetry so bad that reciting it is a mode of torture). Everywhere you go in Adams's imaginary cosmos there are ingenious and hilarious vignettes. Enterprising restaurateurs have created a temporal "bubble" that sits at the very end of all time, so that diners can enjoy a sumptuous meal while watching the ultimate apocalypse in the "Restaurant at the End of the Universe"; one planet's population has evolved into birds to avoid the need to walk on the ground, since shoes had become so expensive; humans are revealed to be the third most important lifeform on Earth, after dolphins and white mice. Before their first trip through hyperspace, Ford warns Arthur Dent that the experience will be "unpleasantly like being drunk." "What's so unpleasant about being drunk?" Arthur asks, to which Ford replies: "Ask a glass of water." Another spaceship travels interstellar distances not via hyperspace but through an "infinite improbability drive"—a brilliant science-fictional conceit that works both as the premise for much surreal humor (since the drive leaves in its wake all manner of bizarre and ill-sorted apparitions) as well as an engagement with the deep logic of space and time, where probability plays as large as part as determinism.

It is surely the case that *Hitchhiker's* works best as a radio drama or novel, for here the imagination can engage in the least-fettered way with Adams's expertly suggestive vistas and tartly engaging characters. It has a great deal to do with the comedy of the work, a tricky matter to discuss since—as everybody knows—a joke explained is no longer funny. In fact, that's not the half of it. To excerpt examples of humor from *Hitchhiker's* does nothing to convey the caliber of the humor of Adams's world, since that humor depends so largely on the spacious, ingenious context in which it occurs. The solvent is charm, a genuinely rare quality in literature, rarer in science fiction, and impossible to fake; but a quality Douglas Adams possessed in large quantities, and with which he infuses the worlds of his creation.

In a last-ditch effort to escape a pair of missiles bearing down on them, the protagonists fire up an infinite improbability drive, turning the missiles—in an infinitely improbable way—into bowl of petunias and a sperm whale. Illustration by James Burton.

A preliminary sketch by artist John Harris for the cover artwork for Ann Leckie's Imperial Radch trilogy, see page 304.

5 THE COMPUTER AGE

As Cold War fears subsided and technology brought us closer to the stars, created worlds became ever more elaborate and the postmodern playfulness of the 1970s gave birth to the fantastical and parodic creations of writers such as Salman Rushdie and Terry Pratchett.

STEPHEN KING

THE DARK TOWER SERIES
(1982–2012)

In King's "Dark Tower" universe lies one of the largest fantasy worlds ever created, and incorporates a wide variety of genres, from fantasy and science fiction to horror and the Western.

Published by Donald M. Grant between 1982 and 2012.

Robert Browning's poem "Childe Roland to the Dark Tower Came" was an inspiration for King's best-selling series.

Although the saga appears to have come to an end, King told *Rolling Stone* magazine in October 2014: "I'm never done with The Dark Tower. . . ."

The Dark Tower series is a collection of seven novels written by Stephen King (b.1947)—an undisputed master of horror, suspense, science fiction, and fantasy—and published between 1982 and 2012. The series artfully blends the traditional themes of fantasy writing with tropes of the Western. The first, and most famous, title in the series is *The Gunslinger* (1982). It nods toward the strange—set in a mysterious place called Mid-world with a desert full of demons—but for the most part, the novel is a mythical version of a classical Western narrative. There's a gunslinger, Roland Deschain, and he's going to kill somebody who is described as "the man in black," who we'll later discover is Randall Flagg.

It is Flagg who holds the key to King's world building in the Dark Tower series, and indeed across his entire oeuvre. While *The Gunslinger* itself is a fairly straightforward book, those that followed over a thirty year period get increasingly longer and more complicated, with massive numbers of characters, a huge world to cover, different creatures and concepts presented, and even a lexicon of terms that needs to be remembered for the story to resonate properly.

Mid-world ostensibly resembles our own world. Or, rather, it's an altered facsimile of it, taking into account both King's and a wider fictional history. A town is destroyed by Captain Tripps, the virus that destroyed the world in *The Stand*; a character comes to Mid-world via Salem's Lot; a major set piece of the series takes place in *The Wizard of Oz*'s Emerald City. It's a strange and disjointed place, which, it would seem, takes in much of other literature. You get the impression that, were he able, King would have gone further with the concept of intertextuality, but much of it has to remain vague. However, some enemies (the Wolves of the Calla) are described in a way that makes it clear they're based on Marvel's Doctor Doom, and they're defeated by throwing Harry Potter's Snitches—or, in this text, sneetches—at them. The man in black is Johnny Cash, but the series' main antagonist is actually The Crimson King, one of King's favorite bands. Of course, the name of the series itself comes from Tolkien's Barad-dûr; individual books in the series take their names from T. S. Eliot and Lewis Carroll.

When, in the series' final books, the characters travel out of Mid-world and into our own reality—meeting with King himself, in a masterful piece of playful metafiction—it becomes clear that the world of the Dark Tower is everything that ever influenced King. All the fiction, cinema, music, and art he sees as an influence is dragged into play, turned into an aspect of the narrative. It's not always smoothly integrated, and it's not always as clear as you'd hope—the intellectual property rights alone ensure that—but it's there. The world is a brain map of King's creativity, and thus both entirely like and unlike anything else ever written.

The rest of King's bibliography is touched by the same influences. Randall Flagg appears in a number of King's novels, often under different names but representing the same individual; many of the characters of the Dark Tower have also appeared in other books, right from the start of King's career. It's a game, sometimes: to be reading a King novel, and trying to find out exactly how he's tied it to his masterplan. And it's something that, in *Nos4atu*, the latest novel published by his son, Joe Hill, has spread: The book features a section that suggests that Hill's own literary universe is implicitly tied into his father's.

Cover painting for the seventh and last book in the Dark Tower series by Michael Whelan, it brings to an end the saga of Roland the Gunslinger as he finally reaches the tower.

TERRY PRATCHETT

THE DISCWORLD SERIES
(1983–2015)

Pratchett's wildly popular Discworld looks, sounds, and smells very much like our own, except that it is carried though space on the back of a giant turtle and populated by a host of colorful characters including bumbling heroes, Death, empowered witches, and self-carrying luggage.

The series is published by several different companies, but the first title, *The Color of Magic*, was published by Colin Smythe Ltd in 1983.

Pratchett was at one point reputed to have been the most shoplifted author in Britain.

On March 12, 2015, the day of Terry Pratchett's death, his Twitter feed posted "Terry took Death's arm and followed him through the doors and on to the black desert under the endless night." Followed by "The End."

When Terry Pratchett's (1948–2015) first Discworld novel, *The Color of Magic*, appeared in 1983, it employed a setting he used in an earlier science-fiction novel, *Strata* (1981). The flat, disc-shaped world was intended to parody Larry Niven's *Ringworld* (1970, page 214), but the idea stuck in his mind and he reused it as the setting for a parody of heroic fantasy. It was to prove so effective and so popular that it would serve as the world in which nearly all of his subsequent novels took place. Discworld became important as a setting that enabled Pratchett to hold a comically distorted mirror to our familiar world, allowing us to laugh while encountering often profound issues. By the time of his death in 2015, Sir Terry, as he became, was one of the most popular authors in the world, largely because the Discworld and its characters had lodged so enduringly in the minds of his readers.

From the start of the first novel we are told that the Discworld rides through space supported on the backs of four elephants who are themselves standing upon the back of a giant turtle, A'Tuin. This hints at ideas found in eastern mythologies, but it is intended to detach the Discworld from our notions of realism and to emphasize that it is a ludicrous place. Here, the turtle and elephants suggest, anything may happen because this is a realm untouched by reality. Nonetheless, while magic is the principal force on the Discworld, it operates in a similar way to the elemental forces in our own world, and is similarly theorized.

Across more than forty novels, a large cast of recurring characters appear. Rincewind, the hopeless magician, was introduced in *The Color of Magic* (1983); Granny Weatherwax and the Witches in *Equal Rites* (1987); Death in *Mort* (1987); Vimes and the City Watch in *Guards! Guards!* (1989); and Tiffany Aching, the young witch in an off-shoot of the Discworld series aimed at a young adult audience, in *The Wee Free Men* (2003). The novels follow a roughly chronological sequence, so that across the books we see characters develop (Vimes is promoted, Granny Weatherwax dies) and new technologies become established (steam trains are introduced in *Raising Steam* [2013]). Thus, it is a dynamic setting.

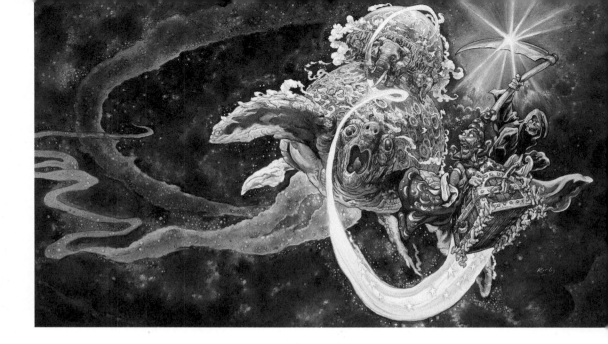

The recurring locations, the Unseen University, the capital city of Ankh-Morpork, the pub that is variously known as The Drum, The Broken Drum, and The Mended Drum, all suggest a solidly realized and consistent landscape. Indeed, there is even a "Mapp" of the city in *The Streets of Ankh-Morpork* (1993). Yet it would be a mistake to imagine that the chronology of the novels and the consistency of the settings imply that Discworld is always the same place.

In fact, as Pratchett said, the point of the Discworld series was always to "have fun with the clichés," and each novel sets out to parody some aspect of popular culture, such as cinema (*Moving Pictures*, 1990), rock music (*Soul Music*, 1994), or journalism (*The Truth*, 2000); attitudes toward other places (Australia in *The Last Continent*, 1998); or features of modern life (the postal service in *Going Postal*, 2004). When writing about Egyptian gods in *Pyramids* (1989), Pratchett's purpose was not to thoroughly research the mythology or to get details of the belief system absolutely right, but to reflect what the person in the street might commonly assume about the subject with all the inconsistencies and absurdities that might imply. It was always necessary that the familiar should be recognizable within the books, whether global politics in *Jingo* (1997), economics in *Making Money* (2007), or conservatism in *Monstrous Regiment* (2003). Therefore, Pratchett had no hesitation in making radical changes to his setting just to suit the story being told or, more accurately, the topic being parodied. Whether it is a new island emerging in *Jingo* or a new social culture in *Pyramids*, Discworld was always and deliberately a fluid setting.

Discworld III by artist Josh Kirby. Kirby's work is unmistakeable to countless Pratchett fans, and he contributed his remarkable illustrations to each book in the series. Kirby died in 2001 and his artwork is reproduced by kind permission of his estate.

Overleaf: The Light Fantastic (1986) by Josh Kirby, showing the wizard Rincewind riding his trusty companion, the intelligent traveling chest Luggage, with Death's adopted daughter Ysabell and Discworld tourist Twoflower.

WILLIAM GIBSON

NEUROMANCER (1984)

Gibson's prescient cyberpunk novel predicts a world where technology is omnipresent and morality nowhere to be found.

First published by Ace (U.S.) and Victor Gollancz Ltd (UK) in 1984.

Neuromancer was the first book—and only debut—to win the Hugo Award, the Nebula Award, and the Philip K. Dick Award.

In 2005, *Time* magazine included it on their list of the 100 best English-language novels.

The novel popularized the term "cyberspace," but Gibson had actually coined the word two years earlier in his short story collection *Burning Chrome*.

Neuromancer was published in 1984 and opens with a bleak, if atmospheric, description. "The sky above the port was the color of television, tuned to a dead channel." Evocative and strangely haunting, this introductory line describes the world's atmosphere in a single breath—a crumbling infrastructure, overwhelmed technology; beautiful and unsettling—all packaged in Gibson's taut, neo-noir prose.

Structurally, William Gibson's (b.1948) seminal cyberpunk work flows like a particularly conspiratorial heist novel. The nominal hero, Case, is a burned out "cowboy," a former hacker who's been stripped of his access to cyberspace after he tried to scam a former employer. He's recruited by Molly, a physically augmented "street samurai," and Armitage, an unstable former black-ops solider, to perform a series of raids. At first, these capers—which take place across real and virtual worlds—seem disconnected, but as the book unfolds, Case and Molly piece together not only the ultimate goal of their actions, but also the true identity—and motivation—of their employer.

Neuromancer begins at Case's lowest point—in a seedy bar in Chiba City, where he's operating, badly, as a petty criminal. A place of flickering lights and dangerous inhabitants—seemingly all back-alleys and dive bars—Chiba City is "like a deranged experiment in Social Darwinism, designed by a bored researcher who kept one thumb permanently on the fast-forward button." Case hustles desperately to stay alive, flitting between one errand and another, buying and selling drugs, guns, information, and even organs.

The inescapable grisliness of "Night City" is intentional—it serves as a "deliberately unsupervised playground for technology." Case is drawn in to the City seeking a chance to repair his ruined nervous system so he can become a hacker again. But with his money and his credit gone, he's now merely another replaceable part in its criminal ecosystem, and he's accelerating rapidly toward self-destruction.

Molly and Armitage save Case from his fate and repair his shattered system so he can hack again. But nothing in *Neuromancer* comes without a price, and now Case is beholden to his enigmatic employer. The team,

now assembled, heads to Boston-Atlanta Metropolitan Axis—the Sprawl. Although more salubrious than Night City, this series of interlinked, domed North American megacities is still far from paradise. If Chiba City is social Darwinism, the Sprawl is capitalism gone mad. The soaring towers of the all-consuming megacorporations tower over the rest of the city, a permanent reminder of who holds the power. As with Chiba City, the Sprawl is a constant hustle, but here the prize is pure profit. Both slickly suited businessmen and the surrealist street gangs target the ordinary people of the Sprawl. All have access to impressive technology, and most are addicted to the fast-paced entertainment of SimStims—exotic virtual reality that lets people share the sensations experienced by their celebrity idols.

From the heady, super-modern heights of the Sprawl, Case and Molly head to Istanbul. If Chiba City is ruthlessly carving out the future and the Sprawl is aggressively defining the "now," Istanbul is where the past and present co-exist, albeit uneasily.

Istanbul's juxtaposition of the sleekly modern—from the airport to the interior of their hotel—and the crumbling, but inescapable past—"crazy walls of patchwork wooden tenements"—is apparent all throughout the city. Case and Molly are joined by a corrupt member of the local secret police, indicating that the political situation is no more settled than the landscape.

From Istanbul, the crew, now accompanied by the sadistic illusionist Peter Riviera, head to *Neuromancer*'s most exotic destination, the space station Freeside. Freeside is "Las Vegas and the Hanging Gardens of Babylon," a playground for the ultra-rich and extremely privileged. Built and completely owned by the Tessier-Ashpool family, Freeside serves as "brothel

The dystopian underworld of Chiba City as imagined by illustrator Josh Godin.

and banking nexus, pleasure dome and free port, border town and spa." An artificial night sky comes complete with fake constellations showing "playing cards, the faces of glass, a top hat." Drones and other invisible servants clean up the clutter, so the wealthy tourists can spend their time completely undisturbed.

Initially, Case and the others remain outside of the space station itself, in a tiny cluster of ships called Zion. Of all the places, Zion is the only one at ease with itself—particularly incredibly given its ramshackle nature. Only parts of Zion have gravity, the rest connected by corridors of freefall. The structure is makeshift, reminding Case of the"'patchwork tenements of Istanbul," but here, they hold together, as if they have found where they belong. Founded by five workers who refused to return to Earth, the people of Zion have made their peace with the complexity of the external world by applying metaphor—everything out there is "Babylon," while within Zion is the love of Jah. Case is a hyperkinetic urbanite and struggles with the langorous pace of Zion, but even he begins to sense—if not appreciate—the peace of this place.

By contrast, Freeside is a slick, and far less comforting, place. The space station has an unusual spindle shape, which leads to complex (and not entirely consistent) gravitational effects. The bulk of Freeside is given over to a hub of hotels, casinos, night clubs, and high-end shopping. The space station contains "outdoor" elements as well, including lakes and a velodrome. Anchoring it all, filling an entire "segment" at one end of Freeside, sits the Villa Straylight, private and impregnable, the home of the Tessier-Ashpool family. The Villa reflects the clan's philosophy: their rigid control of finance, technology, and property through elaborate mechanisms. But it also captures their insanity and their decline, the hubris of their created world is dissolving into dusty relics.

Case's travels through the worlds of *Neuromancer* take him from impeccable hotels to grimy backstreets, from the physical and metaphorical depths of the underground to the heights of corporate rule. Each destination highlights a different way in which humanity relates to both technology and temporality. In Chiba City, hustlers scramble over scraps of data, selling stolen hard disks in a desperate bid to live another day. In the Sprawl, strangely immutable corporations create a rapidly accelerating cacophony of trends, products, and even celebrities. In Istanbul, the past and the present are at constant war. And in the Villa Straylight, the circle completes, with the Tessier-Ashpool clan again using technology in a bid for life—cryogenics to stay young; artificial intelligence to stay financially potent. The same hustle; the same battle against the inexorable approach of time.

In the matrix, however, time does not exist—explaining, to some small degree, Case's obsession with returning to cyberspace. In *Neuromancer*, the matrix is defined loosely, often more in terms of its scale than its aesthetics. Gibson describes his vision of cyberspace as "a consensual hallucination experienced daily by billions . . . a graphic representation of data abstracted from banks of every computer." When Case jacks in—porting his consciousness into cyberspace—he leaves the physical world behind. Aches, soreness, abstract sensations like the passage of time, guilt, or emotional longing: All shed when Case enters cyberspace. *Neuromancer* introduces a mechanism where Case spends much of the book "flipping" back and forth with a VR device, reversing between the abstract vastness of cyberspace and the vigorous physicality of Molly's sensations. With every abrupt change in perception, the reader gets a fraction of what Case must feel—the shift from languorous contemplation of the universal to grubby, painful reality.

Visually, *Neuromancer*'s cyberspace is surprisingly simplistic. Case describes "lines of light ranged in nonspace," but more often than not, data is arranged in geometric patterns. More complex data—an AI, a lethal virus—has more facets, but still moves largely as a flow of patterns.

However, this "unthinkable complexity"—these "bright lattices of logic"—are merely the tip of the iceberg. In Case's interactions with Wintermute, the Tessier-Ashpool's AI, he's transported to a realm that's indistinguishable from the real world. The AI serves up a level of stimulus that, although dreamlike, is rendered in perfect detail. The only absence is imagination: Wintermute can pull images from plugged-in minds, but can't create anything new. In this private cyberspace, Case wanders down a perfect beach in Morocco as well as locations from his own memory. The artistic detail of Wintermute's cyberspace hints at the infinite potential of technology, and its limitless future.

At the end of *Neuromancer*, the matrix reveals two additional facets. The first is that Case's quiet, personal vision—the beach placed in his mind by Wintermute—seems to take on a life of its own, complete with sentient residents. Whether these are fragments of memory or new intelligences is left unexplored. Also left unexplored is Wintermute's cryptic hint that there are other intelligences "like it" out there—and by that, the AI indicates the Centauri System. Despite being a graphic metaphor for the transfer of data, the child of "video games" and military software, cyberspace has extended beyond the reach of humanity—in multiple ways.

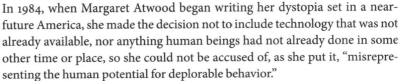

MARGARET ATWOOD

The Handmaid's Tale (1985)

"God is a National Resource" in this remarkably powerful, feminist
dystopian novel about a repressive American theocratic dictatorship.

First published in the
UK by McClelland and
Stewart, 1985.

Atwood dedicated the book
to Mary Webster and Perry
Miller. Mary Webster,
believed by Atwood to have
been one of her ancestors,
was hanged as a witch in
Puritan New England,
but survived.

A 2015 Public Policy Polling
(PPP) national survey
conducted on U.S.
Republican voters found
that fifty-seven percent
wanted to establish
Christianity as the official
national religion, and only
thirty percent were opposed
to the idea, which is
specifically prohibited by
the Constitution.

In 1984, when Margaret Atwood began writing her dystopia set in a near-future America, she made the decision not to include technology that was not already available, nor anything human beings had not already done in some other time or place, so she could not be accused of, as she put it, "misrepresenting the human potential for deplorable behavior."

The transformation of the U.S. into a theocratic dictatorship known as the Republic of Gilead has been brought about by true believers, religious fanatics driven by a determination to establish God's kingdom on Earth, much as the Puritan settlers (who included some of Atwood's ancestors) were determined to do in seventeenth-century New England.

Prior to the beginning of the novel, fundamentalist Christian extremists assassinated the president and Congress, pinning the blame on Islamic terrorists and allowing their army to declare a state of emergency, in which the Constitution is "temporarily" suspended, news is censored, identity cards issued, and, with the new religious rulers in place, new rules imposed. Overnight, women lose the right to have jobs, or bank accounts, or to do anything except submit to the will of their husbands. And all are subject to the rule of the Commanders of the Faith, who claim biblical authority for every act, having abolished any distinction between church and state.

The narrator of *The Handmaid's Tale* is a young woman known only as Offred—"Of Fred"—designated as the legal concubine of a high-ranking Commander whose first name is Fred. Only a few years before, she had a name and a job, a husband and a child, friends, and freedoms she took for granted. But the family left it too late to cross into Canada with fake passports, and now her husband is either dead or in detention, her daughter adopted by a childless couple. The only thing keeping Offred from being shipped off to perform slave labor in "the Colonies" is the possibility she might bear a baby for the Commander and his wife. For another major element driving this bleak vision of the future is that from a multitude of causes—including radiation, pollution, and untreated STDs—there has been a steep drop in human fertility, so women of child-bearing age and proven fertility are very valuable.

The biblical book of Genesis includes the story of Jacob, who married two sisters, Rachel and Leah. When Rachel produced no children, she told Jacob to impregnate her maid, Bilhah: "and she shall bear upon my knees, that I may also have children by her." Thus, under a regime that fears and mistrusts all science, preferring to find the answer to every problem through selective reading of an ancient book, the solution to childlessness, at least in the upper ranks, is to establish Rachel and Leah Centers for the indoctrination of "handmaids" to be assigned to the households of all childless Commanders. (Naturally, the centers are not named after the handmaidens who had Jacob's children, but after his wives.)

In Gilead, society is rigidly hierarchical and divided by gender: Commanders of the Faith at the top; below them the Eyes (secret police), then Angels (soldiers), Guardians (low-level police duties), all male civilians, and all women. Women have no power of their own, and are valued only as wives and the producers of babies. Some unmarried women are assigned other roles by the state—the "Aunts" who indoctrinate and control those who have been selected as potential surrogate mothers and "Marthas" who work as cooks and cleaners. A few women survive by practicing the oldest profession—a brothel known as Jezebel's is permitted to thrive, and the men in power take liberties forbidden to others.

If a handmaid fails to conceive after three different postings she is declared an "Unwoman" and sent off to "the Colonies." This is a euphemism for forced labor camps, where lives are brutal and short. Women likewise become "unwomen" if they refuse to submit, or the men in power have no more use for them.

Women are not the only victims of this repressive, rigidly stratified, coercively heterosexual, white dictatorship. Enemies of the state regularly tortured and then executed include Catholic priests, Quakers, doctors (if

Handmaids are recognized by their red robes, wives dress in blue ones and the "Marthas" (designated cooks and cleaners) wear green. Illustration by Anna and Elena Balbusso.

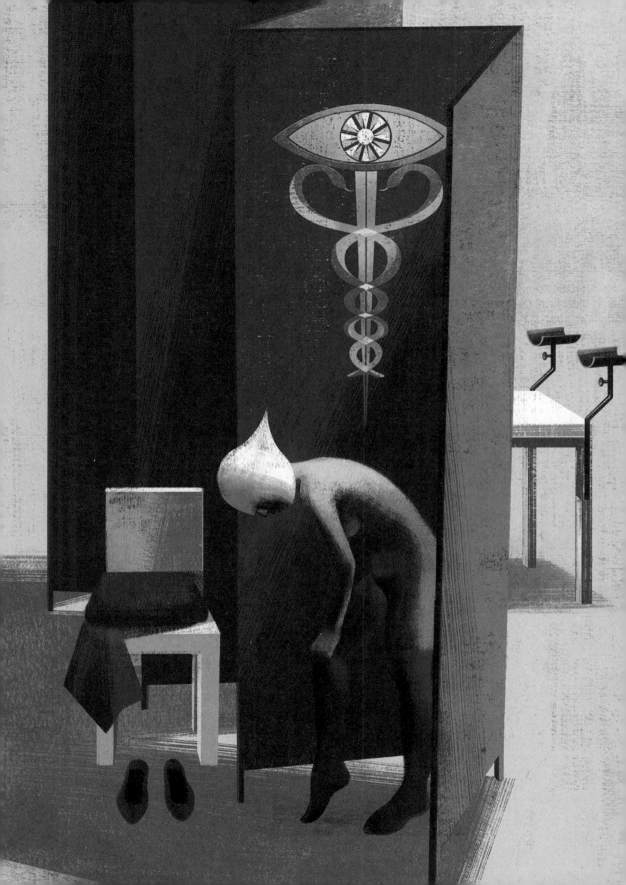

they ever performed an abortion, prescribed contraception, or are accused of having done so), and "gender traitors." African-Americans, called "Children of Ham," have been resettled in distant, underpopulated areas such as North Dakota, now designated a "National Homeland," and Jews were given a choice between conversion and emigration to Israel.

Offred's life as a handmaid is relatively easy, but deeply boring. Most of her time is spent waiting. The occasions when the Commander must attempt to impregnate her are as de-sexualized as intercourse can possibly be ("This is not recreation, even for the Commander. This is serious business. The Commander, too, is doing his duty.") and she wonders if it is worse for his wife, or for her. Her room is as bare as a prison cell, almost everything we would take for granted is classed as a luxury (hand cream) or a sin (reading). She is marked out by her red robes, as the wives are by their blue ones and the Marthas in green. Her daily walk is taken with another handmaid, and they are expected to police each other: If one tries to escape or does anything wrong, the other will be punished, too.

No one is allowed to suggest that a man could be sterile—infertility is always the woman's fault. But of course it is known, and the Commander's wife is desperate enough for a baby to arrange for Offred to spend time alone with Nick, their handsome young chauffeur. Their intimacy, after so much deprivation and misery, is almost enough to reconcile her to her situation. How little it takes, to make someone stop resisting. How easy it is to be distracted.

Although every aspect of this society is supposedly justified by the Word of God, as presented in the Bible, only the Commanders are allowed to read it, and they use it selectively, to say the least. A famous line from Karl Marx, changed to include the expected relationship between women and men, is attributed to St. Paul when repeated to the handmaids-in-training: "From each according to her ability, to each according to his needs."

The city where Offred serves is never named, but it is evidently Cambridge, Massachusetts, home of Harvard University. The university where Margaret Atwood once studied has become the seat of oppression, a detention center, and the site of mass executions.

Atwood has said that one of the elements that inspired her to write *The Handmaid's Tale* was a fascination with how dictatorships work ("not unusual in a person born in 1939, three months after the outbreak of World War II"). She explained: "Nations never build apparently radical forms of government on foundations that aren't there already. The deep foundation of the U.S.— so went my thinking—was not the comparatively recent eighteenth-century Enlightenment structures of the republic, with their talk of equality and their separation of church and state, but the heavy-handed theocracy of seventeenth-century Puritan New England, with its marked bias against women, which would need only the opportunity of a period of social chaos to reassert itself."

During a visit to the gynecologist, the doctor suggests the reason Offred is not yet pregnant might be because Commander is infertile. And since men are not tested, she will be blamed. As a solution he suggests that they have sex instead. Illustration by Anna and Elena Balbusso.

IAIN M. BANKS

THE CULTURE SERIES (1987–2012)

The Culture is a galaxy-spanning civilization composed of several different races (mostly human) and AIs (Artificial Intelligences, known as Minds); the Culture functions as a post-scarcity utopia.

The first four Culture books were written before Iain Banks first achieved publication with *The Wasp Factory* (1984); they were eventually published, by various companies, in the reverse order to that in which they were written.

Banks originally devised the Culture in the early 1970s while still at university. He wanted to write a story in which a bad man fought for a good cause; this would eventually become *Use of Weapons*.

Consider Phlebas is set around 1300 CE; *Surface Detail* is set in 2867 CE; the whole sequence, therefore, covers a period of more than 1,500 years.

The Culture series, ten novels published between 1987 and 2012, was created by Iain M. Banks (1954–2013) as a counterpoint to the conservative American space operas. In those stories, typically, one man saves the universe, restoring order based on the American capitalist system, and operates within a militaristic society in which spaceships are modeled on naval vessels complete with the same chain of command. Banks very carefully subverts every one of those clichés.

His dynamic characters are as likely to be women as men. Women play significant roles in *The State of the Art* (1989), *Use of Weapons* (1990), *Excession* (1996), *Inversions* (1998), *Matter* (2008), *Surface Detail* (2010), and *The Hydrogen Sonata* (2012). Even this isn't the whole story: Throughout, Banks makes it clear it is easy for people to change gender, and practically all do so at least once during their life. This leads to an increase in sexual pleasure while eliminating sexual discrimination. Furthermore, most of what passes for power within the Culture is in the purview of the genderless Minds.

Nor does a lone hero save the universe. Individuals, even individual Minds, play no more than a small part in the shaping of great events, and often have no knowledge of what their precise part might have been or how successful or not it was in the grand scheme of things.

Order is not restored, because order is not threatened. Indeed, order is not an issue, since this is a universe in which change is constant. When the Culture finds itself at war (*Consider Phlebas* [1987], *Excession*, *Look to Windward* [2000]), for instance, the very fact of war is considered an embarrassing failure, which leaves a legacy of guilt. The Culture is a nonracist society in which everyone, human, non-human, or machine intelligence, is equal. It is based on a communist model: Banks said, "Money is a sign of poverty. A [check] book is really a ration book." The Culture, therefore, is a post-scarcity society that has access to all the power needed, and the technological ability to fulfill any need. Out of this has emerged an anarchist system in which there are no hierarchies, no laws, and everyone is free to do as they wish. *The Player of Games* (1988) explicitly states that the only sanction

> They had no kings, no laws, no money and no property, but ... everybody lived like a prince, was well-behaved and lacked for nothing. And these people lived in peace, but they were bored, because paradise can get that way after a time.

An illustration inspired by Banks's The Culture series by Mark Brady.

against any crime is the embarrassment of it being known; but in a post-scarcity society the need for crime is largely removed.

The Culture is portrayed as a utopia, but this is only partly correct. On an individual level, life is utopian. People have an extended lifespan (QiRia in *The Hydrogen Sonata* is ten thousand years old), there are no constraints, no financial worries, sex is invariably wonderful, and built-in drug glands provide an artificial high at a moment's notice. But such an existence can be boring without purpose, so people risk their lives in extreme sports, or become involved in the affairs of other races. On a political level, therefore, the Culture has a more imperial and less utopian aspect.

The Culture is an expression of Banks's atheistic humanism, following what Ken MacLeod calls "pan-sentient utilitarian hedonism": The greater good leads inevitably to the greater pleasure. But again this is not straight-forward. Increasingly, the novels concern the Culture's failure to Sublime, to move to the next level of being, a move equated with death or ascent to heaven. In the later novels in particular, the Culture often finds itself in con-flict with religious symbols: godlike aliens, artificial hells, a demonstrably true religious book.

While outwardly fast-paced space operas are filled with dramatic action, immense artifacts, and great jokes, the Culture asks profound questions about the nature of utopia and of atheism.

BERNARDO ATXAGA

OBABAKOAK (1988)

*A collection of interrelated stories about life and the stories people tell,
including that of the narrator's childhood in an imaginary Basque-speaking
town, featuring a whirlwind of sleuthing, storytelling, and dialogue about
literature and myth-making in "big" and "small" cultures.*

First published by Editorial
Erein in 1988.

Basque or Euskera is a
non-IndoEuropean
language of unknown
origins, possibly the oldest
in Europe, and is spoken
in Spain, France, and the
U.S., Atxaga writes first in
Basque, and translates his
text into Spanish with the
help of his wife.

Obabakoak launched
Atxaga's career outside the
Basque Country when it
received the Spanish Premio
Nacional de Literatura.

Critics have referred to Bernardo Atxaga (b.1951) not just as a Basque novelist, but as *the* Basque novelist, and his writing seeks to evoke his heritage without taking refuge in rose-tinted nostalgia. He was born in the small Basque-speaking village of Asteasu, near San Sebastian, at a time when Basque areas were still reeling from Franco's attempts to eradicate the culture.

In *Obabakoak*—a collection of interrelated stories based in the fictional village of Obaba—Atxaga has transformed the then-rigid borders of Basque identity into an elastic new space, both solid and transient, recognizable and unrecognizable, dark and bright, tempting, appealing, and beckoning to the traveler. "Obabakoak" means both "of the people and things from Obaba" and "Stories from Obaba," and the village is depicted in the stories as experienced by someone: thus, for the young or Romantic it is a "toy valley" or *locus amoenus*; for the marginalized characters, including writers (who take shelter in primordial spaces such as woods, jungles, mountains, or the outskirts), it is violent, full of threats and dark secrets.

Obaba is a small, insignificant place to most people: letters from the big city often do not reach it. Yet, Atxaga does not connect power to size. In his view, like that of a naive painter, everything exists on the same plane and has the same value. Most of the action does not take place in the town center, but at scenic overlooks because, rather than a site to be looked upon, Obaba is a perspective from which the world is perceived. Furthermore, Obaba's borders are extremely permeable, as in a dream—a concept befitting a town whose name stems from the first words of a Basque lullaby ("*oba, oba*" means "hush, hush")—and readers are constantly carried to unknown and unlikely places such as the Amazon jungle.

Furthermore, Atxaga establishes an unbreakable connection between landscape and storytelling. The protagonist of the first story is a geographer who recollects his childhood in Obaba. This image of geographer-writer not only promotes credibility (à la Macondo for Gabriel García Márquez, page 204, Comala for Juan Rulfo, page 192, or Yoknapatawpha County for William Faulkner) but also calls attention to the process of fiction-making,

which is omnipresent in the tales. *Obabakoak* is full of stories and rewritings ("plagiarisms," as the narrator calls them) from the works of many authors such as Borges, Kafka, Celan, Calvino, Perec, Stevenson, Dante, Axular, and Cervantes.

The sleepy Basque-speaking village of Asteasu, near San Sebastian, the inspiration behind Obaba.

And above everything, *Obabakoak* maps the creative process of Bernardo Atxaga. Obaba is a pool into which he dives in order to explore the childhood experiences and mysteries that constituted the humus of his creativity. Thus, his exploration in "Childhoods" (the first section of the book) of the rich tradition of Basque beliefs from Asteasu precedes the series of narratives inspired by writers who influenced the author. The map of Atxaga's creative interior, his inner-life, shows an author who jumps over frontiers between literature and orality, Basque and non-Basque, different audiences and aesthetics—pre-, post-, and modern.

NEIL GAIMAN et al.

THE SANDMAN (1988–2015)

In the groundbreaking comic book saga, the personification of dreams must deal with various challenges and challengers, while approaching his own inevitable fate.

The Sandman: Master of Dreams #1 (© 1999 DC Comics) was written by Neil Gaiman and illustrated by Sam Kieth and Mike Dringenberg. Image courtesy of DC Comics.

Several minor characters from *The Sandman* have spun off into their own series and graphic novels. Gaiman himself wrote several stories about Death, who later appeared in several graphic novels by Jill Thompson.

The Sandman's version of Lucifer, who abdicates from the management of hell in the story "Season of Mists" (issues 21–8, 1990–1), starred in his own series written by Mike Carey, which ran for 75 issues between 2000 and 2006.

The Sandman was originally a minor DC Comics superhero, the alter ego of two crime fighters, Wesley Dodds and Hector Hall. In the late 1980s DC turned to British author Neil Gaiman (b.1960) to reimagine the character as part of DC's Vertigo imprint, focusing on more mature themes and stories.

The Sandman is a story about stories, but, more importantly, it is a story in which stories shape reality, in which there is, in fact, no difference between stories and reality. In this world, cosmology (forget about geography) is shaped by personality. Though there are several fixed settings in *The Sandman*, it's quickly made clear to us that how they appear and operate is a function of the whims of people at their heart. The central character, Dream (the titular Sandman who is known by many other names including Morpheus, Oneiros, and Kai'cul), is the third of seven siblings known as the "Endless," who represent immutable powers that govern the life of every living thing in the universe. But these powers have been given bodies and personalities, which in turn shapes how they present themselves and their realms. So, for example, the oldest Endless sibling, Destiny, is always shown walking through a garden of forking paths, carrying a book from which he reads what is to come. One of Dream's younger siblings, Desire (who is both male and female), meanwhile, lives in a castle shaped like a giant image of her/himself, because Desire is a narcissist. Dream, meanwhile, is the only Endless who plays the role of ruler of his realm properly, complete with a castle, attendants, and even a throne room, because Dream is obsessed with rules and propriety, with the supposed responsibility and demands of his office. But as several of his siblings point out to him, what he perceives as immutable laws are merely his choices. If Dream wanted it, the world of dreams—and thus the world as a whole—could look very different.

Furthermore, Dream—usually appearing as a pale, gangly young man with a mop of unruly dark hair—is only one manifestation of himself. In *Overture* (2015), which acts as a prequel to the events of *The Sandman*, Dream encounters many other aspects of himself, the Dreams of alien races, of animals, or plants, of sentient machines, and of far stranger creatures. Perhaps the only fixed point in the series is his older sister, Death, who nearly always appears as a cheerful, friendly young woman dressed in black jeans and a tank-top. But this, too, is in service of the story's tangled family drama. Death's role is to be the no-nonsense big sister who punctured Dream's self-importance and self-pity. The fact that she is also the calm, friendly face one sees at the end of it all has often been called one of the most striking and compelling aspects of Gaiman's world-building.

It's questionable whether Gaiman could have told a story in which the world is so mutable, so subject to the whims and mood-swings of fractious personalities, in any other medium but comics. The existence of pictures grounds the reader in reality where the written word alone might have left us scrambling for a foothold. The graphic medium also gives Gaiman a freedom that film or television could not have done. *The Sandman* shifts from multi-issue story arcs involving its main characters, to one-off stories whose heroes are sometimes never seen again, in which the Endless play only a supporting role; it also shifts genres, from horror to high

A representation of the many-monikered Sandman, by J. H. Williams III who collaborated with Gaiman on the reboot *Sandman Overture* in 2013.

fantasy to mythology to realist drama, in a way that only the comic-book medium can accommodate, and that is reflected in the shift in artwork styles. The more artistically ambitious Sandman stories, such as *Overture* or "The Kindly Ones" (issues 57–69, 1994–95), use nonrealist styles to convey the strangeness and alienness of their characters and settings. The former (illustrated by J. H. Williams III) breaks free of the restrictions of panels, and even the orientation of the page, to convey the chaos that Dream has unwittingly unleashed on the universe by allowing a "dream vortex" to go unchecked. The latter (illustrated by Marc Hempel, Kein Nowlan, D'Israeli, and others) uses the restriction of a 3x3 grid to illustrate how Dream, despite all his power, has trapped himself in the very rules he holds so dear.

If *The Sandman* is a story in which the characters shape their own world (and thus write their own fate), this is not, in the end, a power reserved only for the Endless, or for stars and other cosmic beings. One of the series' recurring characters is Hob Gadling, an ordinary fourteenth-century Englishman who simply decides not to die, and continues living to the twenty-first century and perhaps even beyond. When Hob asks why Death has spared him, he is told that the choice is ultimately up to him. In the world of *The Sandman*, as in the dreams that he sends to every living creature, it is we who shape and give meaning, we who tell the story.

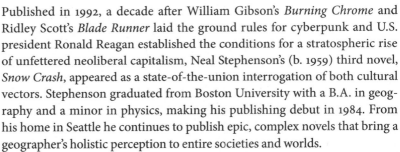

NEAL STEPHENSON

SNOW CRASH (1992)

In a hyper-Balkanized, ultra-franchised near future California an African-American-Korean hacker, Hiro Protagonist, and a fifteen-year-old skateboard Kourier, Y. T., battle the ultimate cyber-conspiracy.

First published by Bantam Books in 1992.

Snow Crash has influenced mainstream culture in everything from the hyper-stylized virtual reality action sequences of *The Matrix* films to the more philosophical notions of *Inception*—an idea as a virus.

While the 1986 computer game *Habitat* first applied the Sanskrit word avatar in a computer or online sense, *Snow Crash* brought the term into mainstream usage. Virtual world geography programs such as Google Earth and Nasa World Wind bear close similarities to the program, Earth, run in *Snow Crash's* Metaverse.

Published in 1992, a decade after William Gibson's *Burning Chrome* and Ridley Scott's *Blade Runner* laid the ground rules for cyberpunk and U.S. president Ronald Reagan established the conditions for a stratospheric rise of unfettered neoliberal capitalism, Neal Stephenson's (b. 1959) third novel, *Snow Crash*, appeared as a state-of-the-union interrogation of both cultural vectors. Stephenson graduated from Boston University with a B.A. in geography and a minor in physics, making his publishing debut in 1984. From his home in Seattle he continues to publish epic, complex novels that bring a geographer's holistic perception to entire societies and worlds.

It is the second decade of the twenty-first century, and the political impulse toward small government has reduced the U.S. to Fedland, where loyal citizens work for a bureaucracy obsessed with micromanaging what little U.S. territory remains. Citizens don't actually live in the U.S., but in L.A.'s Burbclaves, franchised housing developments—micro-nations—protected by MetaCops Unlimited. Or else, like *Snow Crash's* Hiro Protagonist, officially the greatest swordsman in the world, they reside in a converted container unit by the airport with Vitaly Chernobyl, leader singer of The Meltdowns.

Hiro was a cofounder of the Black Sun, the coolest place in the Metaverse, a 2K-HD-3D virtual reality world he co-coded. Now he freelances, uploading data for the Central Intelligence Corporation, an organization formed from a merger of the CIA and the Library of Congress, for which he gets paid per view, and he delivers pizza for Uncle Enzo's CosaNostra Pizza, Incorporated, through which he forms a working partnership with skateboarding Kourier, Y. T., aka Yours Truly—age fifteen, hip, sarcastic, sexually active, and eager to further herself in a place where divisions between country and company, micro-nation and franchise are even less meaningful than the hyper-inflated dollar.

Stephenson's world flicks between a broken L.A. and the Metaverse, a domain of computer avatars foreshadowing Oculus Rift virtual reality and Google Earth, referencing the lightcycle races of *Tron* and anticipating the physics-defying combat of *The Matrix*. Later the action moves to The Raft, a

vast floating refugee city based around a U.S. navy aircraft carrier under the control of megalomaniacal Texan billionaire L. Bob Rife.

Rife controls the infrastructure on which the Internet runs, and forms a distaff alliance with the psychopathic Raven, Fedland, and the Reverend Wayne Bedford's Pearly Gates Pentecostal Church franchise. Variously lined against these forces are Hiro, Y. T., Uncle Enzo's Mafia, Mr. Lee's Greater Hong Kong ("the granddaddy of all FOQNEs" [Franchise-Organized Quasi-National Entities]), and a cybernetic, nuclear-powered dog called Fido.

At the heart of Stephenson's satirical landscape is the duel between a status quo of individuals as free thinking agents in a free market and a vision of mind-controlled human drones created by a virus that crosses the line between biology and programming. The author explores complex theories about the neuro-linguistic origins of civilization and organized religion, extrapolating history as a struggle between rational religions—Judaism, Christianity, Islam, all codified in a Book—and ideas as linguistic viruses capable of physically rewriting the deep structures of the brain. All this is packaged between cartoonishly violent set pieces and knowingly smart dialogue, as befits a world where anyone with their own nuke can be a sovereign state.

Infected by a baroque whirlwind of often surreally prescient ideas, protracted info dumping, and James Cameron-esque cinematic spectacle, *Snow Crash* is, in its intertwining of cutting-edge technological and theological speculation as tools to interrogate the state of contemporary America, cool as snow, confrontational as crashing steel. Ironically, while Stephenson's comedic apotheosis of cyberpunk's first wave went culturally viral, his narrative has itself defeated all attempts to assimilate as the latest L.A. Hollywood franchise.

Graphic artist Igor Sobolevsky's 3D representation of CosaNostra Pizza Delivery Vehicle 2. Stephenson's central character, Hiro Protagonist, delivers pizza for Uncle Enzo's CosaNostra Pizza, Inc.

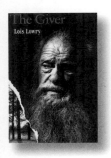

LOIS LOWRY

The Giver (1993)

Lowry's dystopian novel explores individuality, emotion, memory, and morality in a world of "Sameness," which assigns every person and action a time and place.

First published by Houghton Mifflin Company in 1993, *The Giver* is one of the books people most frequently tried to ban in the 1990s—for its depiction of euthanasia.

According to Lowry, the idea of exploring a world made peaceful by abolishing unsettling memories came to her through dealing with the declining faculties of her own aging father.

The death of her older sister, Helen, at twenty-eight, inspired Lowry's first novel, *A Summer to Die* (1977).

Lowry won the Newbery Award (1990) for *Number the Stars*, about the Holocaust, as well as for *The Giver* (1994).

Aimed mainly at a young audience, *The Giver* by Lois Lowry (b.1937) explores serious themes in complex ways. The author was in part inspired to write the story when her elderly father began to suffer dementia, and her thoughts turned to the idea of manipulating memory to avoid recalling distressing thoughts and emotions. Since its publication in 1993, the book has had a controversial reception: celebrated in some quarters for its perceptive exploration of the nature of authority, parents have also repeatedly demanded its removal from school libraries. Lowry herself has noted that she never thought of *The Giver* as dystopian; rather, "it was just a story about a kid making sense of a complicated world."

Nevertheless, the very landscape of the novel lays out the rigid values, culture, and expectations of its "Community." Told from the viewpoint of eleven-year-old Jonas, who will become at the forthcoming "Ceremony of Twelve" the next "Receiver of Memories," we see his world as he has been raised to see it. Every building in the idealized, ordered Community is named according to an obvious function—Birthing Unit, Dwelling Areas, School— except one, the Annex, a small building beside the House of the Old, where Jonas will soon live. The multi-talented Jonas, unquestioningly humble in this world that eschews individuality, initially deeply approves of the order built into his landscape.

Four factors awaken Jonas. First, for reasons never explained, and thus more like fairy-tale arbitrariness than science-fiction extrapolation, Jonas comes to see things "change," first for an instant, then more persistently. Only later does he learn that the visual oddity is color, the absence of which we, seeing through his eyes, had not noticed. Second, and less arbitrarily, Jonas has a slightly erotic dream that leads his parents, smilingly, to initiate him into the life-long regime of a pill a day to suppress "Stirrings." Third, through the hands-on transfer of memories from the older Receiver, now the Giver, Jonas receives knowledge of a world full not only of color but music, joy, weather, pain, dread, agony, loss, and even hills. Only then do we realize that the Community is not only gray and climate-controlled but relentlessly flat.

Fourth, the Community punishes non-conformity—whether intentional, as in disobedience, or accidental, through incapacity—with "Release." The Giver allows Jonas to see a tape of Jonas's father, a "Nurturer," giving Release to the less robust of identical twins, to avoid confusion in the Community. Release, Jonas finally sees, is death by injection. Everything in his perfect world reveals itself as potentially false and cruel.

The Receiver holds all cultural memory, no matter how painful, so that others need not; however, in the rare event that the Community needs venerable wisdom to confront an unanticipated situation, the Receiver can be consulted. Keeping those memories, he lives—in the Annex—alone. When the Receiver begins to "train" Jonas by memory transfer, the Receiver becomes the Giver. But Jonas, too, to soothe a difficult infant "newchild" to sleep, transfers pleasant memories to him. One can be a Giver in more than one way. One can use wisdom in more than one way.

Together, the old and the young Giver devise a disruptive plan to allow Jonas individuality in "Elsewhere," with its hills and weather, and the Community to suffer enough—from the memories that will be released by Jonas's absence—to transcend stultifying perfection. What will happen? Although the book was conceived as freestanding, Lowry later created three companion novels (*Gathering Blue*, 2000, *Messenger*, 2004, and *Son*, 2012) that let that let us know of Jonas's ultimate development and include the wider landscape that the Community seeks to ignore.

PHILIP PULLMAN

HIS DARK MATERIALS (1995–2000)

Pullman's multiverse-spanning trilogy is the story of Lyra Bellaqua,
a young girl who is fated to be a second Eve, and the choices she makes
that will save or doom the worlds.

First published by Scholastic Ltd and Scholastic Ltd/ David Fickling Books (*The Amber Spyglass*) between 1995 and 2000.

Pullman has written several shorter works set in the same world: *Lyra's Oxford* (2003), *Once Upon a Time in the North* (2008) and the forthcoming *Book of Dust*.

Certain passages of *The Amber Spyglass* were cut from the U.S. edition because their implied sexual content was considered inappropriate for a younger audience.

There have been several attempts to ban *His Dark Materials* from libraries and schools. It is the second most challenged literary work in the U.S.

Philip Pullman's (b.1946) *His Dark Materials* trilogy (*Northern Lights*, published in 1995 and entitled *The Golden Compass* in the U.S.; *The Subtle Knife*, 1997; and *The Amber Spyglass*, 2000) has been a publishing phenomenon, selling more than seventeen million copies worldwide and translated into more than forty languages. The series is loved by many—both young and old—for its rich characters and the subtle complexities of its plot, as well as for its engaging re-readability. Although marketed for children and young adults, *His Dark Materials* can be read on many levels. For younger readers, it is a compelling adventure story full of new and beautiful worlds, while older readers will observe a treatise on free will and a sharp critique of religion.

Pullman worked as a teacher for many years and had minor success with his early novels before writing his award-winning series. Inspired by the works of William Blake and John Milton, the trilogy is in many ways a retelling of *Paradise Lost*. In Pullman's own words, "My books are about killing God."

The series begins in Oxford. It is not the Oxford University of our own, less obviously magical, world—for one thing, people in this alternate world are accompanied by daemons, physical manifestations of their souls in animal form—but one that is close enough that we can almost recognize it. It is this feeling of being somewhere that is almost recognizable—almost known, yet not quite home—that characterizes the worlds of this series.

The Golden Compass opens with Lyra hiding in a room that is forbidden to her. She creeps into a wardrobe that is "bigger than she'd thought"— echoing the wardrobe that leads to C. S. Lewis's Narnia (see page 178)—but Lyra's wardrobe doesn't open to a new world. Instead, it is Lyra's own curiosity and quest for knowledge that broadens her world.

When her friend Roger goes missing, she is at first comforted by the appearance of the charming Mrs. Coulter—that is, until Lyra discovers that Mrs. Coulter may be complicit in her friend's kidnapping. With the aid of the alethiometer, her golden compass, Lyra sets out in search for him. And as she journeys to the wildness of the North, she discovers that hers may not be the

only world there is. Place is inherently tied to knowledge in this series. The witches who live in the north of Lyra's world do so because the veil between worlds is thin and their knowledge comes from this proximity. Place is also inherently tied to perspective: "Is this a new world?" one character asks, and is answered, "Not to those born in it." Things look different, depending on where they are seen.

The Subtle Knife (1997) begins in our world, but protagonist Will Parry soon discovers a portal to the world of Cittàgazze. Here he meets Lyra, and becomes the guardian of the subtle knife—the blade that can cut doors through universes. Yet travel between worlds is not without consequences. Each opening causes the loss of Dust, a significant elementary particle. The Church in Lyra's world sees Dust, and the knowledge that accompanies it, as a manifestation of original sin, and wishes to destroy it. But Dust, like knowledge, is necessary.

In *The Amber Spyglass* (2000), yet more worlds are explored. From the land of the dead to that of the elephantine mulefa, Lyra is forced to make her fated choice. But once Lyra's choice is made, the doors between the worlds must be closed—never to be opened again.

Lyra and Pantalaimon, her daemon, meet the armored bear, Iorek Byrnison.

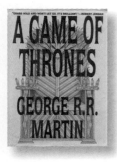

GEORGE R. R. MARTIN

A GAME OF THRONES (1996)

In the world of the Seven Kingdoms, diverse characters play the "game of thrones," a fantastic War of the Roses that can have only one victor.

First published by Bantam Books in 1996.

A Game of Thrones, while critically acclaimed, was not a breakaway hit. Martin's epic took a while to build steam, and sometimes nobody would show up to book signings.

One of Martin's strongest literary influences was Jack Vance, who wrote pulp science-fiction stories, mysteries, and space operas, among other works.

When asked about his dynamic female characters, Martin, who identifies as feminist, said: "You know, I've always considered women to be people."

George R. R. Martin (b.1948), dubbed by many the "American Tolkien," published *A Game of Thrones* in 1996, during a difficult interval for fantasy literature, which was, at the time, struggling to keep up with the wise-cracking chutzpah of urban-fantasy stories. *A Game of Thrones* emerged as a link between worlds, with all the black humor and quick wit of urban fantasy, combined with the scale and drama of an epic story heavily influenced by medieval history. This heady blend of tradition and modernity made the Song of Ice and Fire series a publishing phenomenon that has been translated into over forty-five languages and spawned a hit television spin-off.

A Game of Thrones focuses on the Lord Eddard ("Ned") Stark and his family, Northern outsiders, whose aversion to politics make them essential to the reader's point of view. The novel begins, seductively, with a scene of dark magic that the reader then doubts for the next 600 pages. What were the "Others?" How did they connect to the politics of the Seven Kingdoms, and what was the true focus of this multi-perspective story? What makes the novel so compelling is often what it leaves unsaid.

Martin's first novel divides the story geographically across the "Seven Kingdoms:" from the frozen north and Winterfell, home of the Starks, to the seat of the Iron Throne in King's Landing and the grasslands of Essos. The latter is where Daenerys, another central character and one of the last remaining members of the noble house of Targaryen, comes of age among the Dothraki warriors. Martin's focus here on an adolescent girl—destined to become the powerful "Mother of Dragons"—marks a distinct change from the genre's frequent interest in young male protagonists. He is working in territory that was previously staked out by feminist fantasy authors such as Mercedes Lackey and Tanya Huff, who also produced epic worlds.

Part of the adventure of reading *A Game of Thrones* lies in the way that Martin links place with perspective. Ned Stark's thoughts are always on ice and snow, his son Bran longs for the sky, and Daenerys is tempered by the heat of Essos. Ever since Tolkien added runic clues to his map in *The Hobbit*, cartography has always been essential to the genre. Nowhere is this

more apparent than in *A Game of Thrones*, where ancient families, political factions, and indigenous communities battle for control of overlapping territories. Along with heraldry, mapping is the chief cultural element of the Middle Ages that Martin draws upon in his creation of a mixed feudal society. Rather than romanticizing these systems, *A Game of Thrones* sets out to expose the violence and corruption that underpin them.

Readers are offered glimpses of this dangerous, breathing world through a number of competing perspectives, often separated by culture and geography. Our understanding of the epic map is always incomplete. Canadian fantasy writer Guy Gavriel Kay used the same technique in his *Fionavar* trilogy, and Martin adapts this to a truly massive world. Communities whose fate depends upon mapping—such as the Wildings, on the other side of the Wall—are often those who resist such colonial practices. Martin has cited Hadrian's Wall as an influence for his 300-mile-long, 700-foot-tall "border," but critics such as Michail Zontos have also described it as a metaphor for the American frontier. Your perspective depends upon which side you end up on, and who draws the map around you. The diverse regions of Westeros are accompanied by living languages, developed in meticulous detail by linguist and conlanger David J. Peterson. His Dothraki language (which you can now

Lord Eddard Stark (portrayed by Sean Bean) and his family, kneel before Robert Baratheon (Mark Addy), King of the Seven Kingdoms of Westeros.

take a course on) emerged from only a few words and phrases that Martin had created. What began with Tolkien's working Elvish language—immortal words—has culminated in a series of languages, even dialects, adopted by a range of cultures.

A Game of Thrones begins as an enclosed, Gothic tale, then explodes outward along with the Stark family, taking advantage of its fantastic cartography. Like a darker version of the Pevensies, the Stark children grapple with a hostile landscape, whose dangers and inequalities mirror the structures of late feudalism. Magic remains within the space of the uncanny, always an undertone, while economics and the politics of lineage are the monstrous forces that keep everything turning. Bards are destitute, princesses are pawns, and the maesters, like Jon Snow, "know nothing." Sometimes this ignores the dazzling beauty that was also present during the Middle Ages—the painting, lapidary, verse, and celestial music—but Martin's focus on tragedy reminds us that this is not Disney's Middle Ages. He presents a diverse cast of characters: female translators, disabled boys, sly eunuchs, and queer knights. These people set up camp in our brain, because they err, desire, betray, regret.

Much of the appeal of *A Game of Thrones* has arisen from the idea that it *isn't* a fantasy novel—that it is a more realistic, adult version of a medieval romance. In fact, the opposite is true: *A Game of Thrones* is every inch a fantasy novel, as proven by its imaginative terrain and speculative understanding of magic. The best fantasy novels are full of ambivalent characters, fallible humans (and others), negotiating a world whose powers and origins they can never fully comprehend. The dwarf Tyrion, whose mind is his sword, has an ancestor in David and Leigh Eddings's character of Beldin. Martin has also cited the historical fiction of Maurice Druon as a significant influence, and the personalities in Druon's *The Accursed Kings* series exemplify the paradoxes of the medieval world. They are also trying to understand a wild space whose edges remain unmapped.

Critics often describe loving the series in spite of its dragons, but readers and fans alike know perfectly well that dragons are as old as storytelling itself. Rather than revitalizing a genre for a new audience, *A Game of Thrones* has shown us what fantasy was always capable of, from King Arthur to the Iron Throne.

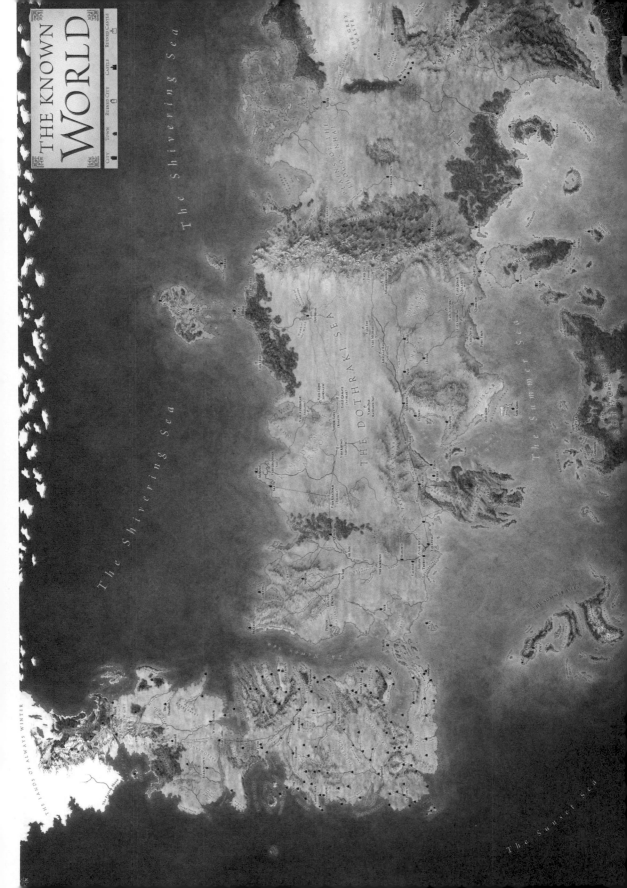

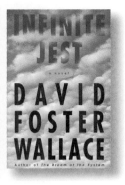

DAVID FOSTER WALLACE

Infinite Jest (1996)

Popular entertainment dominates in David Foster Wallace's immense and complex vision of a future North America, the setting for a story that encompasses addiction, the power of advertising, and tennis.

First published by Little, Brown and Company in 1996.

The book's title is taken from *Hamlet*, its working title was *A Failed Entertainment*.

Wallace wrote many non-fiction and short fiction pieces for newspapers and magazines, as well as the well-received essay collection *A Supposedly Fun Thing I'll Never Do Again* (1997), and a book of short stories titled *Brief Interviews with Hideous Men* (1999).

His last, unfinished novel, *The Pale King*, was published in 2011 and was a finalist for the 2012 Pulitzer Prize.

In the opening scene of *Infinite Jest*, Harold James Incandenza—a competitive teenage tennis player, known as "Hal"—reflects that there's a very good chance that if he makes the finals of the WhataBurger Southwest Junior Invitational tennis tournament on Sunday he'll get to play in front of Venus Williams.

There's nothing particularly surprising about this. It's an average, ordinary scrap of novelistic detail. Why wouldn't Venus Williams be there? And why wouldn't he want to play in front of her? Except that when David Foster Wallace's (1962–2008) astounding work was published in 1996, Williams was only fifteen. She hadn't even played in her first Grand Slam tournament yet. Wallace's casual name-dropping is a bold piece of near-future prognostication, one that marks, or marked, *Infinite Jest* as what it is—a work of science fiction. Though, like all works of art set in the future, it is fated, over time, to become an alternate present instead.

The exact year in which the events of *Infinite Jest* take place is famously hard to pin down. It has been persuasively argued, based on a few carefully gleaned details, that much of the book takes place in 2009, but in the world of *Infinite Jest* years are no longer identified by numbers. The narrative is set in the era of what Wallace calls "subsidized time," in which, every year, a corporation pays to have that year named after one of its products. So among the dates that figure in the timeline of *Infinite Jest* are the Year of the Trial-Size Dove Bar, the Year of the Whisper-Quiet Maytag Dishmaster, and most prominently (you can almost feel Wallace's glee as he types) the Year of the Depend Adult Undergarment.

Infinite Jest isn't known primarily as a work of science fiction, of course. It's better known for its extravagant, ungovernable size—1,088 pages in paperback, counting endnotes—and its enormous literary complexity, which together have turned it into the kind of cult object that young men and women with heavy black spectacles lecture about at cocktail parties: a literary shillelagh for beating one's intellectual rivals into submission. It presents interpretive challenges as serious as James Joyce's *Ulysses* (1922), and it has

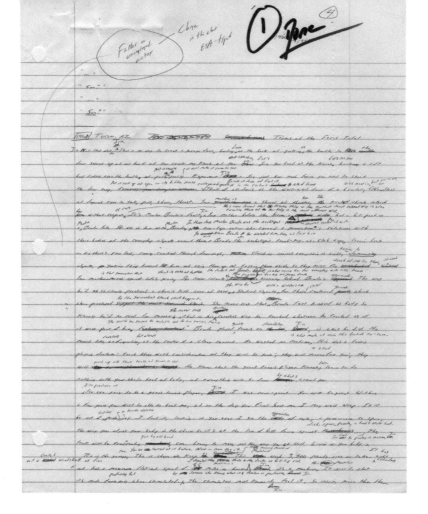

spawned a legion of academic papers, guides, commentaries, spreadsheets, diagrams, and wikis. But the world it takes place in is not our world. *Infinite Jest* is science fiction, just well-scrubbed of any trace of science fiction's pulpy roots. Wallace came to science fiction as a crossover artist from literary fiction, working in the high-art tradition of Thomas Pynchon and Don DeLillo.

But there was something about writing in other worlds that Wallace felt made it easier to get at our own. He liked things to be just slightly askew. His first novel, *The Broom of the System*, was published in 1987, but it's set in 1990. By that time, part of Ohio has been turned into a man-made topographical feature called the Great Ohio Desert. It's meant, apparently, as an immense work of art, "a point of savage reference for the good people of Ohio. A place to fear and love." (It's mostly referred to by its acronym: the G.O.D.)

Wallace wasn't a realist, but he wasn't interested in predicting the future either. He didn't think there would actually be a Great Ohio Desert, in 1990 or ever. He wasn't a world-builder, like J. R. R. Tolkien or Frank Herbert, and he didn't need his fictional otherworlds to be plausible. Rather, time functioned for him as a solvent, a way of making reality more malleable, so that

First page of a handwritten draft of *Infinite Jest*.

he could manipulate it and exaggerate it to express the things he wanted to express. Wallace's science fiction is a form of satire—the future is a place to play in, where he can pull aside the veil and reveal the true nature of things. It's a trick learned from those roots in DeLillo and Pynchon, whose works are veined with science-fictional tropes and plotlines. The Airborne Toxic Event of DeLillo's *White Noise* (1985), for example, wouldn't have looked out of place in *Infinite Jest*.

Infinite Jest has two protagonists. One is Hal, the aforementioned pro-digiously intelligent seventeen-year-old who attends the Enfield Tennis Academy. The other is Don Gately, a recovering Demerol addict and reformed burglar who works at a rehabilitation clinic called Ennet House, located near the tennis academy.

Before he died, Hal's father James, who founded the tennis academy, was the patriarch of a family of eccentric prodigies reminiscent of the Glass family in J. D. Salinger's *Franny and Zooey* (1961). James Incandenza, commonly known merely as Himself, was also an avid amateur filmmaker, and he created a film so addictively entertaining that anyone watching it becomes paralyzed and can pay attention to nothing else, to the point where he or she lapses irredeemably into catatonia. "Whoever saw it," Wallace writes, "wanted nothing else ever in life but to see it again, and then again, and so on." It's like the Monty Python sketch about a joke so funny that everyone who hears it dies from laughing. Before the book begins, Himself has committed suicide by sticking his head in a microwave oven.

Wallace wrote *Infinite Jest* just before the Internet came into its own as a mainstream entertainment medium and, as a result, its world is endowed with Wallace's own homegrown version of an electronic global entertainment network, InterLace. It's more or less a video-on-demand system. People use teleputers, or TPs, to access it, and films are stored on cartridges, not tapes or disks. These inventions weren't just playful whims to Wallace. They exempli-fied the enormous existential challenges that technology now presents to all of us. "Today's person spends way more time in front of screens," he once told the writer David Lipsky. "In fluorescent-lit rooms, in cubicles, being on one end or the other of an electronic data transfer. And what is it to be human and alive and exercise your humanity in that kind of exchange?"

The world of *Infinite Jest* has its own distinctive geopolitics as well. Under the leadership of its president, a former Las Vegas entertainer, usu-ally referred to by Wallace as "Johnny Gentle, Famous Crooner," the U.S. has merged with Mexico and Canada to form a megastate called the Organization of North American Nations. (Again, check the acronym, with its sly wink to the Bible and masturbation shame: O.N.A.N. More glee.) A large part of New England has been partitioned and written off as a massive toxic waste reposi-tory known as the "Great Concavity" (it's a spiritual descendant of the G.O.D. from *The Broom of the System*). Radioactivity from the Great Concavity has given rise to terrifying herds of feral hamsters that scour the Earth, leaving the land behind them bare of all vegetal matter.

This unstable arrangement provides the mechanism for the plot of *Infinite Jest*, to the extent that it has one. The Great Concavity runs along the border of Quebec and, inevitably, pollutants and toxins leach across the border, not to mention feral hamsters. Radical cells of Quebecois separatists oppose the Great Concavity (which they insist on referring to, by Wallacian logic, as the Great Convexity) and, by extension, O.N.A.N. as well, and they'll stop short of nothing, even terrorism, to make their opposition felt. Their weapon of choice? The fatally entertaining film created by James Incandenza, which they spend much of the book trying to get hold of. The film is called, of course, *Infinite Jest*.

Infinite Jest, the novel, is an example of literary maximalism, one of the dominant fictional modes of the 1990s; other examples include DeLillo's *Underworld* (1997) and Zadie Smith's *White Teeth* (2000). As in those works, there's a sense that Wallace is trying to import the multicolored, multilayered fabric of an entire world into his novel intact, leaving nothing out. Not unlike those of *Underworld* and *White Teeth*, the world he's trying to import is one that he's also creating at the same time, detail by detail, hamster by hamster. Writing the book was a gargantuan task. "I've never done something where I've just had to hold so many discrete pieces of information in my head at one time," he told Lipsky. "You ever see *Johnny Mnemonic*? I mean, he gets this sort of data overload, and his ears bleed." It would have been easier, of course, in some ways, to describe the world as it is. Certainly Wallace was up to the task: He was a first-class journalist and essayist as well as a novelist. But, at the time when he wrote *Infinite Jest*, Wallace considered realism to be all but bankrupt, and useless for what he was trying to do. Realism was too easy and familiar for the reader—not shocking enough. He wanted to jolt people out of their comfort zones, so they could make contact with real feelings and raw emotions, and see the world as it is. To do that, he paradoxically had to put them in an unreal world.

Having suffered from clinical depression for decades, Wallace committed suicide in 2008, leaving behind his fiction of another world to help the rest of us survive this one. "Look man," Wallace once told an interviewer, "we'd probably most of us agree that these are dark times, and stupid ones, but do we need fiction that does nothing but dramatize how dark and stupid everything is? In dark times, the definition of good art would seem to be art that locates and applies CPR to those elements of what's human and magical that still live and glow, despite the times' darkness."

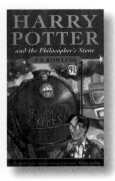

J. K. ROWLING

HARRY POTTER AND THE PHILOSOPHER'S STONE (1997)

Orphaned, unwanted Harry Potter realizes his magical powers at Hogwarts School while battling the evil wizard Voldemort, who seeks the life-giving Philosopher's Stone.

First published by Bloomsbury in 1997.

The Harry Potter series has spawned multiple additional books, including Hogwarts textbooks, the fables read by wizard children (*The Tales of Beedle the Bard*), a short online story by Rowling, and a stage play (*Harry Potter and the Cursed Child*).

Nicholas Flamel, depicted in *Philosopher's Stone* as a friend of Albus Dumbledore, was an actual fourteenth-century scribe who gained a posthumous reputation as an alchemist. His house still stands in Paris, the oldest stone house in the city.

Harry Potter hardly needs an introduction. The series has sold more than 450 million copies worldwide and has been translated into more than seventy languages. Moreover, the world of Harry Potter extends far beyond the books themselves. The blockbuster adaptations are the second highest-grossing film series of all time, and Harry Potter pervades popular culture. From video games to board games, from fan fiction to fan sites, the Harry Potter world and characters have been used and discussed again and again. When J. K. Rowling (b.1965) wrote *Harry Potter and the Philosopher's Stone* in 1997 (published in the U.S. as *Harry Potter and the Sorcerer's Stone*), she sparked one of the greatest and largest fandoms in history.

Perhaps the greatest appeal of the Wizarding World is that it is one both familiar and unfamiliar. Our world is translated into another, parallel world, which operated on rules sometimes similar, sometimes different. Rowling's creation expands through the seven books to reference wizards in differ-ent parts of continental Europe (and the world, in the afterlife of the Harry Potter fandom universe). However, a global presence is not necessary to be transported to a mirror image of our own universe made magical: the place is suburban England; travel is on English trains; schools have classrooms and dormitories. The familiarity of each of these locations is made fresh—sometimes strange—as the reader delights in the intersection—sometimes collision—of the wizarding and Muggle (non-wizarding) existences. The word "utopia" does not quite apply here, but neither is this the "dystopia" popular in contemporary fiction. The neologism "contopia" might suit this world alongside our own, sometimes even within our own, but still function-ing successfully on its own. As Hagrid explains to Harry, wizards keep their world secret because "everyone'd be wantin' magic solutions to their prob-lems. Nah, we're best left alone."

Harry actually begins his life in a wizarding home, but is ushered out of that world and into the life of Muggles with his aunt and uncle, not through a change of location or consciousness, but a traumatic event that he only remembers in dreams. Rowling at first merely suggests the happenings of that

night celebrated by every wizard in England: Voldemort has gone into hiding after spectacularly failing to kill the one-year-old Harry. As Voldemort does manage to kill his parents, Lily and James Potter, "the boy who lived" must be hidden away in the Muggle world. He is subjected to eleven years of privation on Privet Drive with the Dursleys, who are not just aggressively Muggle (partly in response to Aunt Petunia's embarrassment over her sister's magical abilities) but also petty and mean.

As in the *Chronicles of Narnia*, readers are acquainted with the space and environment of wizard life through the eyes of a newcomer. Harry does not understand the flood of letters that are so determined to be opened only by him that hundreds of them follow the Dursleys's escape to a deserted island. The letters are the first of the adapted objects mentioned earlier. These are missives that can fly, squeeze under doors, come down chimneys, and change address at will if the recipient changes locations. Sentient letters are only part of Rowling's versatile system of communication technology—owls are the major means of communication for all wizards. Simple oral instructions from their owners send owls off to carry letters and packages back and forth between wizards, anytime, anywhere. Photographs, newspaper illustrations, and paintings are also forms of communication, conveniently allowing their occupants to move about and even move between frames to convey information to their viewers.

Rupert Grint, Daniel Radcliffe, and Emma Watson play Ron, Harry, and Hermione in Warner Bros' 2001 film adaptation.

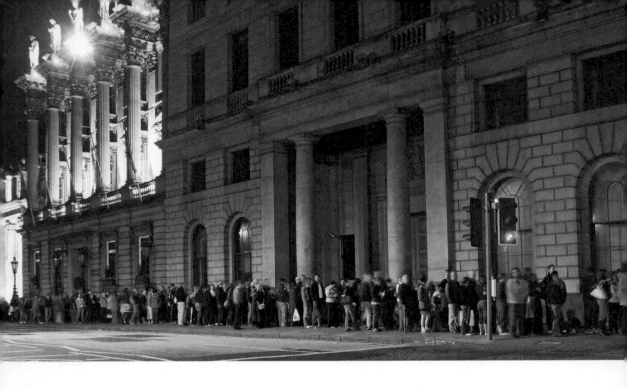

A lengthy queue snakes all the way down Prince's Street into St Andrew's Square in Rowling's adopted Edinburgh at midnight on the day of release for the seventh and last book in the series *Harry Potter and the Deathly Hallows*, July 2007.

Rowling's world is full of objects and practices that possess enhanced capabilities for wizards, showing points at which magic and Muggle technologies morph into something new. Brooms are not cleaning tools at Hogwarts; instead they are, not unlike bicycles, modes of transportation for one or two people and equipment for organized sports. Similarly, the now-famous (and popular tourist photo op at King's Cross Station) Platform 9¾ is only accessed by hurling oneself at the wall between the Muggle train platforms. The Hogwarts Express itself seems to operate just like an ordinary Muggle train, aside from the fact that it has a platform invisible to most of the station's travelers. That last point indicates another practical advantage of this parallel mode of transportation: It is not detectable by Muggles, thus avoiding the necessity of applying "memory" charms to those baffled non-magical humans who would be alarmed at the sight of people flitting about on broomsticks.

The juxtaposition of a train and broomsticks for transportation purposes—as opposed to cars, which are comically mysterious to wizards—exemplifies a feature of Rowling's world that may seem puzzling: A fundamental distinction between our existences is the markedly different capabilities of Muggles and wizards to master, and then manage, the knowledge required to make technology or magic work. We have developed complex mechanical and electronic products and systems external to our beings that control our lives probably more than we like to acknowledge. If a car coughs and stalls, many are helpless in the face of the blinking lights on the dashboard. If a computer screen is suddenly blue and blank, a visit to the electronics store is in store. Witches and wizards, trained for seven years in the magical arts, learn to control certain forces with their own minds and talents to accomplish similar tasks. We flip a switch on a flashlight; illumination springs from a wizard's wand at the sound of "*Lumos!*" After a big meal Molly Weasley waves her wand at the dirty dishes, and they quietly begin to wash themselves in the sink. A mirror does not reflect one's own face, but, as Dumbledore says to Harry, the Mirror of Erised "shows us nothing more or less than the deepest, most desperate desire of our hearts."

It may assumed that the potential scope of a wizard's abilities would bestow unlimited powers, but Rowling has not resorted to that easy way out. For instance, they choose not to exercise complete magical control over their world. One question raised by magical skill is the creation of wealth: Why not conjure up endless supplies of money? Some wizards are wealthier than others (the rich, haughty Malfoys versus the poor but good-hearted Weasleys), but they do not generate gold out of thin air, despite the Philosopher's Stone. Neither is the handling of their wealth what we might expect. One of Harry's first visits in the magical world is with Hagrid to Gringotts Bank, a Dickensian-looking establishment staffed by goblins so nasty they even intimidate Hagrid. We might expect wizards merely to render their money invisible, or enchant it to prevent theft. Instead, Harry enters an institutional setting organized vaguely like Muggle banks, but with special features: Gringotts sits above enchanted passages hundreds of miles beneath London, reached by a goblin driving a sort of miner's cart, with dragons guarding the most precious vaults.

This existence is imbued with magic, but is not effortless, uncomplicated, or free from evil. The world envisioned in *Philosopher's Stone* raises numerous questions addressed throughout the series: How does one negotiate with non-human creatures who also have powers? Can wizards create life? What happens if they try to control Muggle lives? To Rowling's credit, she has conceived rich possibilities, not just for plot purposes, but to explore how we interact with nature, exert power over others, and cooperate in a diverse and sometimes dangerous world.

CHINA MIÉVILLE

THE BAS-LAG CYCLE (2000–04)

The seminal New Weird novels of China Miéville's mold-breaking cycle intermingle urban fantasy, steampunk, science fiction, horror, and surrealism, engrossing readers with visions of wonder and grotesquery.

First published by Macmillan between 2000 and 2004.

Miéville was an avid player of Dungeons and Dragons and other roleplaying games when he was younger and still collects roleplaying bestiaries.

In addition to writing novels and short stories, Miéville also wrote the superhero comic series *Dial H* for DC Comics.

Born in Norwich, England, in 1972 and brought up in London, China Miéville has become a daring and influential voice in speculative fiction, renowned for his sweeping imaginative scope, erudite political perspectives, and richly evocative prose style. His debut novel *King Rat* is a London phantasmagoria—kin to works such as Neil Gaiman's *Neverwhere*—but it was with the publication of *Perdido Street Station* in 2000 that Miéville became a literary sensation. The Arthur C. Clarke award-winning novel and the two sequels that followed, *The Scar* and *Iron Council*, together comprise the Bas-Lag cycle, a trilogy seminal to the literary movement dubbed the "New Weird." Looking back to the weird fiction of the early twentieth-century—a genre most closely associated with H. P. Lovecraft, but which also includes such under-appreciated luminaries as William Hope Hodgson, Clark Ashton Smith, and Algernon Blackwood—the New Weird exists in what the sinister crime-boss Mr. Motley of *Perdido Street Station* would call "the hybrid zone": a liminal space somewhere between existing genres, borrowing liberally from worlds too-often deemed incompatible. In Bas-Lag artificial intelligence and quantum mechanics mix with magic and monsters in a heady, hallucinogenic brew, simmering with unruly potential.

Perdido Street Station takes place entirely in the city of New Crobuzon: a churning industrial megalopolis calling to mind not only Victorian London but also Cairo, the French Quarter of New Orleans, and Mervyn Peake's Gormenghast castle (see page 170). The many districts of Miéville's sprawling, baroquely described city are rendered in loving detail, from the eerie, crime-ridden slums of Bonetown, shadowed by the ribs of some centuries-dead behemoth, to the alchemical laboratories of Brock Marsh, where badger-familiars run errands for masters somewhere between scientists and sorcerers.

Magic—or thaumaturgy, as it is more generally termed in Bas-Lag—suffuses New Crobuzon's labyrinthine streets, but it is treated as a science, obeying its own distinct laws and logic, rather than an unknowable, uncontrollable mythic force.

Ruled in *Perdido Street Station* by Mayor Bentham Rudgutter, and in *Iron Council* by the coldly calculating Mayor Eliza Stem-Fulcher, New Crobuzon is a place of intrigue and everyday brutality. Though nominally a democracy, the city has strongly authoritarian leanings and rapacious colonial ambitions. Disguised militia make the city a gigantic panopticon, plain-clothes agents blending in with the crowd to ruthlessly enforce the will of their masters, while the rails radiating out from the imperialist metropole extend its power to all corners of Rohagi, Bas-Lag's most-described continent. Resistance to the oppressive Fat Sun party seethes throughout *Perdido Street Station* in the form of the righteously seditious newspaper *Runagate Rampant* and the mysterious outlaw and social bandit Jack Half-a-Prayer, only to boil over into open revolution in *Iron Council*, the most overtly political of the Bas-Lag cycle.

Two other cities feature prominently in the Bas-Las cycle. Armada, a pirate-city fashioned from thousands of lashed-together boats, forms the setting of *The Scar*. The quasi-anarchic politics of Armada contrast markedly with the oligarchic corruption and totalitarian tendencies of New Crobuzon: here the various communities of the city jostle for power, debating which direction the flotilla should drift, which seas to sail, which targets to pick. Press-ganged captives and natives of the city co-exist uneasily, while erstwhile slaves and convicts find freedom and a new life on the waves. As in New Crobuzon, each neighborhood of Armada possesses its own unique character, like the lucrative library-district of Booktown, the vampiric fiefdom of Dry Fall, or Clockhouse Spur, the intellectuals' quarter, to name just a few. The eponymous Iron Council of the third book is similarly egalitarian, a "perpetual train" populated by radical train laborers turned renegades, gone rogue into the wilds of Rohagi. The train-city's odyssey across the nightmarish mutant wasteland of the Catacopic Stain and other strange lands forms the heart of Iron Council.

Other cities receive only tantalizing mention. There is Tesh, the City of Crawling Liquid, a place of "moats and glass cats, and the Catoblepas Plain and merchant trawlers and tramp diplomats and the Crying Prince," an economic rival and sometimes military enemy of New Crobuzon; High Cromlech, a macabre metropolis peopled by quick and abdead in intricate castes and ruled by the embalmed thanati; The Gengris, monstrous subaquatic realm of the grindylow, a place of limb-farms and bile workshops and unthinkable weapons; Maru'ahm, with its casino-parliament and cardsharp senators; the crocodile double-city of the Brothers; Shud zar Myron zar Koni, City of Ratjinn, the Witchocracy of the Firewater Straits.

These allusions and countless others give Bas-Lag a feeling of place rarely found in fantasy fiction, a sense of depth and verisimilitude further fostered by the densely layered history Miéville hints at throughout the cycle. Never overburdening readers with heavy-handed exposition, the novels are scattered with allusions and subtle details to past events and political entities.

Overleaf: The massive conurbation of New Crobuzon. Miéville describes its sprawling districts in great detail, from the crime-ridden slums of Bonetown to the laboratories of Brock Marsh. Map by illustrator Lee Moyer.

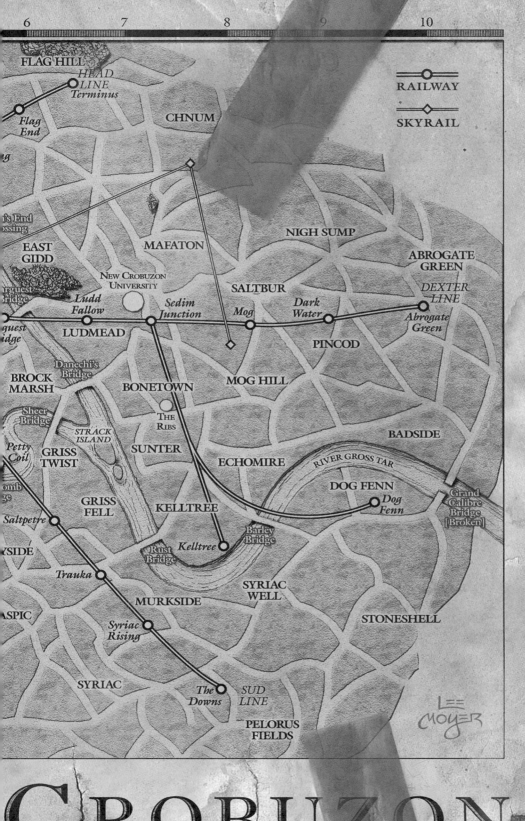

CROBUZON

From piecing together these tidbits we learn of the Ghosthead Empire and their possibility mines; of the bloodsucking Malarial Queendom ruled by the terrifying anophelii, of the Ravening of Bered Kai Nev, the continent across the Swollen Sea; and of the Torque-bombing of Suroch and Jheshull, left in nightmarish ruins. This version of the past—resolutely anti-nostalgic, punctuated with atrocity, shaped by such forces as technology, class, imperialism, and revolution—resonates strongly with Miéville's political outlook and steadfast historical materialism.

A founding member of Left Unity and a founding editor of Salvage, "a quarterly of revolutionary arts and letters," Miéville is an outspoken Marxist and acknowledges the importance of politics in his novels. He wrote his PhD dissertation—now published in book form as *Between Equal Rights*—on Marxism and international law. While a socialist perspective informs the political conflicts and intrigues of Bas-Lag, the novels stubbornly evade reduction, politically or otherwise. Miéville is adamant that his books not be read as allegory. "I'm not a leftist trying to smuggle in my evil message by the nefarious means of fantasy novels," he sardonically insists. "I've invented this world that I think is really cool and I have these really big stories to tell in it and one of the ways that I find to make that interesting is to think about it politically. If you want to do that too, that's fantastic. But if not, isn't this a cool monster?"

Bas-Lag certainly has no shortage of monsters. Miéville scorns the now-clichéd Tolkienian favorites in favor of decidedly less familiar creatures, some culled from mythology, others wholly invented. Instead of orcs, elves, and dwarves, Bas-Lag is peopled with beings such as the beetle-headed khepri, the lumbering, vegetal catcacae, the amphibious, water-shaping vodyanoi, the vulturine garuda, the resilient scabmettlers, and the elegant, enigmatic stiltspear, to name a small handful. Refusing to reduce his characters to stereotypes and assiduously avoiding the monocultural conceits endemic to an unfortunate preponderance of fantasy fiction, Miéville fills Bas-Lag with complex and eccentric characters, often at odds with their own society and customs. Xenians—the non-human inhabitants of Bas-Lag—frequently suffer prejudice and oppression at the hand of human supremacists like the fascist New Quill party. Similarly the Remade, convicted and sentenced by the city's magisters to horrific transformation in the dreaded Punishment Factories, endure the contempt and repugnance of "whole" citizens. Each of the Remade is unique, a chimera of grafted body-parts or machines, their particular mutilations apportioned according to the malignant precepts of an awful poetic justice. These biopolitical horrors exemplify Bas-Lag's fixation on monstrosity in both its fantastic and its societal aspects: the Remade are spectacularly original fantasy monsters and, simultaneously, powerful metaphors for socioeconomic marginalization and exploitation.

Others of Bas-Lag's species occupy a similarly fraught political space, a liminal existence. Take, for example, the khepri, refugees from Bered Kai Nev and its nebulous cataclysm. Inspired by the Egyptian goddess of the same name, khepri resemble human women from the neck down but have the heads of scarab beetles; male khepri are nothing more than oversized insects, imbecilic and necessary only for reproduction. Living in the New Crobuzon ghettos of Kinken and Creekside, the khepri have a fractured spiritual culture, torn between the crushing religious orthodoxy of the Insect Aspect and the more progressive but still-insular following of the Awesome Broodma; this religious division in turn has profound economic implications for the khepri of the two districts. Lin, a khepri herself and one of the protagonists of *Perdido Street Station*, recognizes the shortcomings of both communities and rejects both faiths, while feeling, nonetheless, their ineffable nostalgic tug.

Some of Bas-Lag's monstrous inhabitants are less comprehensible than others. Instead of dragons Bas-Lag gives us monsters like the Weavers, arachnid aestheticians of supreme power and alien intelligence who live only to perfect the beauty of the worldweave, a kind of multidimensional weft of objects, events, and people the Weavers obsessively manipulate. The Weavers exemplify what Miéville, in his theoretical writing, calls the abcanny: an aesthetic affect grounded in a sense of alterity and otherness which he contrasts with the psychological uncanny of Freud. One of the few Weavers encountered in the series dwells beneath New Crobuzon, mercifully dormant, amusing itself with patterns of scissors and crooning a steady stream of lush, stream-of-consciousness poetry. Others of this sublimely unfathomable species have been known to reshape the tapestry of existence more overtly, though no less intelligibly—to destroy whole armies, commit acts of unspeakable atrocity, pretend to be dead, transmute a gun to glass . . . anything to refine the artwork that is the world.

The Weavers are right to see their world as artwork, for Bas-Lag is an imaginative achievement rarely equaled. Though the three Bas-Lag novels have compelling, suspenseful narratives and richly realized characters, it is the setting that lends the cycle its tremendous fascination, a world at once vividly bizarre and yet unnervingly familiar.

JASPER FFORDE

THE EYRE AFFAIR (2001)

The defining feature of the "Thursday Next" series is change. It is an unstable universe, worked through with time paradoxes, alternate histories, peculiar futures, and logical inconsistencies, all cheerfully waved away.

First published by Hodder and Stoughton in 2001.

Fforde's story, *The Well of Lost Plots* (2003), third in the Thursday Next series, won him the Wodehouse prize for comic fiction.

Fforde is the son of John Standish Fforde, the twenty-fourth Chief Cashier for the Bank of England (whose signature appeared on sterling banknotes during his time in office).

The Fforde Ffiesta is an annual event held in Thursday's home town of Swindon, activities include games of "Name That Fruit" and *Hamlet* speed-reading competitions.

London-born writer Jasper Fforde had a twenty-year career in the film industry, before turning his hand to writing. He cites his film career as fueling his imagination and the required global travel brought many opportunities for gathering comic ideas and inspiration for his characters.

Thursday Next, protagonist of *The Eyre Affair* and a subsequent seven titles, is a literary detective (or "LiteraTec") who spends her life hiding inside the plots of unpublished novels. England is a republic, Wales is a socialist republic (there is no United Kingdom), and the outcome of the Napoleonic Wars is continuously in flux due to ongoing issues with French Revisionists.

The alternate universe of Fforde's novels is best introduced through Next's dealings with bureaucracy and the rule of law: the SpecOps forces, dealing with threats and crimes that become stranger the higher the bureaucracy goes. Some elements—particularly the Chronoguard, responsible for dealing with time disturbances—have powers that can alter the past, present, and future. (Fforde neatly establishes that every element in this world is mutable by introducing the banana, a fruit created in the far future and sent back through time to provide early humanity with a superfood.) The various bureaucracies and systems represent doomed attempts to impose order upon chaos, inverting tropes related to genre fiction and dystopian worlds. Vampires and werewolves are an irritating fact of life, and vampire hunting is an unenviable, sometimes soul-destroying job; comedically unethical giant corporations controlling the media are simply a fact of existence.

In this postmodern world where fact can change at any moment, there are strict (if absurd) rules around the interpretation and impact of literature and art. Riots happen as a result of extreme adherence to particular aesthetic movements; free interpretations of literary classics are crimes. Next's background is in enforcing these rules, dealing with forgery and other crimes relating to the written and printed word. Fiction, in Fforde's universe, is a double-edged sword: crucially important but potentially dangerous. When Acheron Hades steals an original manuscript and uses world-hopping technology—developed by Next's uncle in his shed—to open a portal into the

The barriers between reality and fiction are softer than we think; a bit like a frozen lake. Hundreds of people can walk across it, but then one evening a thin spot develops and someone falls through; the hole is frozen over by the following morning.

An illustration by Maggy Roberts, which was intended for the first edition but eventually unused. The creature is Pickwick, Thursday Next's cloned pet dodo.

book itself, he gains the capacity to alter the fiction in ways the author never intended. In a world where stories are the bedrock of social order, this incredibly literal misinterpretation of the text is the ultimate crime.

The Eyre Affair is a story in which the author is not only dead but also occasionally non-existent; characters have agency not just within their own stories but between and outside them, freed to move between worlds and to exist outside the confines of the written narrative. Edward Rochester hosts Japanese tourists at Thornfield while the reader's attention is elsewhere; a minor character from *Martin Chuzzlewit* can not only be liberated from the confines of the original manuscript but also killed in Fforde's "real" world. In his essay "Death of the Author," Roland Barthes wrote that, "A text is . . . a multidimensional space in which a variety of writings, none of them original, blend and clash. The text is a tissue of quotations."

Ultimately *The Eyre Affair* and its sequels hinge on a reimagining of the reader as an active agent of change within the text. Fforde makes the concept of individual interpretation a literal event, creating a world in which other texts by other authors are just as malleable as his own. A reader's intervention can change not just the meaning of a book but the events that take place within it: Thursday Next's imagination and the Prose Portal technology allow her to hop between literary worlds and alter them completely, restoring the writer's original intent or, in the case of *Jane Eyre*, dramatically improving the ending by providing the impetus for the protagonist to return to Thornfield.

CORNELIA FUNKE

INKHEART (2003)

Mortimer Folchart possesses the ability to call characters out of books. In doing so he releases a pair of robbers into the contemporary world, where they create problems that he and his daughter must attempt to resolve by entering books themselves.

First published by Cecilie Dresser Verlag in 2003.

Funke has written more than thirty novels, and her work has been translated into more than twenty-eight languages worldwide.

In 2007, *Inkheart* was voted one of the Teachers' Top 100 Books for Children by the UK's National Education Association.

Prior to becoming an author, Funke worked for three years as a social worker, then as an illustrator of children's books. It was in part her work with children from difficult backgrounds that inspired her to start writing.

Cornelia Funke's Inkheart trilogy is not only a celebration of the love of books and reading, but also a meditation on, and warning about, the potential power of words, blending the grit of the real world with the fantasies that are encased in fictions. The page-turning excitement of this action-packed hybrid has won the series a global audience, selling more than twenty million copies worldwide.

Funke (b.1958) had already established herself as the "J. K. Rowling of Germany" with her previous titles, and her first novel *The Thief Lord* (entitled *Herr der Diebe* in its original German, 2000) almost succeeded in topping the *New York Times'* best-seller list. However it is her award-winning Inkheart series for which she is best known. Here Funke pursues the notion of being "lost in a book" or "living in a book" to its logical extremity with her creation the Inkworld, the world within the pages of *Inkheart*, a book written by one Fenoglio that is itself a story within Funke's own novel.

At the beginning of the novel, twelve-year-old Meggie discovers that her father, Mortimer "Mo" Folchart, has the ability to bring fictional characters to life when he reads aloud. Having learned to his cost that for every character fetched from the page, a person from the real world must enter the book in return, Mo has sworn never to read aloud again. Yet the characters of *Inkheart* that Mo once read into the contemporary world are not content to let him forget the past. Dustfinger seeks to return home to the pages of his story, while the villainous Capricorn and his accomplice Basta attempt to take control by destroying all the existing copies of *Inkheart*. Books, we understand, are powerful objects in both the right and wrong hands.

The tension between the roles of reader and writer becomes ever more apparent in the later titles *Inkspell* (2005) and *Inkdeath* (2007) as the author Fenoglio, living in the fictional world he has created, finds it is constantly changing from his memory of it, while Orpheus, a "silvertongue" like Mo, having written himself into the story, endlessly tinkers with it, creating interpolative pastiche texts, what we might call fan fiction, in which he plays increasingly significant roles. The implication seems to be that, as the theorist

An illustrated map of the Inkworld created by UK publishers of the series, Chicken House.

and philosopher Roland Barthes suggested, once a novel is published, the original author is supplanted by myriad reader-authors. As Mo says:

> Perhaps there's another, much larger story behind the printed one, a story that changes just as our own world does. And the letters on the page tell us only as much as we'd see peering through a keyhole. Perhaps the story in the book is just the lid on a pan; it always stays the same, but underneath there's a whole world that goes on developing and changing like our own.

Critics of the series have argued that, although she raises intriguing questions about the metafictional nature of text, Funke cannot properly answer them because the Inkworld is itself too insubstantial to support a full-scale enquiry into the nature of fiction. Nonetheless, the series continues to win favor with younger readers and *Inkheart* was produced as a movie in 2009.

SUSANNA CLARKE

JONATHAN STRANGE & MR. NORRELL (2004)

Clarke's alternate history, set in England at the time of the Napoleonic Wars, imagines an England in which magic once existed, and is reawakened by the titular magicians.

First published by Bloomsbury in 2004.

Jonathan Strange & Mr Norrell was longlisted for the Man Booker Prize in 2004 and won the Hugo Award for Best Novel in 2005.

Throughout the book, Clarke makes use of footnotes, which are used to outline the backstory and tell the fictional history of English magic, often referencing fictional texts.

Clarke started to write *Jonathan Strange & Mr. Norrell* in 1992, and worked on the novel for more than ten years before submitting it for publication.

A dark blend of nineteenth-century literary tropes and magical adventure, the debut novel of British writer Susanna Clarke (b.1959) has been an enormous best seller since its publication in 2004. Described by Neil Gaiman as "unquestionably the finest English novel of the fantastic written in the last seventy years," *Jonathan Strange & Mr. Norrell* is both critically acclaimed and beloved by many.

At the beginning of the book magic is only barely present in England, or so it seems. There are magicians, certainly, but of a theoretical sort only—gentlemen scholars unable to cast spells. And so England seems to be a magicless, ordinary place. But once the titular practicing magicians do appear, their practice of magic reshapes the nature of England itself—making it a wilder, stranger place. The more magic that is done in England, the more magical England shows itself to be.

For approximately the first third of the book, English magic is in the cold and fidgety hands of Mr. Norrell. He is capable of great and stunning spells— the speaking statues of York cathedral are haunting—but he treats magic as if he must make it a tame thing, regimented and contained, its memory stripped, so that it—and England—no longer remember that they used to belong to John Uskglass, the Raven King. The only exception to this caution is a spell that reverberates throughout the rest of the book—Norrell's summoning of a fairy servant, the gentleman with thistle-down hair, in order to raise Miss Wintertowne, soon to be Lady Pole, from the dead. This magic is strange and terrible, and has dire consequences. Aside from this, as Norrell practices, English magic is something that is staid, businesslike, and would prefer to hide in a library.

Once Jonathan Strange becomes a practicing magician however, English magic is greatly altered. Strange goes to war (taking part in the Napoleonic conflict, in the service of Lord Wellington) and takes magic with him. On the battlefield, Strange learns much magic that was hidden in Norrell's books—spells great enough to speak with the dead, and to rearrange the very geography of Spain.

But while Strange is away remaking Spain via English magic, England itself is being changed by magic as well. Indeed, it is impossible to talk about magic without talking about place, about the way that the presence of magic changes a place, and the ways that places themselves are changed by the presence of magic. The realm of Faerie encroaches England, creeping in by bits and pieces, here and there. The gentleman with the thistle-down hair steals Lady Pole away every night to his palace of Lost-Hope—leaving her exhausted and seemingly mad—and soon begins to steal away one of Sir Pole's servants, Stephen Black, who he plans to make a king. Black witnesses Faerie itself stealing its way into England, layering over streets and places that were once familiar to him, and making them uncanny.

But even then, English magic remains, or so it seems, recognizably English, and in recognizably English hands. This changes, drastically, when the gentleman with the thistle-down hair abducts Strange's wife, Arabella, to Faerie by magic, magic that makes it appear she has died. In his grief, Strange goes to Venice, and then chooses to go mad—madness being a condition that allows an easier window into Faerie. In this self-inflicted madness, Strange is able to literally return magic to England—he throws open the doors between England and everywhere else, and writes magic on the rocks and stones. Magicians spring up in unlikely places and the eye of the Raven King turns to England again.

But while magic is returned to England, Jonathan Strange and Mr. Norrell are taken out of it—cast into eternal darkness through a spell of the gentleman with thistle-down hair. Bound together until they learn the spell to free themselves, they are gone, "Wherever magicians used to go. Behind the sky. On the other side of the rain."

Jim Kay's concept illustration of the Old Starre Inn, the meeting place of the Learned Society of York Magicians.

DAVID MITCHELL

CLOUD ATLAS (2004)

Six different lives interlock in Mitchell's award-winning narrative. Cloud
Atlas *circles the globe and stretches from the nineteenth century to a post-
apocalyptic future, all the time redrawing the boundaries of time, genre,
and language to explore the consequences of humanity's will to power.*

First published by Hodder
and Stoughton in 2004.

Both *Cloud Atlas* and
Mitchell's 2001 novel
number9dream were
shortlisted for the Man
Booker Prize, and *Cloud
Atlas* was additionally
shortlisted for the Nebula
and Arthur C. Clarke
Awards, among others.

The title was inspired by a
piece of music by Japanese
composer Toshi Ichiyanagi:
"I bought the CD just
because of that track's
beautiful title."

The world David Mitchell creates in *Cloud Atlas* is, for much of its duration,
distinctly ours. Running parallel to events, experiences, and phenomena we
know from our own history—slavery, artistic composition, homes for the
elderly—with such care taken to wind them into our reality so that it's almost
disarming when, toward the halfway point of the novel, we're thrown into a
future of clones and post-apocalyptic language.

The structure of the text is its most distinctive feature. It falls into six
nested parts—some would call them individual stories, but that's actually
doing them a disservice, suggesting separation where there actually isn't any.
The flow between them is far deeper than most linked story collections—they
are presented in a way that cuts each of them off at their midpoint, only to
later return to them. So: the first section, which is set in 1850, is both the first
and last section of the book; the second, set in 1931, is the second and penul-
timate; and so on. Each part can't stand on its own because of the structure,
and the structure requires each part in order to work. There's something sym-
biotic going on between the form of the text and each of the parts—more so
than in most novels that adopt this approach.

That structure is, of course, the entire point of the novel. Character and
theme run hand in hand throughout, as Mitchell tells us a story about reincarnation, order, and chaos. Each character in the book is, in some way, a
reincarnation of a character that we have met at another time. That's not to
say we'll always recognize them in each piece, but they're definitely present:
in modes of speech, thoughts, and ideologies, in the events they enact, and
the way that they live. In the 2012 movie adaptation, actors played multiple
parts throughout, throwing that reincarnation theme to the forefront; in the
text, it's rather more subtle than that.

Just as the book loops back on itself, as the characters do the same, so does
the world presented to us. Across the sections—each of them named, each
of them nudging stylistically toward a different genre of fiction and, most
importantly, spanning an enormous (and undisclosed) period of time—we
see that same loop exist on a plot level. We see a world of conquered savagery

at the start, with an American witnessing the slavery of the Maori in New Zealand in the middle of the nineteenth century; then by the end of the novel, having taken in other forms of slavery (to our own identities; to the truth; to time; to the state), we're back in a world that, at a glance, resembles the first presentation, but is, in actuality, a post-apocalyptic future—a future that humanity is a slave to.

It's a world we recognize for much of the book, but that then manages to fall into something entirely different: a future that seems less than plausible— and intentionally so—and that then casts doubt on the text that precedes it. With the concept of reincarnation being so prevalent, it's clear that this is not our world. It's Mitchell's, and it's a world he links together with every novel he has thus far written. They're all tied together, with characters leaping between them, and events in one setting up stories told in another.

The brilliant young composer Robert Frobisher (played by Ben Wishaw), surrounded by pages of his own composition, the "Cloud Atlas Sextet," in a scene from the 2012 film adaptation co-directed by Tom Tykwer and the Wachowskis.

NEVER LET ME GO (2005)

Ishiguro's darkly imagined version of contemporary England hauntingly dramatizes the fragility of life through the fates of a group of students at a seemingly idyllic boarding school.

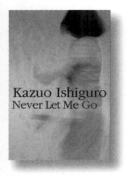

First published by Faber and Faber Ltd in 2005.

Never Let Me Go was shortlisted for the 2005 Booker Prize, the 2006 Arthur C. Clarke Award, and the UK's 2005 National Book Critics Circle Award.

Time magazine included it in its rundown of the one hundred "Best English-language Novels from 1923 to 2005."

The seemingly niche area of "organ-transplant-fantasy" fiction can claim some notable hits. Most would agree with Brian Aldiss, the "Dean of British Science Fiction," that the science-fiction genre, in its modern form, begins with Mary Shelley's *Frankenstein* (1818), in which a brilliant young Swiss scientist puts together a "creature" from a medley of body parts. Similarly, Frederik Pohl also dealt with organ transplantation in his 1964 novel (co-written with Jack Williamson) *The Reefs of Space*. A sardonically dystopian novel in which those branded "risks" to society find themselves incarcerated in "living body banks," reservoirs of limbs and organs to be harvested as the need arises.

These scenarios, however, were fantasy, since medicine had not at that time developed the techniques by which body parts could be successfully transplanted. South-African surgeon Christiaan Barnard performed the world's first heart transplant in 1967. The patient lived for only eighteen days, but a string of ever more successful transplant operations followed, and transplantees were surviving for months, years, and then decades. Science fiction had become medical fact.

Transplant scenarios became commonplace in film and science fiction following Barnard's pioneering surgery. A literary highpoint, well beyond the reach of genre fiction, was reached with Kashuo Ishiguro's (b.1954) highly acclaimed novel, *Never Let Me Go* (adapted into an equally lauded film in 2010). Japanese-born novelist Ishiguro had already received the Booker Prize in 1989 for *The Remains of the Day* and *Never Let Me Go* was shortlisted for the same award. *Time* magazine went on to name it the best novel of 2005.

The story opens in what appears to be an idyllic English boarding school called Hailsham, located in the bucolic Norfolk countryside. Mysteriously, none of the Hailsham children seem to have parents or family, and live in the care of "guardians." Their education is sparse and suited for no kind of examination, or even productive post-school life, the principal focus is on their physical health. Nonetheless, the children develop friendships and, as they grow up, loving relationships.

As the narrative continues the truth emerges. The children have been created in laboratories as living organ banks for specific owners ("normals"), of whom they are clones ("doubles"). Some of the young people, now they know the truth, rebel. Others seek ways to postpone the fate that awaits them. Others embark on desperate searches for their "normals."

The novel in its last section depicts the pathos of the donors' (as they are called) lives, as parts are clipped off them, until they "complete" (when they are used up and disposed of). The clones come to understand, more acutely than their normal "receivers," the nature of the humanity they are doomed never to possess, of mortality, and—most presciently—what is evolving outside the school:

> . . . a new world coming rapidly. More scientific, efficient, yes. More cures for the old sicknesses. Very good. But a harsh, cruel, world. And I saw a little girl, her eyes tightly closed, holding to her breast the old kind world, one that she knew in her heart could not remain, and she was holding it and pleading, never to let her go.

Ironically, the children and the adult donors they become are merely a transitional remedy. Already, in their adulthood, they are being overtaken by new medical "advances."

However one labels it (and Robert Heinlein's description of "SF" as "speculative fiction," rather than "science fiction," seems appropriate here) Ishiguro's is rightly regarded as one of the twenty-first century's greatest works of literary fiction.

Ham House in Richmond, Surrey, U.K., doubled as the idyllic boarding school in a 2010 film adaptation directed by Mark Romanek, with a screenplay by Alex Garland.

NGŨGĨ WA THIONG'O

WIZARD OF THE CROW (2006)

Ngũgĩ's absurdist satire on postcolonial kleptocracy is set in Aburiria,
a fictitious African dictatorship whose tyrant is challenged by a self-styled
wizard and his lover.

The novel, whose English version is more than 760 pages long, was originally published in four volumes in Gikuyu as *Murogi wa Kagogo*. Returning to Kenya, for the launch of volume I, in 2004 after Moi's rule ended Ngũgĩ and his wife suffered a brutal attack.

Ngũgĩ's first novel in Gikuyu, *Devil on the Cross* (1980), was written in prison on toilet paper (the wizard finds a man reading it aloud in a bar to a spellbound crowd).

The Free Republic of Aburiria owes most to Ngũgĩ's (b.1938) native Kenya—particularly the twenty-four-year dictatorship of Daniel arap Moi (1978–2002), under whose vice-presidency Ngũgĩ was detained for a year without trial in 1977, and his books banned. By the time this prisoner of conscience emerged from Kamiti Maximum Security Prison in December 1978, Moi was head of state.

In *Wizard of the Crow*, "the Ruler" is a supreme kleptocrat ("A loot-a continua") whose hubristic goal is to build Africa's tallest skyscraper. His western suits are patched with big cats' fur. Yet the allusions stretch to despots far beyond Kenya, from Mobutu and Idi Amin to Marcos and Pinochet. As Ngũgĩ wrote in an afterword to the novel, published in his own English translation in 2006, he drew on his exile in London in the 1980s, when he campaigned to free political prisoners from Kenyan and other dungeons—hence the novel's atmosphere of paranoia about the "M5" secret police. The Ruler's sycophantic ministers go to extreme lengths to keep enemies under surveillance. One minister has his eyes "enlarged to the size of electric bulbs," while his rival's ears are made "larger than a rabbit's." There is "almost a comic element, except that they're so dangerous," the author said of his targets. Asked how he approached them, Ngũgĩ responded with his own question: "How do you satirize someone like Moi, who says he wants all his ministers to be parrots?"

Ngũgĩ's answer was to break with the early realism of novels such as *A Grain of Wheat* (1967) and *Petals of Blood* (1977), which he wrote in English as James Ngũgĩ. When, in the late-1970s, he renounced his Christian name and staged peasant theater in Gikuyu—the language of Kenya's largest ethnic group—the prison sentence that resulted strengthened his resolve to write fiction only in his mother tongue. *Wizard of the Crow* was written in part to be read aloud in bars and *matatus* (taxis).

Despite echoes of the great Latin-American dictatorship novels of Augusto Roa Bastos, Gabriel García Márquez, and Carlos Fuentes, this grotesque, scatological universe feels closer to Alfred Jarry's *Ubu Roi* (1896)—the

292

Why did Africa let Europe cart away millions of Africa's souls from the continent to the four corners of the wind? How could Europe lord it over a continent ten times its size? ... How did we arrive at this, that the best leader is the one that knows how to beg for a share of what he has already given away at the price of a broken tool? Where is the future of Africa?

Kenya's President Daniel arap Moi as Chancellor at a graduation ceremony at the University of Nairobi, 1972.

Macbeth parody that presaged the Theater of the Absurd—whose foul usurper is propelled by omnivorous greed. There may also be a nod to the bloating cadaver in Eugène Ionesco's play *Amédée* (1954): the Ruler, having outlived his usefulness to his cold war western allies, balloons like a putrid corpse and births Baby Democracy, a cynical façade of multi-party politics. In an era of globalization, aid, and the "war on terror," the Ruler "missed the cold war, when he could play one side against the other," but finds ample pretext to crack down on opponents: "What I did before against communists, I can do again against terrorists."

The political satire has a counterpoint in a transcendent world of resistance heroes that recalls Ngũgĩ's childhood. His father was forced off his land by British settlers. Ngũgĩ's mother was jailed for three months in a colonial jail when his elder brother joined the Mau Mau army. Another brother died in World War II, while another, who was deaf and mute, was shot dead by a British soldier for failing to hear the order to halt. The fog of rumor, spin, and mythic invincibility that surrounds the eponymous wizard and his lover harks back to Mau Mau heroes and their heirs.

Some imagery is biblical; the Bible was the first book Ngũgĩ read in his mother tongue—though to speak it at school was punishable with the cane. He later found in Brecht's poetry an "extraordinary optimism about the capacity of human beings to change their environment" —an optimism this novel ultimately shares.

MICHAEL CHABON

THE YIDDISH POLICEMEN'S UNION (2007)

A detective story set on an Alaskan island where Jewish refugees have created a vibrant, complex, Yiddish-speaking metropolis, now on the eve of its destruction.

First published by HarperCollins in 2007.

The Yiddish Policemen's Union won three major science fiction awards: the Hugo, the Nebula, and the Locus Award for Best Novel of the Year.

Yiddish is a hybrid of Hebrew and medieval German, written in an alphabet based on Hebrew. At its height it had an estimated 11 million speakers, which dropped to perhaps a quarter of a million in America by the end of the twentieth century, but it is now undergoing something of a renaissance, and being taught in universities.

"Nine months Landsman's been flopping at the Hotel Zamenhof without any of his fellow residents managing to get themselves murdered. Now somebody has put a bullet in the brain of the occupant of 208, a yid who was calling himself Emanuel Lasker."

The first lines of Michael Chabon's (b.1963) fourth novel announces it as a detective story in the tradition of Raymond Chandler. But the mean streets Meyer Landsman must travel are not in Chandler's Los Angeles, or any other American city, for "Landsman is the most decorated *shammes* in the District of Sitka."

In our world, Sitka, located on Baranof Island and the south half of Chichagof Island in the Alexander Archipelago of Alaska, has a population of little more than 9,000, although in terms of land area, it is the largest city-borough in the United States. In Chabon's alternate world, it is the Federal District of Sitka, offered as a temporary refuge for Jews fleeing Nazi rule in Europe, and then to Jewish settlers in Palestine after their newborn State of Israel was destroyed in the Arab-Israeli War of 1948. But now, after sixty years, the big, booming, metropolis created by the settlers—"a pinnacle of Jewish civilization in the north, people say"—will revert to the State of Alaska, and the more than two million Jewish, Yiddish-speaking inhabitants will lose their home. Published in 2007, *The Yiddish Policemen's Union* unites the detective story with the strand of science fiction known as the alternate world. Such stories generally start from the notion of there being one decisive moment at which the history of the world we know is changed: A significant figure is assassinated (or not), or an important battle is won by the other side. It is difficult to pinpoint just one change to our history that would have led with any kind of inevitability to the vivid and compelling northern city he depicts, but Chabon begins with the proposal made by Secretary of the Interior Harold Ickes in November 1938 that Alaska could be used as a haven for Jewish refugees from Germany. (Since it was then a territory, not a state, the usual immigration quotas would not apply.) In reality, the proposal received little support from anyone, but in Chabon's counter-factual history,

My Saturday Night. My Saturday night is like a microwave burrito. Very tough to ruin something that starts out so bad to begin with.

Meyer Landsman: "the most decorated *shammes* in the District of Sitka." Illustration by Nate Williams.

the sudden, accidental death of Alaska's non-voting delegate to the House of Representatives allows it to be pushed through in 1941. Millions are saved from the Nazis' "final solution" and the war in Europe only ends in 1946 when the atom bomb is dropped on Berlin.

The original seed for the novel was planted by Chabon's discovery of a copy of *Say it in Yiddish* (1958), edited by Beatrice and Uriel Weinreich, published as part of a series of phrase books for travelers: "I could neither understand nor stop considering, stop wondering and dreaming about, the intended nature and purpose of the book . . . At what time in the history of the world had there been a place of the kind that the Weinreichs' work implied, a place where not only the doctors and waiters and trolley conductors spoke Yiddish, but also the airline clerks, travel agents, ferry captains, and casino employees?" In the same essay ("Imaginary Homelands"), Chabon wrote about his feeling of being a writer in exile, not only as an American Jew, but as a lover of genre fiction: "Because when you are talking . . . about lands that can be found only in the imagination, you are really speaking my language—my *mamaloshen*."

SUZANNE COLLINS

THE HUNGER GAMES (2008)

Collins's wildly successful Hunger Games series is set apart from a wealth of YA imitators by its powerful female protagonist and searing vision of an unsettling dystopian future that revolves around a deadly reality TV show.

First published by Scholastic Press in 2008.

Collins began her career in the 1990s writing for television, specializing in scripting children's shows for the Nickelodeon network; and something of the dramatic pace and focus of the best screenwriting is evident in her novels.

We discover in the trilogy that the name "Panem" comes from the Latin phrase *panem et circenses*, which means "bread and circuses." It derives from Ancient Rome, as a cynical summary of the way governments pacify the mass population by giving them the basics of food and gladiatorial entertainment.

The dystopian adventure trilogy made up of *The Hunger Games* (2008), *Catching Fire* (2009), and *Mockingjay* (2010) is one of the twenty-first-century's best-selling works of fiction and it's not hard to see why. The novels revolve around the intriguing premise of a savage television game show in which teens from different parts of the country are confined in a forested area and compelled to fight one another until only one is left alive. The outline of this horrifying idea has been seen before in Koushun Takami's *Battle Royale* (1999), but Suzanne Collins' epic tale builds into something greater than the sum of its narrative parts: an interrogation of questions of political and social freedom, its appeal, and its costs.

The Hunger Games is set in a post-apocalyptic version of America called "Panem" consisting of twelve districts. The wealthiest is the high-tech city of the Capitol, the seat of the oppressive government. The other districts exist in grinding poverty. Long ago, the districts rebelled against control by the Capitol, but the revolt was violently suppressed and a thirteenth district supposedly destroyed. Now an annual gladiatorial "Hunger Games" is staged to remind the districts of their subjugation with violent spectacle and entertainment. One teen boy and one teen girl are chosen from each district by lottery as "tributes," and brought to the Capitol to fight in the televised games. The winner's district is rewarded with food and other supplies.

Katniss comes from District 12, where life is unusually hard even by Panem standards, and starvation common. The first novel is the most grippingly plotted, building an impressive narrative momentum as we wonder how she can survive the violent arena in which she finds herself. The two subsequent books broaden and deepen the focus of the story, encompassing the nature of friendship and loyalty, the difference between love and friendship and the need for independence—issues core to the lives of the book's "Young Adult" demographic.

Each rural district is dedicated to one industry: agriculture in one, mining in another, fishing in a coastal district, and so on. On one hand this is a little hard to picture—it's never quite explained how these goods are

transported across Panem to the Capitol on the scale that would be required, given the general poverty; or how distant District 12 can be a short train ride from the Capitol. But in another sense the landscape works very well. It symbolically externalizes two things that shape people's sense of their place in their real world. One is the sharp contrast between the way the rich and the rest of us live. The other is the general sense of surveillance. To walk down a road after reading these books is to feel the nagging sense that your every step is being watched by spy-tech. Collins's creation literalizes and externalizes the senses shared by teens everywhere: the unfairness of arbitrary authority, the oppressiveness of being watched all the time, the importance of friendship, and the need to fight back.

Panem is a terrifying land, sharply divided between the superficially utopian high-tech Capitol and the dirt-poor districts, but that doesn't diminish its appeal. On the contrary, though perhaps counterintuitively, dystopia exerts a more powerful grip upon the imagination than utopia, since it has more conflict and therefore more drama, which provides far more imaginative potential than the static staleness of social perfection.

Jennifer Lawrence stars as the powerful central character, Katniss Everdeen in the 2012 Lionsgate film adaptation of the first book in the series, directed by Gary Ross with a screenplay adapted by Collins.

HARUKI MURAKAMI

1Q84 (2009–10)

This shifting and complex narrative vigorously demonstrates the power of the novel, describing the closely intertwined fates of two people through themes of murder, religion, family, and love.

First published by Shinchosa Publishing Ltd between 2009 and 2010.

The first printing of the novel sold out in a single day and sales had reached one million copies within a month.

In 2009, Murakami was presented with the Jerusalem Prize, a literary award given to writers whose work deals with freedom, society, politics, and government. Murakami attended the ceremony, but spoke harshly of Israeli policies.

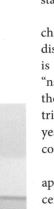

Haruki Murakami (b.1949) has been creating "other worlds" in his fictional landscape for decades. His characters jump into apparently bottomless wells, ride down metaphysical elevators, descend into subterranean caverns beneath the Tokyo subway system, or simply wander too far out into the woods. Next thing they know, they are in an "other world." This parallel-world structure, which has been prominent particularly since Murakami's second novel, *Pinball, 1973* (1980), alternates between the physical and metaphysical worlds (or consciousness and unconsciousness), between the activities of parallel characters in the story, or both.

In the early days of his career, Murakami was known (and sometimes criticized) for creating heroes who were too "detached" from the societies in which they lived. That changed dramatically after the "Aum incident" of March 20, 1995, in which members of the religious cult Aum Shinrikyo released the lethal nerve agent Sarin into various Tokyo subway trains and stations during the morning rush hour.

Murakami's work had always been tinged with a certain spiritualism; his characters enter into the "other world" not for kicks, but in search of self-discovery, and sometimes for self-preservation. Their goal, then and now, is to preserve a unique core identity—what Murakami now terms the "narrative" (*monogatari*)—against the harmful, even obliterating effects of the prefabricated, groupist identity offered by contemporary postindustrialist society. Accordingly, the culprits in Murakami novels in those early years had generally been politicians backed by their soul-sucking, mass-consumerist utopian social systems.

In the years that followed the Aum incident, Murakami cautiously approached the topic of religion, and particularly the Aum Shinrikyo, perceiving among its members people seeking what he himself sought: an alternative to the premade identity narratives offered by contemporary Japanese society. He interviewed victims of the incident, and then members of the cult itself and, while he did not share the latters' radical nihilism, he seems to have recognized in them a desire for something more spiritual than the consumerist model could offer. He toyed with religion in his short fiction—notably in "All children of the gods dance" (2000)—and finally explored the formation of religious cults in *1Q84* (2009–10).

1Q84 explores questions of fate/determinism and free will through the movements of its two protagonists, Aomame and Tengo, who met as children, drawn together (though they did not know it) by their shared sense of alienation both from their parents and from the other children who surrounded them. Aomame, as the daughter of religious proselytes, was embarrassed by the very public demonstrations of faith (such as praying aloud before meals) her religion obliged her to make before her classmates; Tengo was ashamed of his father's equally zealous devotion to the government-owned broadcasting agency, NHK, for which he collected monthly "dues," dragging Tengo along on Sundays.

Even as children, readers learn through flashback scenes, Tengo and Aomame seem to recognize that some bond exists between them. One day, ten-year-old Aomame suddenly grasps Tengo's hand and looks into his eyes. No words are spoken between the two, but from this moment Aomame appears to feel that Tengo is her soul mate, and she stubbornly waits for fate to bring them back together. "What I want is for the two of us to meet somewhere by chance one day," she tells a friend. Later in the same conversation she asserts the possibility that "everything's decided in advance and we *pretend* we're making choices. Free will may be an illusion."

Aomame's willingness to accept fate is put to the test when she unwittingly steps into the latest of Murakami's magical wonderlands, which she decides to call 1Q84, a grim joke based on the year in which the story is set—1984—with "Q" standing for question mark. 1Q84 is very nearly the same as 1984, yet just a little sinister: The police carry automatic weapons in place of the revolvers she is used to; two moons hang in the sky, where before there had been only one; and certain events appear to be controlled by "the Little People," spirits who rule the metaphysical "other world" and take an active interest in the affairs of humankind. Less like gods than mischievous wood sprites, the Little People appear to lay claim to the fate of Aomame and Tengo and, more importantly, to the fate of the child they have conceived.

It is for the sake of this child that Aomame decides, at long last, that she will escape 1Q84 and the unwanted influence of the Little People. Although warned that either she or Tengo must perish in order for the other to escape, Aomame determines that she and Tengo must *both* survive in order to nurture and protect their child. It is at this point that she breaks faith with fate and declares her own free will. "I am not just some passive being mixed up in this because someone else willed it," she says to herself. "I chose to be here of my own free will." This declaration marks her independence from the ruthless zealotry of her parents, a break with her tightly controlled past. In the wider context of Murakami's fiction, it is a reaffirmation of the inner "narrative," and the individual's right to determine her or his own destiny.

Believers of the doomsday cult Aum Shinrikyo at their temporary facility on July 20, 1990, in Namino, Kumamoto, Japan.

WU MING-YI

THE MAN WITH THE COMPOUND EYES (2011)

A folk-inspired fantasy parallels hard political and ecological realities in a tale of a boy determined to defy his destiny.

The Man with the Compound Eyes was first published in Taiwan in 2011 by Summer Festival. The above edition was published by ThinKingdom (2016).

In Taiwan, Wu Ming-Yi is also well known for his nonfiction books on butterflies, *The Book of Lost Butterflies* (2000) and *The Dao of Butterflies* (2003), which he also designed and illustrated.

Wu Ming-Yi (b.1971) is a man of many talents, turning his creative attention variously to writing, painting, and photography. Professionally he is no less multifaceted: he lectures in literature and creative writing at National Dong Hwa University in Hualien County, Taiwan, publishes on lepidoptery, and tirelessly raises awareness as an environmental activist. And it is this commitment to ecology that informs his metafictional parable, *The Man with the Compound Eyes* (first published in Mandarin in 2011, and in its English translation in 2013), an environmental-disaster novel set in the near future on the island of Taiwan.

Like Haruki Murakami (page 298) and David Mitchell (page 288), Wu combines hard facts and richly detailed fantasy. As author and critic Tash Aw observes, his story hovers "over the precipice of wild imagination before retreating to minutiae about Taiwanese fauna or whale-hunting." The environmental disaster depicted is anthropogenic and all too realistic. Discarded plastic swirling around in the Great Pacific Trash Vortex—an enormous gyre of sludge and debris that is hard to map, but that conservative estimates have placed at more than 270,000 square miles wide—forms a giant, floating trash mountain that crashes into Taiwan's east coast, ruining hundreds of miles of shoreline. Two of the clean-up volunteers, Dahu and Hafay, are indigenous islanders. They relearn how to live an off-the-grid, no-garbage lifestyle and teach it to others, including Detlev, a German geologist, and his friend Sara, a Norwegian marine biologist studying the ecological impact of the trash tsunami. In this way, the storylines of the individual protagonists tangle together into a narrative of collective environmental action.

The imaginary and real are also bound together by the disaster, entwining Atile'i, a denizen of an imaginary Polynesian atoll called Wayo Wayo, into the story, too. Wayo Wayo is so resource-poor that the islanders have had to impose a drastic restriction on family size, and all second sons, like Atile'i, are sent into the sea as sacrifices to the Sea God at fifteen years of age. Atile'i, however, is determined to defy his destiny and become the first to survive the

Suitably fantastic fold-out artwork from the Mandarin edition by artist Zhang You-ran.

cull. Soon after he departs his island home, he sights a pod of whales, avatars of the spirits of all the second sons who have perished at sea. But instead of joining them, Atile'i becomes caught up on the floating trash mountain, and the sea soon hurls him, along with tons of refuse, onto Taiwan's eastern shore. There, he meets Alice, who takes him on a trip to the mountains, where she believes her Danish husband Thom and son Toto went missing on a rock-climbing and insect-gathering expedition.

What happened to Thom and Toto? It seems only the "Man with the Compound Eyes" knows, a persona the reader only learns about through a reported conversation between Thom and the man himself as the former lies dying at the base of a cliff. The Man with the Compound Eyes can be understood as a symbol of individual points of view contained within a collective perspective. Like an insect's, the man's eyes are composed of ommatidia forming a kind of video mosaic, and creating a transcendent image of nature. The Man with the Compound Eyes exists to encourage the reader to step outside him or herself and see the world through nonhuman eyes.

We later discover that Toto died of a snakebite four years before the trash tsunami, and the story about the climbing and bug-collecting expedition was concocted by Alice to work through the trauma of the loss of her only son. She tells Atile'i that she is writing a novel called *The Man with the Compound Eyes* and, in so doing, reveals herself to the reader as the one who has woven all the narrative strands of the novel together into a metafictional parable about the power of the imagination to reflect and refract worlds within worlds, projecting what is and might be.

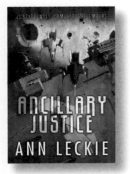

ANN LECKIE

THE IMPERIAL RADCH TRILOGY
(2013–15)

Starting with a remarkable debut novel that won every major science-fiction award in its first year of publication, the Imperial Radch trilogy takes a powerful approach to gender and sexuality.

First published by Orbit between 2013 and 2015.

Ancillary Justice is the first in Leckie's Imperial Radch trilogy, followed by *Ancillary Sword* (2014) and *Ancillary Mercy* (2015).

Ancillary Justice won the 2014 Hugo Award for Best Novel as well as the Nebula Award, the Arthur C. Clarke Award, and the BSFA Award.

Readers worldwide have created a wealth of fan art of the Radchaii and Ancillary characters. Significantly, most fan artists choose to depict Breq, Anaander Mianaii, and others as androgynous or ambiguously gendered.

Ann Leckie (b.1966) grew up reading science fiction and fantasy throughout her childhood in St. Louis, Missouri, but it wasn't until the birth of her children in 1996 and 2000 that she found the motivation to begin work on her conceptually ambitious Imperial Radch trilogy, which tells the story of an AI trapped in a human body in a genderless galactic empire on the brink of civil war. The trilogy combines the operatic scope of Iain M. Banks's Culture novels with the intimate explorations of humans as social animals found in Ursula K. Le Guin's most-loved books. Leckie's writing has drawn comparisons to both, but it is the power of her storytelling that makes her approach to gender and sexuality much more than a gimmick.

Throughout, gender is conspicuous—chiefly by its absence. It is a literary decision, underlined on every page by the use of "she" as a neutral, universal pronoun. In English, "she" is almost never a neutral pronoun. "He," by contrast, is still used synonymously with "men and, as an afterthought, women." "She" is specific; "he" is universal. We're so used to assuming the masculine default in culture that if every character in the trilogy were referred to as "he," it would be easy to assume that they were all men and boys—which would hardly distinguish the trilogy from a great deal of pulpier science fiction.

The narrative arc of the series, however, is not about gender. It breaks new ground in storytelling precisely because it is not about the gender binary. For Breq, the protagonist and viewpoint character, gender is not a concern for the quite simple reason that Breq is a fragment of the consciousness of a two-thousand-year-old warship, built by an imperial civilization which happens not to draw clear distinctions between "people with and without penises." Readers experience a great deal of experimental science fiction through the eyes of outsiders, but Breq is part of the machine of the Radch (the conquering empire)—quite literally.

Leckie drops us into the middle of a struggle between the warring factions of a tyrant, Mianaii, who is able to clone herself and divide her consciousness between multiple bodies that have now turned on one another. The books manage, masterfully, to concern themselves with intimate questions

of identity while at the same time they illuminate empire, colonization, and conquest on a galactic scale. The world's very strangeness, from the customs of Radch citizens—who are obsessed with crockery and never show their naked hands in public—to the in-depth exploration of postgender, posthuman love relationships, is thrown into sharp relief by its relentless familiarity. It's still about who conquers, who is conquered, who is sleeping with whom, who respects social norms, who disobeys her parents, and what the neighbors will think of it all.

For Breq, the trauma and the drama are an embodiment itself. Breq is the last surviving human ancillary of the destroyed warship, and the strangeness of being confined to one fragile human body leaves her little time to concern herself with the genital specifics of that body, or of anyone else's. Without the familiar signifiers, Breq and her crewmates still manage to wage war, fall in love, betray and rescue one another, and wrestle with the complexities of conquest and social justice. That is the real wonder at the core of the Imperial Radch series: It demonstrates that gender itself is not essential to a good story.

More than anything, Leckie's trilogy is fun—a classic, rollicking space opera. Breq could, in many ways, be the heroic soldier-protagonist familiar in science fiction: brave, deeply moral, conflicted, forced to confront the barbarity of the system of which she is a part as she meets alien ambassadors, kicks down doors and launches missiles at enemy spaceships. She manages to be all this and more without being limited or defined by gender—which is precisely what makes the Radch series a story for our times.

The three covers of the Imperial Radch trilogy are composed of one large artwork by the artist John Harris.

NNEDI OKORAFOR

LAGOON (2014)

Okorafor's portrayal of Lagos before, during, and after an alien invasion is both a biting commentary on current Nigeria as well as a fast-paced futuristic adventure.

First published by Hodder & Stoughton in 2014.

The novel was initially titled "Lagos" but this was changed to *Lagoon*, not only to avoid the controversy of nomenclature, but also to more intimately capture the dominance of water in all parts of the story.

Lagoon is the English translation of "Lagos," which is what the Portuguese called the city in the fifteenth century.

Science fiction has long been assumed to be a purely Western genre. As noted by Nnedi Okorafor (b.1974) herself, there is a sense in which the perception of African reading audiences as being more interested in reality-based stories than ones dominated by technology has become needlessly pervasive. This makes writers and publishers reluctant to produce work of this kind, and audiences hostile to them. As she said first in a Nebula Award blog post:

> …I think getting African audiences to open up to science fiction will take some finesse. True African science fiction, which is different from what Western audiences are used to consuming, needs to be written/filmed and made available first….[O]ne will have to deliberately combine the concept of 'art as a tool for social commentary and change' and entertainment. The root of the technology, cultural shifts, sentiments, concerns, characters, way of speaking, needs that drive the story must first and foremost be endemically African. Along with the unfamiliar, must come the familiar …a gradual ascent. A whisper to a shout. A ghostly woman in the night to a full blown alien invasion in the middle of Imo State that only a frustrated plantain chip seller named Chukwudi can stop.

This background is necessary to understand the novel, which was written after that interview, half as an intervention and half in protest against a denigrating portrayal of Nigeria and Nigerians in Neil Blomkamp's 2009 South African sci-fi/alien-invasion thriller, *District 9*. How do we change the negative perception of Africa to one of an exciting, dynamic place, important enough to warrant something as phenomenal as an alien invasion? How do we make audiences receptive to it?

Lagoon's main plot begins when a hip-hop artist from Ghana on a post-performance stroll (Anthony), a Nigerian soldier with a bloody nose (Agu), and a marine biologist with domestic violence issues (Adaora) chance upon each other at Bar Beach at the exact moment when an alien invasion of Lagos begins. Their abduction and eventual excretion by the body of water

The stilt houses of Makoko shantytown on the edges of the Lagos Lagoon, Nigeria.

set the mood for a rollercoaster plot of events that upend not just their individual lives but those of the whole nation and the sub-region, adding a more creative disorder to a place already defined by chaos.

But why Lagos? The author insists we ask "why not?" The city is the most populated in Nigeria and one of the largest in the world: a cosmopolitan sprawl of humans, concrete, and tar, and, for a while, the capital city of Nigeria. Bar Beach, where much of the plot takes place, is the country's most famous outlet to the Atlantic Ocean, foregrounding a skyline of private high-rise buildings for upper- and middle-class Nigerians. As well, it accommodates the dregs of that society within it: prostitutes, informants, religious scam artists, miscreants, and security officials, among others. In the 1970s and 1980s, the beach hosted a number of public executions of robbers sentenced to death by the military government. This combination of a grotesque history and a social backdrop that the beachfront provides keeps the story exciting from start to finish, along with the activities, intentions, and behaviors of the visiting, shape-shifting aliens.

But far from being a merely didactic intervention and protest, *Lagoon* weaves itself beautifully into a fast-paced suspenseful narrative, absorbing in its realistic characterization, language (with which many non-Nigerian readers might inevitably struggle: Pidgin English is a creole formed organically from the many years of interaction of Portuguese and English with Nigeria's many languages), diverse range of voices and perspectives, brilliant writing, and the powerful imagination of the writer, to whom Nigeria is as much a fertile fantasyland as it is a real, conscious entity, and a home.

SALMAN RUSHDIE

TWO YEARS EIGHT MONTHS AND TWENTY-EIGHT NIGHTS
(2015)

Malevolent jinn leave the realm of Peristan to interfere in human affairs in Salman Rushdie's half-fanciful, half-journalistic treatment of contemporary global chaos.

First published by Random House (U.S.) and Jonathan Cape (U.K.) in 2015.

Iran's Ayatollah Khomeini famously issued a fatwa against Rushdie after the 1988 publication of *The Satanic Verses;* numerous death threats and attempted assassinations forced the author into hiding for a year.

"Dunya" is the Arabic word for "world" and has trickled into a number of languages including Persian, Turkish, Urdu, and Hindi. It refers specifically to the temporal world, as opposed to the spiritual realm or hereafter.

It is rare for contemporary works of literary fiction to take on magical worlds beyond our own; in this recent novel, Salman Rushdie (b.1947) brings the reader to Peristan, or Fairyland, the realm of the jinn. This somewhat chaotic tale also takes on the dismal state of current world affairs, attributing it to the malign influence of these supernatural beings who have transgressed the barrier between our two worlds.

The novel begins in medieval Spain, during the time of the so-called *Convivencia,* when people of monotheistic faiths lived together in more-or-less harmony under Muslim rule. The great rationalist Muslim philosopher Ibn Rushd (usually known in English as Averroes) is working on his rebuttal to the anti-philosophical screed of his predecessor Al-Ghazali, at a moment when religious fanaticism is ascendant and Ibn Rushd's promulgation of Aristotelian philosophy is viewed with skepticism. One day, a jinnia—a genie princess called Dunia, among other names—arrives at his door. Dunia slips into the world of men and women from Peristan, and then into Ibn Rushd's bed. Together they originate a race called the Duniazat—human beings without earlobes and with slightly magical propensities.

Along with his rambunctious, irreverent style, Rushdie is best-known for his public disputes with certain bastions of conservative Islam. While this novel, like all of Rushdie's novels, despises fundamentalism, it makes loving use of the rich Islamic cultural tradition. Jinn are mentioned in the Koran and appear throughout doctrine, folk Islam, and works of art and literature. They are made of smoke and fire, but can assume corporeal form; they inhabit a kind of parallel world, slipping in and out of human affairs, usually to make mischief. They range in representation and, in this novel, from fearsome to feckless: "They live in the moment, have no grand designs, and are easily distracted." Peristan, the home of the jinn, manifests their obsession with "the patterning of things which only civilization provides; it was a place of formal gardens, elegantly terraced, with cascading streams of water." Despite these idylls, jinn cannot seem to stop themselves from interfering in human affairs.

We meet the present-day descendants of Ibn Rushd and Dunia's brood at a moment when environmental chaos, corruption, and fanaticism have cast the human world into a period of darkness. As we learn, the upheavals, or "strangenesses" of the modern day are the result of jinn interloping in the human realm—sinister jinn who are power-mad and obsessed with mayhem. Seeking revenge for the death of her father at the hands of these bad jinn, Dunia reenters the human world and enlists her descendants to fight them: Geronimo the kindly gardener, the hapless graphic novelist Jimmy Kapoor, and a harridan named Teresa Saca, are three among others in a large cast of characters, some of whom appear briefly and pass quickly out of the book. The heroes are up against "jinn parasites," who are unleashed among the populace to commit horrors taken straight from the headlines; these parasites are "eating people's faces in Miami," or "stoning women to death in desert places," or "shooting passenger aircraft out of the sky." The human realm turns out to be particularly susceptible to the jinn brand of chaos: "the craziness unleashed upon our ancestors by the jinn," the narrator writes, "was the craziness that also waited inside every human heart."

The novel ends on an optimistic note; the narrator reveals that he or she is writing from some thousand years in the future, after "men and women returned to their senses, order and civility were everywhere restored, economies began to function, crops to be harvested, factory wheels to turn." No one is "gulled" any longer by "those antique, defunct belief systems." Most importantly, Dunia has sealed the cracks between Peristan and the human realm, risking no chance of further conflagration. But, even in this enlightened age, the novel concludes, human beings sometimes yearn for the troublesome magic that once enlivened a thousand and one nights.

A nineteenth-century engraving shows the twelfth-century scholar and philosopher Ibn Rushd (Averroes) condemned by Islamic theologians for the temerity of his ideas.

CONTRIBUTOR BIOGRAPHIES

LAURA MILLER – GENERAL EDITOR
New York–based journalist and critic. Miller was a cofounder of Salon.com, where she worked as an editor and writer for twenty years, and is now a books and culture columnist at *Slate*. Her work has appeared in *The New Yorker, Harper's, The Guardian,* and *The New York Times Book Review,* where she wrote the "Last Word" column for two years. She is the author of *The Magician's Book: A Skeptic's Adventures in Narnia* (2008) and editor of *The Salon.com Reader's Guide to Contemporary Authors* (2000).
Page 178

JES BATTIS
Coeditor of *Mastering the Game of Thrones* (2015) and author of the Occult Special Investigator series and Parallel Parks series (as Bailey Cunningham). He teaches in the Department of English at Kwantlen Polytechnic University, Vancouver. His research focuses on the medieval period and eighteenth century, with interests in pop culture and LGBTQ history.
Page 264

LAWRENCE BATTERSBY
Scottish freelance writer who has lived in Paris for the past twenty years. Battersby writes in different forms including short stories and poetry, and has recently completed a historical novel set in nineteenth-century Spain.
Page 60

MATTHEW CHENEY
Author of *Blood: Stories* (2016) and academic work on Samuel R. Delany among others. He is currently a PhD candidate at the University of New Hampshire.
Pages 196 & 220

NOEL CHEVALIER
Associate professor of English at Luther College, University of Regina, Saskatchewan. His teaching and research interests include literary responses to the Bible and literary representations of eighteenth-century pirates.
Page 70

JOHN CLUTE
Canadian writer of science fiction and fantasy criticism, currently based in the UK. Clute's novel *Appleseed* was a *New York Times* "Notable Book" in 2002. He is currently working on the third edition of *The Encyclopedia of Science Fiction*.
Page 214

GARY DALKIN
UK-based writer and editor. Former judge of the Arthur C. Clarke Award and founder of the International New Media Writing Prize, Dalkin is a contributor to *Writing Magazine, Amazing Stories,* and *Shoreline of Infinity*. Recent projects include Andrew David Barker's *Dead Leaves* and the anthology *Improbable Botany*.
Pages 124, 184, 216, & 258

RICHARD ERLICH
Emeritus professor in English at Miami University, Ohio, since his retirement in 2006, Erlich is best known for his scholarship on the works of Ursula K. Le Guin.
Pages 28 & 174.

PETER FITTING
Emeritus professor of French and Cinema Studies at the University of Toronto. Fitting is author of numerous articles on science fiction, fantasy, and utopia. He is also author of the anthology *Subterranean Worlds: A Critical Anthology* (2004).
Page 78

ANDREW R. GEORGE

George teaches Akkadian and Sumerian language and literature at SOAS, University of London, where he is professor of Babylonian. He is author of *The Babylonian Gilgamesh Epic: Introduction, Critical Edition, and Cuneiform Texts* (2003), and a prize-winning translation of *The Epic of Gilgamesh* (2000).
Page 16

LEV GROSSMAN

Journalist, novelist, and book critic for *Time Magazine*. *The New York Times* describes Grossman as "among this country's smartest and most reliable critics." His novels include *Warp, Codex, The Magicians, The Magician King*, and *The Magician's Land*.
Page 268

MARY HAMILTON

Game designer and executive editor for audience at *The Guardian*. Hamilton describes herself as a storyteller, a writer, and a news junkie.
Page 282

ROBERT HOLDEN

Australia-based lecturer, curator, and historian, and the author of over thirty books. Holden has received awards from the Literature Board of the Australia Council, held a Mitchell Library Fellowship and has spoken at numerous conferences in Australia and at the Universities of Oxford and Cambridge.
Page 136

NICK HOLDSTOCK

Edinburgh-based fiction writer and essayist. Holdstock is the author of *The Tree That Bleeds: A Uighur Town on the Edge* (2011), a study of life in China's Xinjiang province, the nonfiction book *China's Forgotten People* (2015), and the novel *The Casualties* (2015).
Page 222

KAT HOWARD

Kat Howard lives in New Hampshire. Her short fiction has been nominated for the World Fantasy Award, anthologized in several collections, and performed on NPR. Her debut novel, *Roses and Rot*, was published in 2016.
Pages 262 & 286

MAYA JAGGI

An award-winning cultural journalist, literary critic, and festival director in London. For a decade Jaggi was a long-form arts profile writer for *The Guardian*. Her 2012 honorary doctorate from the UK's Open University was for "extending the map of international writing." She has judged international literary awards, and holds degrees from Oxford University and the London School of Economics.
Page 292

LYDIA KIESLING

San Francisco–based writer and editor of literary website The Millions. She is a member of the National Book Critics Circle and her work has appeared in *The Guardian*, *The New York Times Magazine*, Slate, and Salon.com.
Page 308

PAUL KINCAID

Paul Kincaid has received both the Thomas Clareson Award and the Best Non-Fiction Award from the British Science Fiction Association. He has published two books of essays and has recently completed a book on Iain M. Banks for the University of Illinois Press.
Page 252

REYES LÁZARO

Associate professor of Spanish and Portuguese at Smith College, Massachusetts. Lázaro holds a PhD in Spanish and Portuguese and a Masters in Philosophy from University of Massachusetts, Amherst, and a BA in Philosophy from the Universidad de Deusto, Bilbao, Spain.
Pages 62 & 254

ANN MORGAN

Writer and editor from London. Morgan's first book, *Reading the World: Confessions of a Literary Explorer* (2015), grew out of a project she undertook to spend a year reading a book from every country on Earth. Her debut novel, *Beside Myself*, was published in January 2016.
Pages 156 & 224

MAHVESH MURAD
Book critic and editor from Karachi, Pakistan. Murad is also host of the interview podcast Midnight in Karachi on Tor.com, and editor of the *Apex Book of World* SF *4*.
Pages 206, 208, & 226

JONATHAN NEWELL
PhD candidate in English Literature at the University of British Columbia, specializing in weird fiction. He has published articles on China Miéville, George R. R. Martin, and others in journals including *Horror Studies*, *Science Fiction Studies*, and *Studies in Gothic Fiction*.
Page 276

JEFF NUNOKAWA
Professor of English at Princeton University, New Jersey. Nunokawa has written widely on nineteenth-century literature and is the author of *The Afterlife of Property* (1994) and *Tame Passions of Wilde: Styles of Manageable Desire* (2003). His most recent project is *Note Book*, a collection of his writings on Facebook.
Page 198

ABIGAIL NUSSBAUM
Columnist and book critic based in Israel. Nussbaum has written columns for *Progressive Scan* and was reviews editor for *Strange Horizons* for four years. She was a contributor to the third edition of *The Encyclopedia of Science Fiction*, and has been nominated for a British Science Fiction Association award.
Pages 166 & 256

MARGARET J. OAKES
Professor of English at Furman University, South Carolina, and contributor to *Reading Harry Potter* (2003) and *Reading Harry Potter Again* (2009). Oakes's research interests are in early modern British poetry and children's fantasy literature.
Page 272

LAURIE PENNY
Columnist and author, Nieman Fellow at Harvard University, and contributing editor at *New Statesman*. Penny has written for *The Guardian* and *New Statesman*, and is the author of several books including *Unspeakable Things*

(2014), *Cybersexism* (2013), and *Meat Market: Female Flesh Under Capitalism* (2011).
Page 304

ANDREW H. PLAKS
Literary critic and researcher, focusing on Chinese and Japanese classical literature. Plaks was previously a Professor at Princeton University, New Jersey, and now lectures at the Hebrew University of Jerusalem.
Page 58

ERIC RABKIN
Professor emeritus of English language and literature at the University of Michigan whose specialties include fantasy and science fiction.
Pages 164 & 260

ADAM ROBERTS
British science-fiction writer and professor of nineteenth-century literature at Royal Holloway, University of London.
Pages 138, 194, 204, 232, & 296

DAVID SEED
Professor of English at Liverpool University. Seed specializes in science fiction, Cold War culture and spy fiction, and the interface between fiction and film.
Page 162

TOM SHIPPEY
Emeritus professor of Saint Louis University, his publications include *The Road to Middle-earth* (4 expanded editions, 1982 to 2004), *Beowulf: The Critical Heritage* (1998), *The Shadow-Walkers* (2005), and *Hard Reading: Learning from Science Fiction* (2016). He currently reviews fantasy and science fiction for *The Wall Street Journal*.
Pages 18, 22, 30, 34, 36, 40, 44, 48, 52, 54, 64, 68, 74, 96, & 188

JARED SHURIN
Shurin has edited over a dozen anthologies on topics ranging from mummies to Dickens. He has been a finalist for the Shirley Jackson and Hugo Awards, and twice won the British Fantasy Award for Non-Fiction. He is also the editor of Pornokitsch, a pop culture website.
Pages 210, 218, & 244

SHARON SIEBER

Professor of Spanish at Idaho State University. Sieber's research focuses on Latin American and twentieth-century Spanish literature.

Page 192

JAMES SMYTHE

London-based novelist and creative writing teacher. Smythe regularly writes for *The Guardian* and his novels include *The Testimony, The Explorer, The Machine,* and the *Australia Trilogy.*

Pages 238 & 288

MAUREEN SPELLER

A critic and reviewer of science fiction and fantasy. Speller is senior reviews editor at *Strange Horizons* and assistant editor of *Foundation: The International Review of Science Fiction.*

Pages 240 & 284

DARRYL STERK

Assistant professor of translation at National Taiwan University, specializing in the representation of Taiwan's aboriginal peoples in film and fiction.

Page 302

MATTHEW STRECHER

Professor of Japanese literature in the Faculty of Liberal Arts, Sophia University, Tokyo. Strecher is a specialist in contemporary Japanese literature and is the author of several books on Haruki Murakami, including *The Forbidden Worlds of Haruki Murakami* (2014).

Page 298

JOHN SUTHERLAND

Journalist, author, and professor of modern English at University College London. His books include *How to Read a Novel: A User's Guide* (2006), *Curiosities of Literature: A Feast for Book Lovers* (2008), and *Magic Moments: Life-Changing Encounters with Books, Film, Music...* (2008). He is a regular contributor to *The Guardian, The New Statesman* and *The London Review of Books.*

Pages 80, 82, 88, 94, 100, 104, 106, 108, 110, 116, 130, 132, 140, 212, & 290

ANDREW TAYLOR

Freelance writer and journalist based in the UK. He read English at Oxford University and his books include *God's Fugitive: The Life of C. M. Doughty* (1999), *The Pocket Guide to Poets and Poetry* (2011), *Walking Wounded: The Life and Poetry of Vernon Scannell* (2013), and *Books that changed the World* (2014).

Pages 134, 144, 148, 154, 170, & 200

KOLA TUBOSUN

Writer, critic, and language professor, Tubosun recently coedited a collection of essays on African linguistics. His work has appeared in various publications, including the *International Literary Quarterly, Aké Review, The Guardian,* and *The Maple Tree Literary Supplement.*

Page 306

LISA TUTTLE

Lisa Tuttle is an award-winning author of horror, fantasy, and science fiction. Her novels include *Windhaven* (written with George R. R. Martin) and *The Curious Affair of the Somnambulist and the Psychic Thief* (2016). Her nonfiction includes the *Encyclopedia of Feminism* (1986) and *Writing Fantasy and Science Fiction* (2001).

Pages 186, 230, 248, & 294

BENJAMIN WIDISS

Widiss teaches literature at Hamilton College, New York. He is the author of *Obscure Invitations: The Persistence of the Author in Twentieth-Century American Literature* (2011), and is currently working on a monograph *Flirting with Embodiment: Textual Metaphors and Textual Presences in Contemporary Narrative.*

Page 158

INDEX

CREDITS

Every effort has been made to trace copyright holders and to obtain their permission for the use of copyright material. The publisher apologizes for any errors or omissions in the following list and would be grateful if notified of any corrections that should be incorporated in future reprints or editions of this book.

Nineteen Eighty-Four by George Orwell (Copyright © George Orwell, 1948) Reprinted by permission of Bill Hamilton as the Literary Executor of the Estate of the Late Sonia Brownell Orwell.

The Bloody Chamber by Angela Carter. Published by Vintage, 2006. Copyright © Angela Carter. Reproduced by permission of the Estate of Angela Carter c/o Rogers, Coleridge & White Ltd., 20 Powis Mews, London W11 1JN

Ace Books, 1984, 244. Alamy Stock Photo: © 2nd Collection 64; © A. T. Willett 164, 165; © AF archive 179, 197, 219, 238, 263, 265, 289; © AF Fotografie 125; © Age Fotostock 255; © Agencja Fotograficzna Caro 298; © Alpha Historica 188; © Antiques & Collectables 75; © Artepics 23; © Brother Luck 308; © CH Collection 130; © Chronicle 309; © Classic Image 4, 22, 101; © Craig Stennett 252; © DPA Picture Alliance 284; © Everett Collection Historical 174, 184, 186, 204, 216; © Frans Lemmens 307; © Frederick Wood Art 36; © Gary Doak 288; © GL Archive 64, 74; © Granger, NYC. 28, 46, 66, 81, 86, 89, 90, 91, 196; © Heritage Image Partnership Ltd 35, 38, 42, 50, 63, 97, 140; © Ian Dagnall Computing 52; © Interfoto 99,140, 212; © Jaguar 296; © Jeff Morgan 16 240; © Jeremy Sutton-Hibbert 272; © Kathy deWitt 262, 282; © Keystone Pictures USA 293; © Lebrecht Music and Arts Photo Library 76, 83, 102, 103; © Liam White / Alamy Stock Photo 226; © Liszt Collection 41; © Marco Destefanis 292; © Mary Evans Picture Library 53, 59, 60, 71, 157; © Moviestore collection Ltd 115; © Painting 27, 40; © Pako Mera 258; © Peter Barritt 95; © Photos 12 131; © Pictorial Press

Ltd 80, 85, 87, 111, 117, 119, 144, 158, 164, 175, 209, 261; © Picture Library 31; © Prisma Archivio 168, 228; © Shaun Higson 248; © SOTK2011 231; © Steve Taylor ARPS 128; © The National Trust Photo Library 291; © Walker Art Library 122; © WENN Ltd 218, 264, 294; © World History Archive 25, 187; © ZUMA Press, Inc. 193, 232, 244, 273. Bridgeman Art Library: © Birmingham Museums and Art Gallery / Bridgeman Images 45; © Gallery Oldham, UK / Bridgeman Images 20; © Royal Library, Copenhagen, Denmark / Bridgeman Images 37; Bibliotheque des Arts Decoratifs, Paris, France / Archives Charmet / Bridgeman Images 56; De Agostini Picture Library / Bridgeman Images 61; Musee d'Art Thomas Henry, Cherbourg, France / Bridgeman Images 33; Private Collection / Bridgeman Images 127; Private Collection / Photo © Christie's Images / Bridgeman Images. Gnome Press, 1950 185; Private Collection / Photo © Peter Nahum at The Leicester Galleries, London / Bridgeman Images 55; Private Collection / Photo © The Maas Gallery, London / Bridgeman Images 14; Pushkin Museum, Moscow, Russia / Bridgeman Images 19; Yale Center for British Art, Paul Mellon Fund, USA / Bridgeman Images 65; Private Collection / Photo © The Maas Gallery, London / Bridgeman Images 6. Ballantine Books 186, 214. Bantam Books, 220, 258, 264. Copyright © BBC Photo Library 233. Bloomsbury, 272, 286. © Mark J. Brady / www.mjb-graphics.co.uk 253. © Colleen Corradi Brannigan/ www.cittainvisibili.com 217. © Anne de Brunhoff, 1978 222. © Edgar Rice Burroughs, Inc. 132, 133. © Jonathan Burton 2011. Illustration from The Folio Society edition of *The Hitchhiker's Guide to the Galaxy* by Douglas Adams. All editions from The Folio Society are available exclusively at www.foliosociety.com 234. © Sam Caldwell, 'The Castle' (2014), watercolour and graphite 141. Cecilie Dresser Verlag, 2003, 284. Chatto & Windus, 1932, 148. Inkspell map © Carol Lawson 2005, reproduced with permission of Chicken House Ltd. All rights reserved 285. Colin Smythe Ltd., 1983, 240. Cover designed by Will Staehle and reproduced with permission of www.unusualcorporation.com 294. © Rebekah Naomi Cox 211. From: *The Sandman: Master of Dreams* #1 © 1999 DC Comics. Written by Neil Gaiman and illustrated by Sam Kieth and Mike Dringenberg. Courtesy of DC Comics. 256. Delacorte, 1969, 212. Used by permission of Samuel R. Delany and his agents, Henry Morrison, Inc. Copyright © 1969, 2016 by Samuel R. Delany. Image supply: Royal

Books Inc. 221. © Carles Domènech 254. Donald M. Grant, 1982, 238. Doubleday & Company, Inc., 208, 230. E. P. Dutton, 1924, 138. Editions Denoël, 1975, 222. Editorial Erein, 1988. 254. Editorial Sudamericana, 1967, 204. Editorial Sur, 1941, 158. Einaudi, 1972, 216. Marion Ettlinger/Corbis Outline 268. Eyre and Spottiswoode, 1950, 170. Faber & Faber Ltd. 2005, 290. Farrar & Rinehart, Inc., 1942, 162. © Finn Dean 2013. Illustrations from The Folio Society edition of *Brave New World* by Aldous Huxley. All editions from The Folio Society are available exclusively at www.foliosociety.com 149, 152. Fondo de Cultura Económica, 1955, 192. G. P. Putnam's Sons, 1962, 198. Geoffrey Bles Limited, 1950, 178. George Allen & Unwin, 1954, 188. Getty Images: © Bettmann 69, 135; © Buyenlarge 120; © Carl Mydans 198; © Cristina Monaro 139; © David Cooper 290; © DEA / A. de Gregorio 49; © DEA / G. Dagli Orti 17; © DEA Picture Library 29; © Fox Photos / Stringer 151; © Jack Mitchell 220; © Kean Collection / Staff 78; © Leemage 79; © Mondadori Portfolio 201; © Movie Poster Image Art 195; © Paco Junquera 192; © Philippe HUPP 208; © Photo by Leo Matiz/Leo Matiz Foundation Mexico/Getty Images) 205; © Portland Press Herald 260; © Raymond Kleboe / Stringer 170; © SFX Magazine 276; © The Asahi Shimbun 301; © Ulf Andersen 256; © Ullstein Bild 138; © Universal Images Group 48; © William Vandivert / The LIFE Picture Collection 213; © Javier Moreno/DPA/Getty Images 160. Courtesy www.maygibbs.org © The Northcott Society and the Cerebral Palsy Alliance, 2016 136 (top & bottom), 137. Gollancz, 1979, 226. © Ben Gonzales 210. Grayson & Grayson, 1952, 184. Copyright © Marian Wood Kolisch 206. Copyright © Ursula K. Le Guin 207. Harcourt Brace Jovanovich, 1973 218. © Penguin Random House, image used courtesy of George R.R. Martin, 267. Illustrations by John Harris, commissioned by Lauren Panepinto of Little Brown (US). www.alisoneldred.com 236, 305. Harvill Secker, 2006 292. Image courtesy: John Hay Library and Special Collections Brown University. Accession number: A32500. 147. Image courtesy: John Hay Library and Special Collections Brown University. Accession number: A55361. 145. Heinemann, 1962 196. Hodder & Stoughton, 2001 282. Hodder & Stoughton, 2014 306. Houghton Mifflin Company, 1993 260. © IWM (Art.IWM ART LD 2905) 199. A. C. McClurg & Co.,1922. 132. Hodder & Stoughton, 2004 288. © Tove Jansson 166 (top & bottom), 167. Jonathan Cape, 2015 308.

© Josh Godin, sour.org 245. © Artist Igor Karash, 2012. Illustration from the Folio Society edition of The Bloody Chamber and Other Stories by Angela Carter. All editions from The Folio Society are available exclusively at www.foliosociety.com 227. Drawing by Jim Kay for Jonathan Strange and Mr Norrell. Courtesy of BBC/Cuba Pictures/Feel Films, www.alisoneldred.com 287. © Josh Kirby Estate / www.joshkirbyart.com 241, 242. Illustrations by Pauline Baynes, copyright © C.S. Lewis Pte. Ltd. 1950. Reprinted by permission. 180, 182. Library of Congress Prints and Photographs Division Washington, D.C. 20540 USA. LOT 11735 134. Little, Brown & Company, 1996 268. Macmillan UK (1987) 252. Macmillan, 200 276. © Maggy Roberts, www.thepaintednet.com 283. © Werner Bischof/Magnum Photos 223. © Paul Marquis, pmarq.com 215. © Joe Mazza – Brave Lux 306. McClelland & Stewart, 1985 248. © Lee Moyer, www.leemoyer.com 278. Orbit Books 304. Pan Books, 1979 232. Pantheon Books, 1979, 134. Parnassus Press, 1968, 206. Pax, 1977, 224, 225. Images by Mervyn Peake reprinted by permission of Peters Fraser & Dunlop (www.petersfraserdunlop.com) on behalf of the Estate of Mervyn Peake 171, 173. Image supplied by Harry Ransom Center, The University of Texas at Austin and used with permission of the David Foster Wallace Trust. 269. Used with permission of Edward Relph. 163. René Julliard, 1963 200. Scala House Press, 2004 156. Scholastic Ltd, 1995 262. Scholastic Press, 2008 296. Secker & Warburg, 1949 174. Illustrations from The Folio Society edition of The Handmaid's Tale by Margaret Atwood © Anna and Elena Balbusso 2012. All editions from The Folio Society are available exclusively at www.foliosociety.com 249, 250. Shinchosa Publishing Ltd., 2009 298. © Snap Stills/REX/Shutterstock 297. © Igor Sobolevsky 259. © Peter Stubbs, www.edinphoto.org.uk 274. © ThinKingDom Media Group Ltd.2016 302. "MS. Tolkien Drawings (fol.1) ORTHANC" © The Tolkien Estate. Image supplied by the Bodleian Library. 189. Viking Press, 1968 210. © 2009 Jarle Vines 224. © Michael Whelan www.michaelwhelan.com 239. Widawnictwo Ministerstwa Obrony Narodowej, 1961 194. © Nate Williams 295. © J. H. Williams III 257. © Zhang You-ran 303.

Conceived and produced by
Elwin Street Productions Limited
14 Clerkenwell Green
London, EC1R ODP

www.elwinstreet.com

First published in North America, November 2016 by
Black Dog & Leventhal Publishers

Black Dog & Leventhal Publishers
Hachette Book Group
1290 Avenue of the Americas
New York, NY 10104
www.hachettebookgroup.com
www.blackdogandleventhal.com

Cover illustration and design by Jim Tierney
Cover copyright © 2016 by Hachette Book Group, Inc.
Text design by Peter Ross / Counterpunch Inc.

ISBN: 978-0-316-31638-5 (hardcover), 978-0-316-54773-4 (ebook)

Printed in China
10 9 8 7 6 5 4 3 2 1